MICHELANGELO

MICHELANGELO

Trewin Copplestone

BARNES
& NOBLE
BOOKS
NEW YORK

This edition published by
Barnes & Noble, Inc.
By arrangement with
Regency House Publishing Ltd.

ISBN 0-7607-5837-9

1 3 5 7 9 10 8 6 4 2

Printed in China
by Sino Publishing House Ltd.

Contents

Preface

To celebrate the fourth centenary of Michelangelo's death in 1564, a volume was published which surveyed his entire life's work. It was 600 pages long, with more than 1,000 illustrations. It measured 14.5 x 11in (37 x 28cm) and weighed 12lb (5.5kg) – a weighty tome by any reckoning – both physically and intellectually.

As the preface to the book notes, Michelangelo has the most extensive bibliography of any artist in history and more books studying his life and works are still being written. It is reasonable to ask why yet another? – and, specifically, why this one? Perhaps two reasons might be offered. Firstly and most obviously, there is a demand for books on Michelangelo which will continue to be met. This is not because earlier books are out of date, factually unreliable, or visually inadequate. The truth is that great artists remain interesting and simple curiosity is a quality most human beings possess. In most people's minds, Michelangelo has always been an enigma and his achievements are without parallel. This is the first reason for writing.

The second, less obvious perhaps, is that every historical figure is perceived differently over the course of decades and centuries, judged by different criteria, while facts not previously known continue to emerge and offer fresh interpretations or new food for thought. Society and fashion continues to change as well as perceptions of art. We not only prefer the modern idiomatic language of our own time, we also like to feel a part of the society to which we belong. Michelangelo does not change but books about him do and we like books that are comprehensible in a modern age.

Over more than four centuries the understanding and knowledge of Michelangelo and his work has indeed changed. Facts supplied by Vasari, Michelangelo's friend and first biographer, or Condivi, a pupil and biographer, have subsequently been proved inaccurate in some details and misleading in others, while efforts to set the record straight have led to even more confusion.

A graphic example of how perceptions change is when the 19th-century French painter Paul Delaroche saw his first photograph: his comment was 'From today art is dead'. An unconscionable time dying, one might think; but he had a point in that presentational painting had received a shock and reflection was necessary.

Almost every biography of any great figure in history is subject to factual inaccuracies and with the passage of time mistakes are inevitably compounded. After five centuries, the task of untangling fact from fiction, while it may be a reasonable, even enthralling, academic excercise, becomes less important than the wish to convey the character and atmosphere of the historical period in which the artist lived. Following on from this, there is the desire to assess and analyze the artist's significance from a contemporary and personal point of view – which is what all writers, with varying degrees of effectiveness, inevitably try to do.

Underlying all this, however, is an even more important reason for a study of Michelangelo, other than the analysis of an artist's achievement. Of the many thousands of artists in history, most are of interest primarily to the academic and the historian. Some artists, however, have been able to convey a sharp visual impression of a period – a flavour, a feeling of nostalgia for a particular time in history. A few – remarkably few – it may be said, provide more profoundly demanding and inspiring visual insights concerning their society, its conventions and beliefs. Moreover, their work has managed to transcend time and remain as fresh and inspiring to subsequent generations as it was when it was first created. Michelangelo will continue to fascinate: more than any artist he reflected the times in which he lived and established a climate of culture that would inspire and evolve to this day. More than any other single figure of the Italian Renaissance, Michelangelo deserves never to be forgotten.

There is another small point to make, and I am making it here after the book has been completed. One may start a project when one believes that it is reasonable to undertake it. I believed I knew enough about the man, having been a student of his work all my life, to write about him. I was wrong: such genius is immeasurable and I am exhausted with the task. I hope that you will think it was worth the effort: I have said all I can.

The half-millennium from 1500 to the present, it is often claimed, constitutes the legacy of Renaissance influence. For this reason, before embarking on the central story of Michelangelo's art, it is important to

Preface

suggest background material which would be useful when reading this book, to explore further the history of the time. For this reason, not only has a suggested reading list been included, but in the course of the text, references to specific titles by other authors have also been indicated.

The above considerations, together with others not yet mentioned, have suggested that to undertake a straightforward chronological approach, which attempts to absorb every aspect of a complicated and diverse story in a continuous narrative, would inevitably introduce digressions and diversions of a confusing and irritating nature. In order to avoid this, the main textual content has been divided into three sections: the story of Michelangelo's life as it fits into the Renaissance scene; a biography of the Renaissance, which sets the location and time; and the nature and quality of Michelangelo's work and the circumstances in which he produced it.

These divisions, however, present one more problem: there are other members of the cast, their lives important because of their association with Michelangelo, who will inevitably be a distraction but are of peripheral interest. Similarly, there are groups and factions, circumstances and events, which will require elaboration, and minor figures of limited but relevant importance also to be included.

To prevent unnecessary intrusion upon the main narrative, and to provide informative digressions for those who need them, a system of 'boxes', clearly identified and isolated, have been introduced, which can be skipped or studied according to the fancy of the reader. They are located where they are of most use rather than where they correspond to the text. Some of the figures involved are of interest in a much wider context, one that takes them beyond the confines of Michelangelo's story; a number of them have been included in the book list and are referenced where necessary.

There is one further point to be made concerning structure. Each section and sub-section is self-contained; this means that if any reader knows everything they feel they need to know about, say, the Renaissance or the technique of fresco painting, they will be able to skip these pages.

But, and this is the crux of the matter: everything that is in the text is there only because it is part of the Michelangelo story, discernibly relevant to a greater or lesser degree. The book is intended to be a comprehensive survey of the greatest artist of the Renaissance, his life, his art and his times.

OPPOSITE

Head of Michelangelo by Daniele da Volterra *(c.1529–1566)*

Bronze, 35in (89cm) in height

Introduction

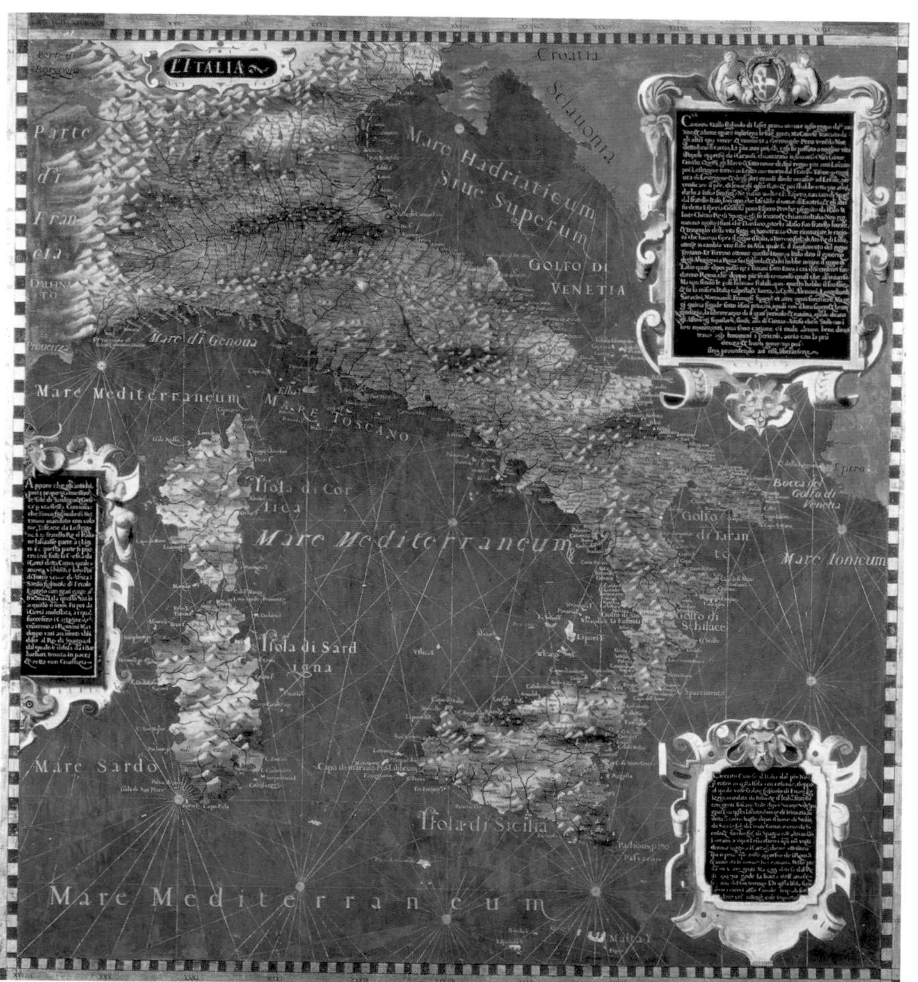

There are many reasons why Michelangelo poses more than the usual challenge to the biographer. He was a figure of unique significance at a seminal stage of European history. He was regarded by his contemporaries, by the time he was in his early 20s, as a figure of almost 'divine' stature, to which even his greatest contemporaries, Leonardo da Vinci or Raphael, could not hope to aspire. He was a living myth and so he has remained – a solitary, brooding presence, far removed from the usual role expected of an artist.

To place him within the context of an ordinary life is hardly possible. To consider him living an artist's life, as is commonly understood today, would be to distort any real understanding of his place as an artist alive during the Italian Renaissance. It should also be said that his patrons, with whom he dealt on a daily basis, were far from ordinary citizens; for a young man from a less than privileged background to be on first name terms with popes was more than unusual. From his mid-teens onwards, he was a contributor to the higher levels of Italian culture. Italy, too, was no ordinary country – officially it was not a country at all in the way that we would understand the term today.

Michelangelo

Michelangelo's artistic and cultural achievement encompassed a Platonist philosophy allied to a strong Christian faith. This, in a complicated, mercurial, difficult, argumentative and powerful personality, quick to take offence, suggests that there was more to Michelangelo's character than could be said of any artist of any discipline at any period in history.

His life and work requires the investigation of many social, political and artistic aspects present in the growing 15th- and 16th-century Italian Renaissance, rather more factors than would impinge on the life of an artist, even that of a recognized genius. When examining the life of Rembrandt van Rijn, life in 17th-century Holland is not as highly relevant although, inevitably, it would have shaped Rembrandt's character and influenced his expression of the human spirit in his deeply moving portraits. More significantly for our study, he did not have an appreciable influence on Dutch 17th-century culture or social life. Nor, to move to another time and place, does J.M.W. Turner's revolutionary and visionary interpretation of European landscape demand a special study of early Victorian England.

The Italian Renaissance, on the other hand, in all its aspects, is of great significance in the life of Michelangelo and the understanding of his work. Conversely, and equally importantly, it is not conceivable that the Italian Renaissance could adequately be examined and understood without the inclusion of Michelangelo's massive contribution to that culture.

Since renaissance means 'rebirth', and the Renaissance is a period of history, the implication must be that it is the rebirth of an earlier period, and that indeed is what the name is intended to indicate. Baldly stated, that earlier period consists of the pre-Christian civilization of classical Greece and Imperial Rome and we are consequently obliged to make a broader sweep of historical study than might have been anticipated.

History is not, of course, the simple division of time which identifies when particular societies or civilizations existed; it is a slow, often imperceptible process of change only recognized in retrospect. The Renaissance was not described as such until the later 19th century; although the word was used somewhat earlier, its first appearances in literature were in Michelet's *Renaissance* (1855), and the great work of Jacob Burckhardt published in German in 1860, *The Civilization of the*

OPPOSITE
Map of 16th-century Italy by Stefano Bonsignori and Egnazio Danti
Sala delle Carte Geografiche,Palazzo Vecchio, Florence

Period of the Renaissance in Italy, and translated into English in 1878. Other early works include Walter Pater's *Renaissance: Studies in Art and Poetry* (1873) and J.A. Symonds' *The Renaissance in Italy* (7 volumes 1875–86), and others published at the same time on the European continent. Studies of the life and works of Michelangelo in the context of the Renaissance appeared in the 1870s.

Any reasonable study of the Renaissance will not only involve the history of the whole of Europe from the Middle Ages to the 15th and 16th centuries, but will also require a look at the entire history of Western society and, properly, the prehistory that influenced its formation. History is a continuous process and we are in the middle of it; however, it is evident that a comprehensive study of history is impossible in a book of this nature, with its focus as the work of one artist; but it is essential to look both backwards and forwards in placing Michelangelo in his context.

The study of an artist – even one as singularly important as Michelangelo – cannot justify the in-depth examination of the whole of Western civilization without distorting the balance of the study, and this will not be attempted here; but it is a salutary reminder of the unity of all cultures that the question should arise – and a particular indication of the difficulties that Michelangelo almost uniquely presents. Think again, perhaps, of Rembrandt and Turner; neither would demand a history of the world as a prologue to their lives.

Although Italy was not a unified country with an overall government during the whole period we are considering, it was one of the richer – if not the richest – and more commercially successful areas of Europe. It provoked the envy and avarice of European countries with organized monarchies such as France, Germany, England and Spain. Each, at some time during the period, had ambitions of conquest in Italian territory and are consequently part of the Italian Renaissance story.

The Renaissance, as many will recall, was also a period of the great explorers, by land and sea, during which the possibilities of a global society were beginning to emerge. Continents other than Europe were revealed, exerting an influence, cultural and commercial, as well as providing opportunities for expansion and exploitation. As a result of the rapid and widespread discoveries of such explorers, who could be regarded as unwitting commercial travellers from Europe, rapid steps were taken in international trade; the great ports of Europe also became its greatest cities. The adventures of such heroes as Christopher Columbus (1451–1506), Vasco da

OPPOSITE

Amerigo Vespucci *(artist unknown)*

Uffizi, Florence

Vespucci was sent by Lorenzo de' Medici, Michelangelo's mentor, to Seville where he met Christopher Columbus, recently returned from his first expedition. Inspired by Columbus Vespucci made several voyages of exploration to the New World between 1497 and 1504. He is believed to be the inspiration for naming America.

LEFT

Christopher Columbus,
by Sebastiano del Piombo

Metropolitan Museum of Art, New York

Columbus, like Vespucci, is known for his contribution to the great age of discovery in the Renaissance.

Introduction

OPPOSITE
***The Sistine Chapel Ceiling: The Creation of Adam** (1510)*
Fresco
Vatican Museums and Galleries, Rome

Gama (1469–1524) and Amerigo Vespucci (1451–1512) reveal an exciting and important element of the Renaissance, and since all of them died before Michelangelo, their discoveries are part of his age. Of course, this is not to say that the Eastern world was unknown; the riches of Venice give ample evidence of its connection with the Orient.

When Michelangelo was born, at the beginning of the last quarter of the 15th century, Italy was fractured into independent republics. These were centred in the most important cities, mainly in the northern third of the country. As time passed, what had been city republics (independent city states dominating nearby smaller towns and controlling the countryside around them) came to be controlled by powerful, ambitious or militant figures and were transformed into 'dukedoms' or even small kingdoms. Consequently, Michelangelo was predominently a citizen of the Florentine republic and only in a general sense one of Italy.

To examine the man and his achievements effectively, we must also consider, in broad perspective, the state of the arts before and during Michelangelo's lifetime. Some reference to the period after his death will also be necessary, since his influence is evident in the succeeding period in the artistic styles of Mannerism and Baroque.

A number of major social and political circumstances, dramatic and influential events, and cultural conditions that require even more discussion, will have to be incorporated into the main study of Michelangelo's career. These will be included where they are essential and where they are significant in Michelangelo's life.

However, it should be recognized that we are looking at a society that had little direct functional or structural relationship to present-day society. The Renaissance is over. To think, for instance, of the artists of the Renaissance in terms of how artists live today will be neither informative nor accurate. It would also be to ignore the power of the Roman Catholic Church and its vast administrative organization, which was to remain supremely dominant until the Reformation and the growth of Protestantism which followed, usually pinpointed as 1517, following Martin Luther's Wittenberg Theses. Such had been the power of the church, and its domination of society, that before this point, such a challenge would not have been possible.

Introduction

It should not be assumed that Italy was at peace throughout the Renaissance. The truth is very different and, although it will not be constantly referred to, it would be wise to remember that the threat of conflict was ever-present and affected any commission in which Michelangelo might have been engaged. A sense of imminent danger must have occupied the thoughts of most of the population going about their daily lives, and though the full causes of Italy's internecine tensions are too peripheral to be examined here, they will be discussed where, in the progress of Michelangelo's life, they come to the surface.

One underlying historical influence of continuing importance was the often unacknowledged effect of the two conflicting loyalties, that of Guelph (Church) and Ghibelline (Empire), that were present in Italy. Their influence upon the city states is important and a great deal of the destructive internecine conflict, and even ochlocracy, had its origins here.

In Italy the Renaissance took a different form and character from its manifestations in other countries. Italy was a united country only in its physical form and language. Its history throughout the Roman Empire, and its expansion through Europe, gave it an identity which, from the medieval period, divided it into small separate communities centred around the growing wealth of the cities. Indeed, by the time of the Renaissance, the notion of the city state in Italy was being compared with those of ancient Greece. Some were republics (such as Florence for most of the time), some were dukedoms (which included Milan under the Visconti and Sforzas), dominated by one family. The only two larger states that existed by the time Michelangelo had reached matuity were the Kingdom of Naples, which occupied the lower half of Italy (the foot and lower leg), and the Papal States which stretched, from the beginning of the 16th century, like a garter across the middle. Different both in its natural location and organizationally, Venice has a special role in the history of the period, but lies mostly outside our main concern.

It is in the smaller northern city states that the Renaissance, differently and effectively, flourished, and Florence, Michelangelo's family city, was one of the most significant.

It has already been indicated that there were internecine conflicts, political struggles, persecutions, brutality, unprincipled conduct, and local warfare throughout the land, in the city states and within and without the Church of Rome. Furthermore, the power and influence wielded by the church leaders, and uniquely by the popes, at all levels of Italian society, bears little relationship to that which obtains today. Throughout the Renaissance, the unique power of the Church, in the absence of a national government, gave to the popes a measure of autocratic power which they were not slow to exploit. The fact that Michelangelo was a devoted and thinking Christian, as well as a Platonist, had a great effect upon his life and art. To understand the man, however, we must recognize the power – even of life and death – concentrated in the hands of the papacy, particularly as, in Michelangelo's case, it was so directly influential throughout his life and in his work.

To understand Michelangelo in the context of his society is valuable, but it leads to a more important issue – his individual artistic achievement and its place in the history of art. This raises the crucial question of the relevance to later generations of all the art of the past.

We can explain, by reference to writings, the reverence and even awe in which any artist is held in his day: we can consider his character, his technical abilities as a sculptor, painter or architect, and we can even examine and appreciate his own aesthetic value. But to what degree can these interest and effectively inspire us today? Can we share, or even comprehend, his feelings and intentions? In the case of Michelangelo, does the enormous scale and scope of his painting and sculpture create such overwhelming admiration that the intended message of its content is obscured? Is the question now 'How could he have done it?' and not 'What has he said?' To what degree can his values be of importance to present societies around the world? Does his Christianity, expressed in specifically related images, impress people of other faiths? Does his architecture have a special personal message? Does the art of a great Renaissance figure actually affect us as emotionally or intellectually as it did his contemporaries? How relevant is his art today?

While these questions are appropriate and relevant there is no general answer to them that will fully satisfy all, or even many, observers. The message of Christian art is Christianity. Christianity is a faith – one that inspired Michelangelo. If you are not a Christian, then one dimension of importance is certainly removed,

although intellectual interest may still exist. But there may be other factors important in each observer. There can be few who, having seen the powerful images Michelangelo created on the Sistine Chapel ceiling, in the Vatican, Rome, do not feel that humanity alone, through the talent of an artist, can offer much inspiration and evoke a pure aesthetic response.

We may, for instance, be awed by Michelangelo's paintings of the ceiling and end wall of the Sistine Chapel, which depict episodes and figures from the Christian Bible, both Old and New Testaments; but will they, or can they, buttress our Christian faith in an age which is increasingly seeing all religion from a different perspective? What effect or meaning do they have today? Many of the elements depicted have obscure connotations that would be recognized by biblical scholars; but most people seeing the works today will not be familiar with their content.

Is Michelangelo's art only accessible to Christians? Or is the drawing, design, colour, composition enough in itself? It would not have been sufficient for his contemporaries; indeed it was for interpretative strength in visual terms that he was so admired and revered. It is doubtful if more than a handful of those who visit the Sistine Chapel today, many of different races and faiths, have much notion of its original inspiration or are moved by its Christian message.

The amount of discussion that remains is a measure of Michelangelo's stature. He was a powerful creative force by any definition and one of the greatest masters of Western art; his achievement was immense and, although it is certain that much of his message will escape many present-day observers, that which remains is powerful and impressive.

Michelangelo is one of the few artists who absolutely demands, nearly half a millennium after his death, our attention today. His art is still relevant, not because the message it sends to present generations is necessarily that which he intended, but because all art, of whatever discipline, is an expression of the human spirit. Art in whatever form it takes may be interesting, informative and attractive but without being deeply affecting. This requires a quality of creative perception that can transcend the intended message and transport it into philosophical realms. One may feel that intellectual mountains are being moved and thoughts disturbed or

St. Peter's, Rome

The façade was by Carlo Maderna from 1606–12 and the piazza and colonnade by Gian Lorenzo Bernini from 1655–67. The view from the piazza, as this illustration reveals, tends to diminish the role and importance of the dome because of the magnificent contained space created by Bernini and even more by the addition of the heavy façade not intended by Michelangelo in his last plan. The dome can only be effectively viewed from the approach road about a quarter of a mile away.

uplifted without understanding how this has been achieved. This is so with Michelangelo's work and to such an extent that has rarely been achieved before or since. One does not necessarily have to know the story to feel the emotion.

Michelangelo's life, though relatively uncomplicated, was not uneventful. He did not marry and had no close partners or friends to intrude upon his work until later in life. As already mentioned, it was his work rather than the accident of his birth for which he was admired and respected. His time was spent mainly in Florence and Rome, with short intervals in other cities, such as Bologna and Venice. Unlike many of his contemporaries he did not leave Italy.

Most of his work centred around sculpture, with two major painting contracts for the Sistine Chapel and, later in his life, important architectural commissions in Rome. Although he worked for private patrons, notably the Medici family, his principle employers were popes, two of whom were also Medici. He responded to most offers of work, especially sculpture, with enthusiasm; but clients, particularly the popes, were capricious, changing their minds frequently and attempting to renegotiate his

The Ponte Vecchio (Old Bridge), Florence

As its name suggests, this is a medieval structure in origin and has served Florence, with modifications, over the centuries. One feature that attracts visitors is that the bridge continues the early practice of having small shops along its length and which attractively overhang the river Arno.

contracts after he had already begun work. This caused Michelangelo bitter frustration, though he was not slow to vent his anger and discontent. But the popes, who held all the power, after all, were less than conciliatory and Michelangelo grumbled on in vain.

Human cultural history does not, as already mentioned, divide itself conveniently into the periods by which it is subsequently identified, but slides gently or swiftly, constructively or destructively, towards the names by which it becomes convenient to know them. Michelangelo is commonly regarded as the great late master of the High Renaissance, the last living member of the super-triumvirate who, with Leonardo da Vinci and Raphael, were a part of the Mannerist period which succeeded the Renaissance and also to some degree precursors of the Baroque. Elements of all three 'styles' can be discerned in Michelangelo's work and something will be said of these at an appropriate stage.

As a prelude to the examination of Michelangelo's life and work, some consideration of the characteristics of art will be useful. The creative process itself is easily identified; someone wants to create something and does so. But what form it takes, where it is located and what

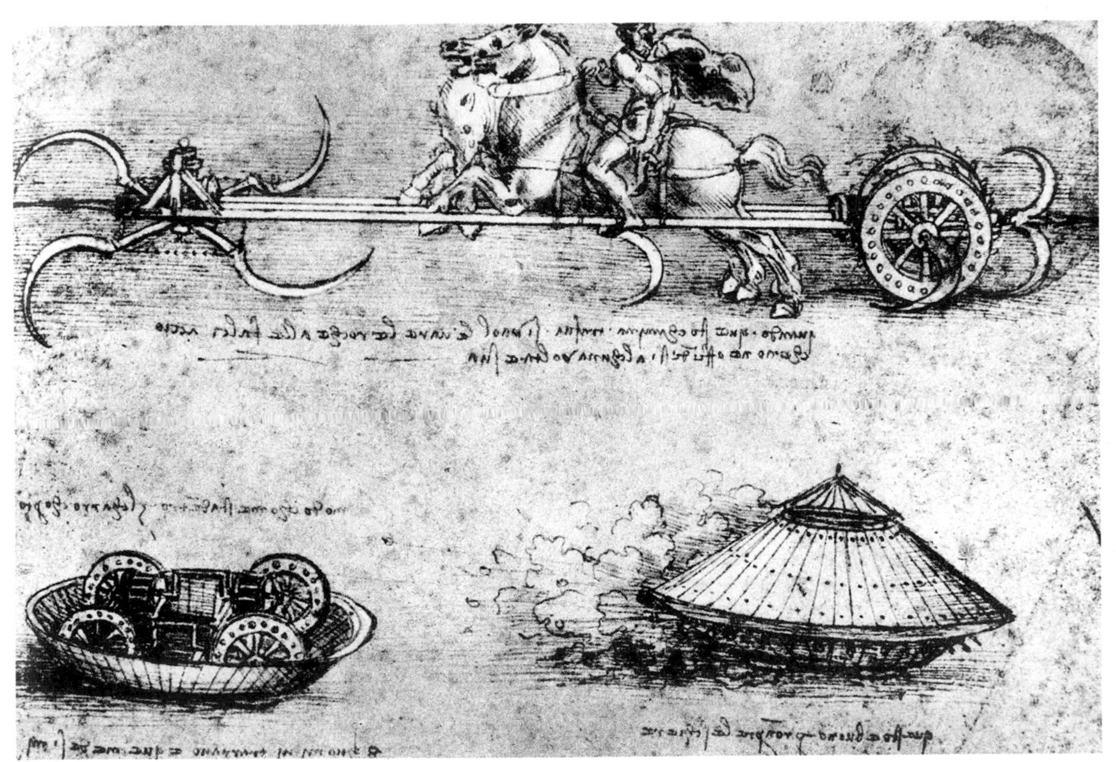

LEFT

Drawings of inventions by Leonardo da Vinci

The upper drawing is a rather gruesome contraption which consists of a chariot with shafts geared to the wheels and with scythes attached. These effectively mow down the infantry as it progresses. Below are two drawings of a submarine invented by Leonardo and said by some to be potentially operable.

OPPOSITE

A bronze medal of Michelangelo by Leone Leoni (1509–90)

A Tuscan engraver and medallist, Leoni's sculpture for the Escorial in Spain is his most famous, but he completed a number of medals of famous men and some artists. His last years were spent in Milan, working on a Medici tomb for the cathedral.

David (with the adjacent figures of Hercules and Cacus)
Piazza della Signoria, Florence

This copy of one of Michelangelo's most famous sculptures has occupied the pedestal made for the original since the late 19th century. The sculpture itself is now in the Galleria dell' Accademia.

activates and inspires it are the important issues. Here we are concerned with what are generally termed the visual arts – painting, sculpture and architectural design. Each has different characteristics.

Architecture differs from the other visual arts in that it is initiated by a clear, practical, functioning, social need. The form it takes is dictated by the use to which it will be put and the structural demands will determine its scale and volume. In fact, what might be described as the 'art percentage' is what it will look like inside and out. In most buildings it has to be admitted that this is minimal and often unconscious. Where the art percentage becomes significant is when the building is considered to be an important expression of a cultural condition; that it says something about its use and its users as well as the ambitions and standards of society.

Before moving on to the other arts, there is another point of impact which affects most of what we shall be considering. The building will also say something about the quality of its designer. During the period preceding the Renaissance, churches and cathedrals were designed, in the main, by anonymous craftsmen, master builders and masons, and it was not until the Renaissance that

the term 'architect' was adopted. When that happened, and it happened concurrently in the case of the other arts, the name of the creator became important in a way that had not existed previously. In architecture, it became a building by Bramante or Raphael and said something about them as well. The visual arts became personalized in their public recognition.

The practical social necessity, although the essential creative motivation in architecture, is not found in the other visual art forms. They have their being in a different need – that of creation – a motive that is of a distant, even prehistorical origin. John Ruskin, in his Lectures on Architecture (1854), made a pertinent observation: 'No person who is not a great sculptor or painter can be an architect. If he is not a sculptor or painter, he can only be a builder.' The point that he is making, with characteristic boldness, is that architecture carries an important element of aestheticism which the architect must be capable of embracing.

The other visual arts are not of identical character either. Traditional painting, with which we are concerned, operates on a two-dimensional surface in which the paint is transformed into an image. The surface is chosen for convenience and effectiveness and the transformation is accomplished by the use of colour mixed with a drying adhesive. These elements are not significant to the message or the created image – intention, imagination and technique are the vital factors. With sculpture, on the other hand, a three-dimensional object is created in which the quality and character of the whole volume is involved: materials, scale and technique are implicit in the message or created image which has a physical identity. A sculptured figure carries a different message from a painted one. Since Michelangelo created both sculpture and painting it is important to recognize this fact.

These matters will be examined further when individual examples will also be considered. All the different factors come together in the eventual work and it is located, temporarily or permanently, in a specific site; a church, a palace, a home, a public building or a dark cellar. The work does not change but its effectiveness and appropriateness does. One does not need to labour this point and it is obvious that much but not all of the visual art created is intended for a specific or general type of location. Consequently, creators will

OPPOSITE

The Doge's Palace, Venice

An oligarchy of families existed in Venice from which the Doge was elected to act as chief magistrate of the city. His palace is an important and magnificent Renaissance building and is illustrated here an example of the art and architecture that existed in the Venetian republic at this time. It is very different from that of Rome and reflects the opulence and luxury that was a feature of Venice and had come from oriental influences, mainly through trade.

Michelangelo visited Venice but the republic was peripheral to his life. But in a general survey of the artists of the Renaissance, Venetians, such as the Bellini family, Mantegna, Giorgione, Veronese, Tintoretto and Titian figure large, Andrea Palladio giving his name to an architectural style.

Introduction

OPPOSITE

Study of five figures by Michelangelo

Pen and ink on paper

Musée Condé, Chantilly, France

Michelangelo made a large number of drawings, some as studies of the human body, for which he had a particular reverence, and others as sketches for particular compositions. The figures are either nude so that the underlying muscular structure can be studied or clothed to capture the effect of drapery over form. Among the drawings there are none that make a similar study of landscape or weather effects. As will be noted, when landscape does appear in his paintings it is barely touched upon. It should not be forgotten that he was essentially a sculptor and even his paintings have an element of this in their make-up.

develop their conception of it with this in mind.

This indicates that some works of art arise from nothing more than a personal need to create: everyone today is familiar with the notion of the penniless artist in a garret, painting or sculpting and perhaps hoping to be discovered. It has become almost the archetypical description of the artist that his/her work is not created for a location or as a commission. It arises only from the desire or compulsion to create it – to express a response to a question. In consequence, a purity of intention, absence of external commercial pressure, a direct expression of the painter's or sculptor's imagination and vision may be invested.

It was not so in the Renaissance period. The visual arts almost always had a patron and a purpose, which introduces a different element. In Michelangelo's time most work was commissioned either, and most frequently, by the Church, or by wealthy members of ducal families or successful merchants. It was not intended for the pure enjoyment of the viewer or the satisfaction of the artist but to send a message of religious importance or satisfy the ambition or pride of a wealthy patron. This art did not arise from the pure simple need of the creator to create. It was essentially intended for general or limited public instruction, or a specific section of it, and had a practical purpose for the patron who commissioned it. In this sense it was commercial art, as we would understand it today. If, to this extent, we regard Michelangelo as a kind of commercial artist, it adds a singular dimension to the consideration of his art. In the case of the Catholic Church, the art it commissioned was intended to instruct and inspire the worshippers – or so it would have been claimed; but examination suggests that the pride and ambition of the popes, and its manifestation, should not be excluded from the reckoning. It also follows that in much of his work Michelangelo was a proselytizer or publicist for Christianity.

The artist (painter, sculptor or architect), who was deeply religious, could immediately and effectively respond to such a call from a prelate. Of course the result would reflect the character and ability of the creator but it gave him a motivation as he had a subject he knew something, even a great deal, about and for which he might have the deepest respect and the desire to promote. This suggests that the artist believed in the

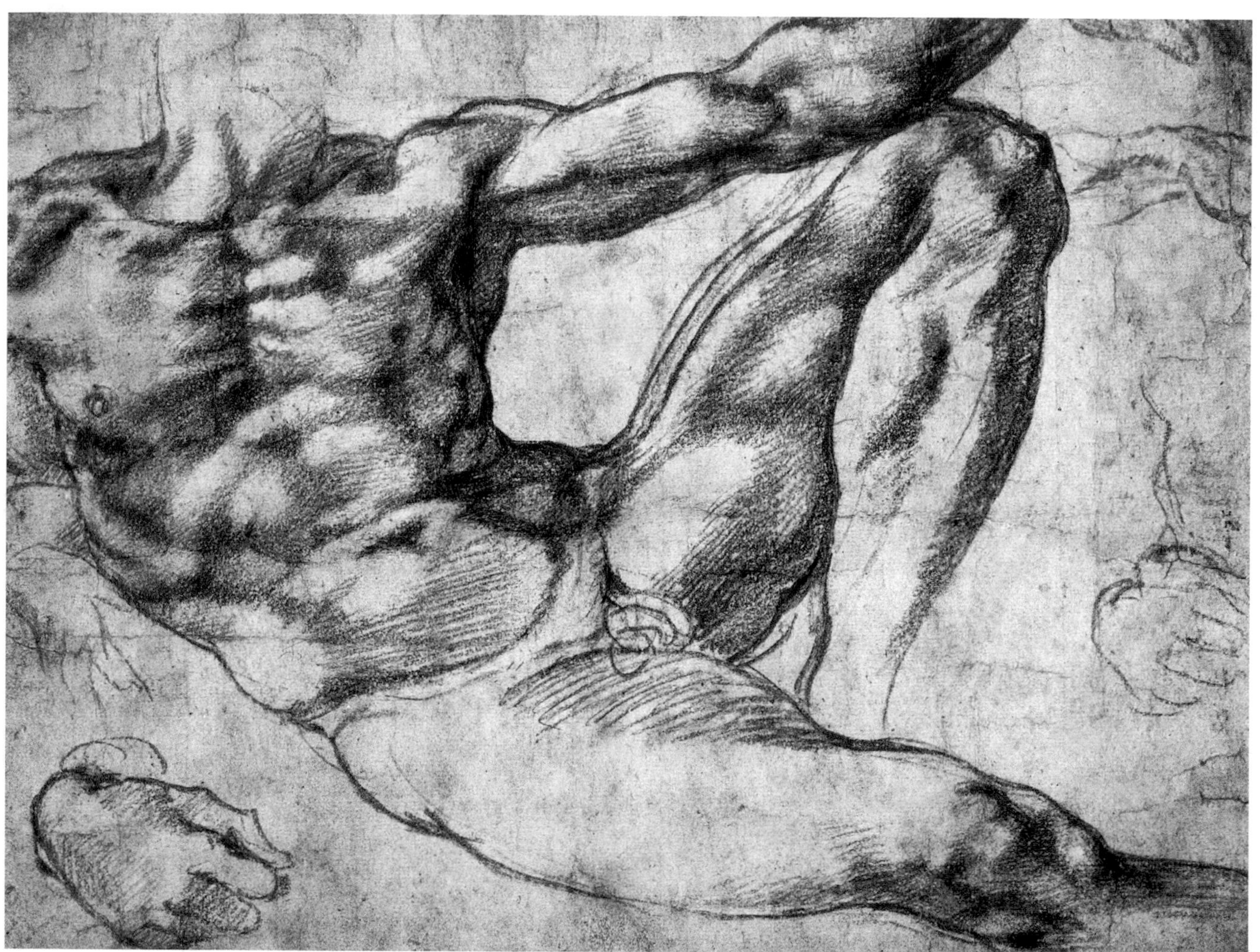

OPPOSITE

Study for The Creation of Adam on the Sistine Chapel ceiling

Red chalk on paper

British Museum, London

The hand in the lower left-hand corner, although detached, is in the position it finally adopts in the finished panel on the Sistine ceiling (see page 278–79).

LEFT

Study of male figure

Black chalk on paper

This drawing appears to be a study for a subject in a painting since it concentrates on the relationship of the arms, which had perhaps been causing Michelangelo some difficulty.

potential efficacy of his art; that it would work, making people more religious or even envious as a result.

In the Renaissance this led to repercussions of which Michelangelo's work is an example. The extensive knowledge, effective imagination and accomplished technique of the best artists resulted in their being in constant demand and consequently under great creative pressure. It is not surprising that many, like Michelangelo, though secure in their social milieu, were stressed, often physically and emotionally, by the demands that patrons placed upon them and that they placed upon themselves. When, as in Michelangelo's case, this was accompanied by a difficult temperament and sustained by a high level of artistic self-belief, stormy times were likely to ensue.

It has already been noted that the creative process obviously precedes the work and it follows that its success can only be established in retrospect. What happens if the work fails to win approval when it is finished? What would have been the result if this had happened to the painting of the Sistine ceiling, after four years of physically demanding work? What would have happened to the great block of stone if the gigantic statue of *David* had been reviled ? This could have happened – as will be evident later on.

This is an important question for the period and the answer is revealing of the significance that those involved in art, from patron to practitioner, placed upon intellectual values; the history and civilization of classical Greece and Rome, the teaching and moral precepts of the Church and the Bible; the qualities of intellect in the contemporary philosophers which were the common currency of intellectual and artistic Renaissance man. The Sistine Chapel paintings (page 266 et seq.) were so universally admired because Michelangelo knew exactly what he was creating, for whom and why, as did his contemporaries. Artists were a major part of the intellectual and creative culture of the day, and few were contracted without the patron knowing exactly what he could expect.

Michelangelo was in constant demand because his clients knew that his powerful genius was likely to rub off on them. And of course it did: we know a number of Renaissance figures primarily as patrons of Michelangelo or other reputed artists of the day. It might be noted that such a role is no longer a part of present-day society.

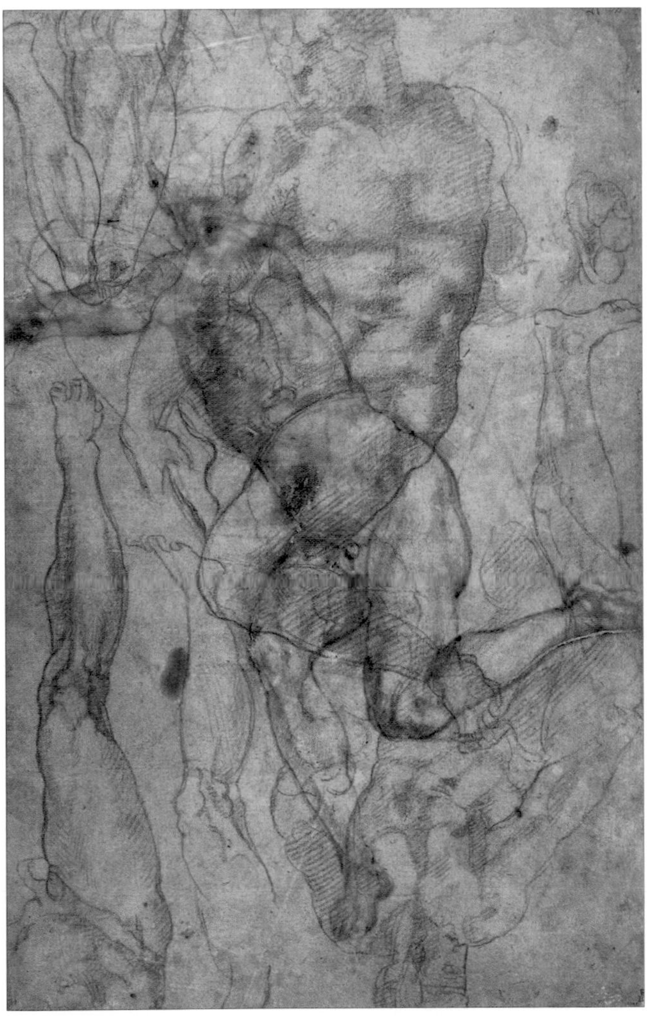

Figure study
Red chalk
British Museum, London

Chapter One

The Story of Michelangelo's Life

Michelangelo Buonarroti (Michelagniolo di Ludovici di Leonardo di Buonarroti Simoni) was born on 6 March 1475 at Caprese (now called Caprese Michelangelo), about 35 miles (56km) to the south-east of Florence, in Florentine territory. He came from an old Florentine family of the Guelph faction, noble but poor, which was barely able to survive on the income its small estate produced. Ludovico, Michelangelo's father, held the powerful if temporary post of *podesta* (resident chief magistrate) of the adjoining towns of Caprese and Chiusi in the Casentino. This lasted for six months from the autumn of 1474 by which time Michelangelo, his second son, was born. Michelangelo's mother, Francesca, was the daughter of Neri di Miniato del Sera and Bonda Rucellai and came from a good Florentine family. Ludovico kept records of family events and writes of his son's birth as follows:

I record that on this day the 6 March 1474 [by present dating 1475] *a son was born to me: I gave him the name of Michelagnolo and he was born on Monday morning before 4 or 5 o'clock, and he was born when I was Podesta at Caprese, and he was born in Caprese ... He was baptized on the 8th day of the same month in the church of San Giovanni of Caprese ...*

Ludovico, on the termination of his office, returned to Florence and the child was given to a woman of Settignano to wet nurse, Settignano, a village outside Florence, being near to the Buonarroti villa. She was married to a marble worker and Michelangelo later claimed that he had imbibed his passion for sculpture along with his foster mother's milk.

Ludovico placed his son, while still very young, in a school run by Francesco da Urbino where, although he made some general progress, began to reveal something of his eventual great talent, spending more time drawing and painting than studying at his desk. Young as he was, he also liked to seek out artists and have discussions with them. This displeased his father who had no wish for his son to become an artist; indeed he hoped that he would 'go into trade', as it would now be expressed, and rescue the family fortunes in the Florentine silk and wool industry.

Michelangelo's mother died when he was six, after bearing three further boys. His elder brother, Leonardo, became a Dominican monk in 1490, when Michelangelo was in his mid-teens, largely through the influence of

Savonarola's preaching. As a result, Michelangelo, at the age of 15, essentially became a replacement for Leonardo as the eldest son of the family, with all the responsibility that this entailed.

The failure of his unattractive brothers to understand or respect Michelangelo's genius must have contributed to his sense of isolation, but he continued to support them all his life, which demonstrated his strong feelings of duty towards his family. His recognized role as second in importance in the family probably accounts for his desire to improve their position in society and to be excessively conscious of any minor attacks on his own dignity. He was a proud, solitary spirit carrying a heavy load of care. It is probable that his early life is linked to his development as one of the most passionate, difficult to understand though creative forces in Western history.

Michelangelo also seems to have inherited his political republicanism from his Guelph family background. Through most of its history Florence had been allied to the Guelph or Church party and was the most important city in the territory of Tuscany, which also includes the cities of Siena, Lucca and Pisa. The most fertile area is along the valley of the Arno and most of the Tuscan landscape is undulating, except for the area around Lucca, Florence and Arezzo. The origins of Tuscany lie in the ancient state of Etruria, the centre of Etruscan art and civilization from around 500 BC; this had been annexed by Rome by the end of the 3rd century BC, when it was somewhat larger than the present-day Tuscany. Although it is no longer a state or a recognized official separate entity, it was a highly significant part of Renaissance Italy and the centre of Florentine power and influence.

While he was a Guelph Florentine, Michelangelo was therefore also a Tuscan. The Tuscan dialect is remarkable for its idiomatic purity and its adoption by Petrarch and Dante probably resulted in it becoming the literary language of Italy. It also gave Florence a particular singularity: Pisa and Siena did not participate in the artistic and intellectual climate of the Renaissance with the same enthusiasm as Florence, which gave her the uniquely important role she holds in Renaissance history.

Thus was Michelangelo's cultural inheritance and his knowledge and experience widened to encompass a larger cultural world as he attained heroic status. He began as a Florentine and a Tuscan and ended up, along

with Leonardo, as a quintessential Renaissance man.

What gives him the final advantage over his fellow luminaries, Leonardo da Vinci and Raphael, was that he lived to within three weeks of his 90th birthday and for 45 years after they had died. In addition, his art was unique and his determination indestructible.

As we trace Michelangelo's early rise to fame it will be evident that there were gaps in his early education, important and unusual as it was, and that to become the man he was by middle age he had to develop social skills which are not usually discussed, since they are not thought to be of sufficient importance. Through his contacts with the Medici family he would have learned much of the social etiquette of the day, though coming from what might be called middle-class or minor gentry, he was, as we shall see, already more than a little conscious of his place in society.

His patrons certainly influenced him – both positively and negatively – and included a number of popes from rival families, a certain source of conflict in Renaissance times. He also had contact with a number of his famous contemporaries and had personal friends among the nobility, though his patrons in Florence and Rome were

At the beginning of a survey of Michelangelo's life, it is useful to remind the reader of his background and a view of the Tuscan countyside surrounding Florence appears suitable. It is also an image to retain when one examines his work. However, the beauty of a landscape was not what inspired Michelangelo. His life's work was concentrated on the human form and the world about him was of only passing interest.

RIGHT
Figure Study
Black chalk on paper
British Museum, London

OPPOSITE
The Dream of Human Life *(c. 1533)*
Black chalk on paper
Courtauld Gallery, London

not close friends. It was not until later in life that he met two people who were to mean a great deal to him, and in fact contributed significantly to his personal fulfilment and happiness

Success and fame created two contrary images of Michelangelo: the mythical hero verging on the divine and the antisocial 'avaricious heretic'. Subsequent generations have tended to elevate rather than diminish his reputation and the antisocial part of his nature has been replaced by an appreciation of him as a strong, passionate, caring but difficult genius. The first printed appreciation of his work seems to have been his inclusion in a list of the best Tuscan sculptors of 1504 when he was 29.

The process of deification began in about 1540 and the first printed volume on Michelangelo appeared in 1549; in following years the two best-known early biographers, Giorgio Vasari (1550) and Ascanio Condivi (1553) produced their volumes, with Vasari's second edition, revised, appearing in 1568. A *Funeral Oration* by Varchi came in 1564, which contained a short biography. All these are available still and while Vasari's is the most lively and informative, it is part of a larger volume tracing the lives of other important artists. Condivi's is possibly the most factually reliable since he was a pupil of Michelangelo and the biography may have been partly dictated by him.

The difficulty of assessing Michelangelo's real character still remains. The evidence that he was difficult and 'touchy' seems clear, but the descriptions of a 'spirit in turmoil' and 'avaricious heretic' do not ring true. The later revelation of his poems through their publication in 1863 and nearly 500 of his letters in 1875 (400th anniversary of his birth) together reveal him as a generous and noble man.

The life of a painter, sculptor, architect, scientist, inventor or gardener may be interesting, but even a garden must be wrested from the wilderness and given time to grow. Michelangelo's life has been traced, checked and argued over; elements such as his sexual orientation have been questioned, together with where he went and how and for whom he worked; but in the end it is the works that speak for themselves. In any event, since his life was largely spent creating great sculptural or pictorial works his leisure time must have been very limited. For instance, he spent four years

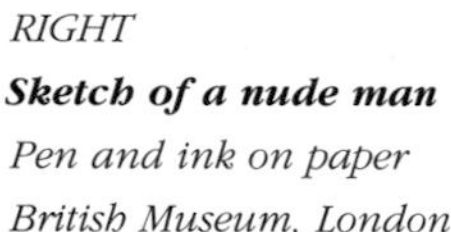

RIGHT
Sketch of a nude man
Pen and ink on paper
British Museum, London

OPPOSITE
Study of Vanity
Pen and ink on paper
British Museum, London

The drawings on these and the preceding two pages effectively illustrate Michelangelo's preoccupations. It should be born in mind that behind the effective rendering of any subject in paint, and particularly the human figure which was Michelangelo's abiding interest, studies were necessary to prepare the perfect image to which all painters aspire. When one recalls the power of Michelangelo's imagery as it emerges, it is his emotional assurance that dominates.

painting the Sistine Chapel ceiling and nearly six working on the *Last Judgment* on the end wall of the chapel some 30 years later. He worked, ate and slept, met a few people, was harassed by popes, revered by his public and travelled to and from his workshop, in the meantime creating one of the great works of Christian belief. His life was so consumed by work that leisure was not a major feature. When not actually working on a specific contract, he was making studies of new projects, drawing the human body, and spending not a little time obtaining the raw materials of his craft, including large blocks of marble. But this does not mean that he was a virtual hermit. He knew many people, although not intimately, was revered by his fellow citizens, was celebrated whenever he appeared, and was highly rewarded for his work.

The role of the artist in Renaissance society is not typified in Michelangelo. As his work and temperament set him apart, so did his rewards. The fees he received should have made him rich were it not for his family who were a constant drain on his pocket. He differed from others of his calling in that Renaissance artists typically received payment from their positions as part of

RIGHT

Façade of Santa Maria Novella, Florence, by Leon Battista Alberti

Alberti was both a practical architect and a theorist. His De Re Aedificatoria *is an outline of classical architectural design with suggestions on its application to the Renaissance. The façade of Santa Maria Novella (1458–70) represents an interesting mix of classical elements on a medieval base.*

OPPOSITE

The Holy Trinity with the Virgin and St. John by Tommaso Masaccio

(1425–28)

Fresco

Santa Maria Novella, Florence

Masaccio's importance in the development of Renaissance painting, despite his short life, was eulogized by Giorgio Vasari, who links him with Giotto and ultimately with Michelangelo, Vasari's hero. *(See page 59).*

the entourage of the great courts where most of their needs would have been provided for them. (Michelangelo's period of early association with the Medici court is an example.) The benefit such rulers received in exchange was the kudos of having famous artists, writers and philosophers attached to their courts and basking in reflected glory.

Michelangelo appears not to have been seduced by this way of life and kept very much to himself. The fact that he was employed for much of his life by popes and nobles in various disciplines, and that most of the contracts were for large paintings or sculptural groups destined for religious locations, also set him apart.

As a sculptor he spent many months at the Carrara marble quarries searching for suitable stone for his large sculptural figures. In short, tracing his daily life is not, in fact, singularly exciting but examining his work provides a highly fascinating, deeply moving insight into the nature of creativity. For him, the pleasures of social contact were a distraction from the main purpose of life.

He was what would now be described as a young achiever. From his early 20s he was already regarded as a master, a phenomenon, a 16th-century equivalent of a

Francesco Granacci (1469/70–1543)

A capable but uninspired follower of Domenico Ghirlandaio, and a pale reflection of his master. Perhaps his principle claim to remembrance is his close and continuing friendship with Michelangelo. On one occasion Michelangelo supplied him with a design for the high altar for a convent – a gesture which surely implied close friendship. Unfortunately, the panel is lost. Giorgio Vasari described Granacci as one who disliked effort, who gave some exercise to his handwork but little to his mind.

movie star. He would have been constantly photographed had cameras and paparazzi existed in his day. He seems to have had none of the diffidence that so frequently afflicts the young. He believed in himself, questioned himself, and was viewed by his contemporaries in Florence with something akin to awe. He was not only a passionate creative force, he was also recognized and respected as such, even as he walked the streets of Florence.

THE BEGINNING

Despite the strong opposition of his father (both Vasari and Condivi claimed that they sometimes came to blows), Michelangelo had clearly decided early in life that he would become an artist and, realizing this, and on the advice of friends, his father relented and made the wise decision to send his son as a paid apprentice to a master in Florence.

This was the usual first step on the artistic ladder, and depending on the apprentice's skill and the regard the master had for him, the apprentice could expect to graduate from cleaning up and mixing colours to assisting the master with actual commissions.

Michelangelo became a paid apprentice on 1 April 1488, at the age of 13. His father Ludovico recorded the contract:

I, Ludovico di Leonardo di Buonarrota place Michelagnolo my son with Domenico and Davit, sons of Tommaso Currado, for the three following years, with these agreements: that the said Michelagnolo shall remain with the above for the said time, to learn to paint and to exercise himself therein, and to do what the above may desire, and that the said Domenico and Davit are bound to pay him, during these three years 24 florins as per agreement: the first year six florins: the second year eight florins: and the third year ten florins: together the sum of 96 livres.

Michelangelo had been introduced by his friend, Francesco Granacci, about five years his elder, an assistant in one of the foremost painter's workshops in Florence, that of Domenico Ghirlandaio, whose original name was Domenico di Tommaso Bigordi. His adopted name reflects the craftsman tradition of a goldsmith and maker of metal garlands or *ghirlandi*. However, his chief interest lay in religious frescoes, but his ambition to paint the complete walls surrounding Florence was unfulfilled. The Davit mentioned was Domenico's brother and partner in the workshop.

Michelangelo later profited from his early acquaintance with the demanding technique of fresco when he was commissioned to paint the Sistine Chapel ceiling, having witnessed, during his time with Ghirlandaio, the whole process as Ghirlandaio worked on frescoes in the church of Santa Maria Novella in Florence, which had been given a new façade by Leon Battista Alberti just before Michelangelo was born and which contained Masaccio's great and significant painting of the Trinity (page 45). Michelangelo must have been employed as an assistant and may have even had a hand in the Ghirlandaio painting.

Michelangelo showed obvious ability from the start although he had no great respect for Ghirlandaio who, at the end of his first year, suggested that he join the school of sculpture in the new Academy of Art opened by Lorenzo de' Medici in the gardens of the Medici Palace, close to the piazza and monastery of San Marco, where Savonarola, who was to have an influence on Florence, Michelangelo and the history of the period, would become a friar in 1490 and prior the

DOMENICO GHIRLANDAIO
(DOMENICO DI TOMMASO BIGORDI)
c.1449–94

Ghirlandaio was the most famous of a family of accomplished painters in Florence at the turn of the 16th century, where they had a flourishing workshop and took on apprentices, among them Michelangelo.

During the Middle Ages religious subjects had been presented in a way that was remote from the lives of ordinary people. Ghirlandaio was popular in that he depicted the lives of the affluent classes of the Renaissance in his religious paintings, which was probably the result of his interest in Flemish art. His particular importance to Michelangelo is that he facilitated his introduction to painting and his membership of the Medici School.

Ghirlandaio's Florentine frescoes include *Scenes from the Life of St. Francis* in the Sassetta Chapel in Santa Trinità (1482–85) and *Scenes from the Life of St. John the Baptist and the Virgin* (1486–90) for the choir of Santa Maria Novella, which also contains Massaccio's Trinity. He was one of the painters to contribute frescoes to the newly built Sistine Chapel in Rome in 1481.

OPPOSITE

Giuliano de' Medici as Melchior, by Benozzo di Lese di Sandro Gozzoli

(c.1460)

Fresco

Palazzo Medici-Riccardi, Florence

From the Journey of the Magi cycle in the chapel.

following year. Michelangelo's time as a painting student of Ghirlandaio abruptly ended in 1489 and, to his great delight, he began his study of sculpture in the Medici Academy.

THE MEDICI EXPERIENCE

The Medici dynasty played an important part throughout most of Michelangelo's life and work and a brief digression to consider the history of the family, particularly its relationship with Florence and Michelangelo, is of obvious relevance.

The family name appears as early as the late 12th century and legend has it that the house was founded by the hero Perseus who cut off the head of the gorgon Medusa and gave it to Athene. Benvenuto Cellini's figure of Perseus holding the head of Medusa was placed in the Loggia dei Lanzi in the Piazza della Signoria, Florence, as a symbol of the victory of the Medici over the city.

The first clear family member to emerge was Salvestro, who led a revolt in Florence in 1378 which gained him great public popularity and permanently linked the Medici name with the city of Florence.

However, it was Cosimo de' Medici (1389–1464) who cemented the association. He became known as *pater patriae*, 'father of the fatherland', and achieved what is theoretically impossible; he became absolute ruler of Florence while it remained a republic devoted to its liberty. He assumed no office, suborned no form of government and always adopted the appearance and demeanour of a courteous private citizen. He had a great affection for the arts, was devoted to his business (wool and banking), and maintained a friendly association with the papal court. As the result of a conspiracy by a rival family, the Albizzi, he was exiled for a period but returned in 1434. For the next three centuries the Medici family played an integral part in the history of Florence.

After Cosimo's return he took control of Florentine affairs by exiling, by consent, his citizen rivals to all parts of the country. Nevertheless, he did not assume the role of a tyrant prince, as happened in other cities, but consolidated his power by control of an elected magistracy which retained office for periods of five years. It should be noted that he also devised the magistracy system to suit his needs; but it also suited the republicans – and it worked.

Cosimo's regal and generous patronage of arts and

Angelo Poliziano (1454–94)
One of the group of philosophers and writers assembled by Lorenzo the Magnificent to whom he had dedicated his translation of a part of Homer's *Iliad.* He left behind a body of poetry in Greek and Latin and was appointed tutor to the family of Lorenzo de' Medici. His principle interest here is that he took Michelangelo under his wing and transmitted his interest in Humanism to the young student. As noted elsewhere, he was one of many who were greatly affected by Savonarola's preaching.

letters gave him the effective status of a royal ruler without any suggestion of tyranny. In addition to his own palace in Florence he built other palatial villas in nearby cities and in the countryside and built the church of San Lorenzo in Florence, the location of much of Michelangelo's Florentine work. He was the patron of many artists, including Donatello, Ghiberti, Brunelleschi and Lucca della Robbia. He acquired many ancient Greek and Latin documents and at his own expense opened the first public library at San Marco, began the study of Platonic philosophy, and arranged to have the young Marsilio Ficino trained in philosophy and Greek in order to have the complete works of Plato available in Latin, while through Ficino the Platonic Academy was formed.

While listening to the Latin version of one of Plato's dialogues, Cosimo died on 1 August 1464 at the age of 75. The title of *pater patriae* was certainly justified.

But the Medici role, as defined by Cosimo, seemed unlikely to survive when his son, Piero (1416–69), succeeded him. Known as 'the Gouty', Piero managed to quell one plot against his leadership but showed none of his father's abilities or interests and died five years later leaving two sons, Lorenzo (1449–92) and Giuliano.

Lorenzo, the elder, quickly asumed the reins of power and founded what became the most highly admired and publicized private court of the Renaissance. Eventually known as 'the Magnificent' he began, without Cosimo's financial ability but great determination, to carry on Cosimo's astute political policy. Moreover, he had nobler

Marsilio Ficino (1433–99)

A philosopher and scholar, Ficino was born near Florence and was a member of the Renaissance Platonist school. Since his father, a physician, was a friend of Cosimo de' Medici, the young Marsilio was encouraged and supported by Cosimo in his studies, and became the head of the Platonic Academy. Ficino studied both Latin and Greek and devoted most of his later life to the translation and interpretation of Plato and his followers. Like other philosophers and intellectuals of his day, he was much involved with the Christian/pagan dichotomy and produced his own modernized version of Platonic philosophy. His influence steadily widened in Italy and Europe and close association with Lorenzo de' Medici (the Magnificent), Cosimo's grandson, who had been his pupil, caused his retirement when the Medici were expelled in 1494 Michelangelo's Platonist passion was inspired by the writings of Ficino, Pico della Mirandola and other philosophers in the Florentine Platonic Academy.

OPPOSITE
Angelo Poliziano with his pupil Giuliano de' Medici
Detail of a fresco by Domenico Ghirlandaio
Santa Maria Novella, Florence

LEFT
Marsilio Ficino, Humanist leader of the Neo-Platonic Academy in Florence
Detail of a fresco by Domenico Ghirlandaio
Santa Maria Novella, Florence

political beliefs and ambitions and his devotion to the arts and literature was as strong if not stronger than Cosimo's. He also had a passionate and less cautious temperament and was more capable of tyrannical behaviour.

Not surprisingly he acquired a number of enemies, including the Pazzi family (see page 54) and Pope Sixtus IV, who excommunicated him; but with the help of the king of Aragon he emerged as complete master of Florence. He further manipulated the magistracy to the extent that he ended up with a council of 70, which

Pico della Mirandola (1463–94)

Born in Mirandola, a small independent territory near Ferrara, and son of the prince of the area, Pico became a philosopher and exponent of Platonism and is highly regarded as an important Renaissance scholar.

He was a precocious child and studied law at Bologna, Aristotelian philosophy at Padua and learned Hebrew, Aramaic and Arabic. He visited Florence and Paris and in Rome proposed to defend 900 Christian theses in a public disputation in 1486, although this was banned by Pope Innocent VIII on the grounds that some were heretical.

He was allowed to settle in Florence at the request of Lorenzo de' Medici and joined the Platonic Academy where he remained, apart from short trips to Ferrara, for the rest of his short life. Despite his early death, his philosophical writings and his reputation as a philosopher, exploring and reconciling the philosophies of Plato and Aristotle, have made him an important figure in the development of Platonist Christian studies.

In his last years he came under the influence of Savonarola and remained a Christian. His influence upon the Platonic Academy and upon the developing Neo-Platonism was significant. Michelangelo was at the Medici School during this time.

ensured his personal security. Florence was still nominally a republic but Lorenzo was in charge of everything – virtually a tyrant. In many ways he exemplified Machiavelli's *Prince*, but as one commentator, the writer Guicciardini observed: 'If Florence was to have a tyrant, she could never have found a better or more pleasant one.'

However, Lorenzo is historically best remembered for his great contribution to letters and the arts, although his effect on Florentine industry, commerce and public works was enormous. The parity that citizens enjoy today was entirely absent during the Middle Ages and into the early beginnings of the Renaissance, but a development towards equality of citizenship began under Lorenzo in Florence, where it was taken further than in any other city in the world.

Lorenzo appointed able citizens from all levels of society to the highest posts and even the peasants in the fields were well regarded and prospered. Lorenzo and the Medici family became known throughout Italy and Lorenzo became an international influence on Italian affairs. It might be said that Lorenzo's motives were not entirely without self-interest – but Florentine society worked, and the pragmatic approach certainly proved itself. Lorenzo remains one of the most admired figures of the Renaissance. Moreover, he had the good sense to sponsor Michelangelo.

The one significant point that should be drawn from this brief examination of the Medici is that there is no representative parallel to be found today of the unique cultural, intellectual, political and social climate and power that Lorenzo created through intelligent but often unprincipled behaviour, as well as commercial and political intrigue. It was not a dictatorship either in name or in fact and functioned on persuasion rather than force.

In addition to the many works of art and classical writings that he had inherited from his grandfather, Cosimo, Lorenzo the Magnificent had formed his own unique collection comprising specimens of ancient sculpture, paintings and engravings which were made available to students. He had noticed that sculpture had been neglected when compared with painting, and had made a special sculptural collection (to Michelangelo's later delight), which he placed in a school under the guidance of a sculptor, Bertoldo di Giovanni (1420–91), who had been a pupil of Donatello (see page 58).

OPPOSITE

Pico della Mirandola by Botticelli

Fresco

Louvre, Paris

The Pazzi Conspiracy

This is a typical and unpleasant example of the kind of bloodthirsty intrigue not uncommon in Renaissance Italy.

The Pazzi were Florentine patricians, like their rivals the Medici, and also like them had consolidated their social position through architectural patronage (e.g. Brunelleschi's Pazzi Chapel in the Church of Santa Croce). Believing themselves under threat from the Medici, and encouraged by Pope Sixtus IV (who built the Sistine Chapel), they concluded that they would have to rid Florence of Medici tyranny, as they would have described it.

Their plan involved killing both Lorenzo the Magnificent and his brother Giuliano, and was simple and ingenious. They were to be attacked when at their most vulnerable – while attending mass, and at the moment of the Elevation of the Host. Who would do the killing? The priest, of course – he was nearest. In the event, Francesco de' Pazzi succeeded in stabbing Giuliano to death but Lorenzo escaped with a throat wound, rallied Medici support, and the conspirators were themselves killed. The effect was to increase Medici support. Niccolò Machiavelli's account is interesting and revealing:

Jacopo de' Pazzi's body was dragged naked through the street by the noose with which he had been hanged; then he was thrown into the Arno, the waters of which were at their highest. Truly a great example of fortune, to see a man of such wealth fall into such unprosperity with such ruin and such contempt.

The Foundling Hospital (Ospedale degli Innocenti) *1419*

The Florentine Silk Guild determined to build a safe asylum for the abandoned children of the city and asked Filippo Brunelleschi (1377–1446), one of their members, to present a design which resulted in his first formal presentation. Its portico, with round arches on monolithic Corinthian columns and giant pilasters, became the hallmark of his style. The present building, though basically Brunelleschi's personal vision, was completed over a period of time and in the end carried elements other than those intended by Brunelleschi.

Donatello had been born in Florence and became the most important master sculptor of the early Renaissance. With regard to Michelangelo, Donatello's primary significance is twofold. He was the first sculptor whose work Michelangelo directly studied and which he came to revere. Secondly, and most significantly, he was the first since classical times to make free-standing, complete and independent statues, which was a departure from the tradition of earlier Christian church sculpture. Michelangelo was later to follow his lead, making both free-standing and architecturally-related sculpture – including some with architectural elements which he had designed himself.

It seems that Michelangelo was initially instructed in modelling, but he quickly turned to carving in marble; the first attempt is believed to have been a mask of a faun in the late Roman style which is now in the Bargello Museum of Florence.

Another early example of his carving is a white marble relief depicting the *Battle of the Centaurs* (pages 164–65). This small-scale work showing a number of human figures in energetic athletic poses is both an early indication of Michelangelo's primary interest, the human form (especially the male), and his precocious ability as a sculptor. The influence of Bertoldo can also be discerned in this student work.

It is reported that Lorenzo sent for Michelangelo's father, who had expressed disgust that his son was becoming a 'stone carver', but later so effectively modified his views that he offered his services to Lorenzo, with those of his whole family, with the most exaggerated expressions of gratitude. As a result, Michelangelo became a resident of the palace and met the important scholars, philosophers and statesmen who were part of Lorenzo's entourage. He was now able to study under the most favourable circumstances and was given special individual treatment.

The famous philosopher, Angelo Poliziano (see page 50), aparently took him under his intellectual wing and introduced Michelangelo to classical philosophy, with particular emphasis on Plato and Platonism, which subsequently became a central part of Michelangelo's intellectual life. While at the school, Michelangelo also read the works of the Italian poets, Boccaccio, Petrarch and especially Dante.

Another of influence to the young Michelangelo at

OPPOSITE

Sketches of babies and cherubs by Michelangelo

Pen and ink on paper

British Museum, London

Bertoldo di Giovanni (1454–94)

Bertoldo was a pupil of Donatello and completed the work on the pulpits of San Lorenzo left unfinished by Donatello. Bertoldo was a close friend of Lorenzo the Magnificent and was in charge of the Medici School where Michelangelo was a pupil. Not a great deal of his work remains and most consists of bronzes, reflecting the influence of Donatello. He was a link with the past where Michelangelo was concerned, since Donatello, with Verrocchio, were responsible for developing early Renaissance sculpture.

The equestrian figure of Gattamelata by Donatello *(1453)*
Bronze
Piazza del Santo, Padua

DONATELLO (DONATO DI NICCOLÒ BARDI) C.1386–1466

Trained first as a goldsmith and later in the studio of the sculptor Ghiberti, Donatello was one of the most significant sculptors of the early Renaissance. His contemporaries included the painter Masaccio and the architect Brunelleschi, whom he accompanied to Rome to study the classical forms seminal to the development of art during the 15th century in Italy; with Brunelleschi's architecture and Donatello's sculpture we encounter the quintessential Renaissance spirit. Donatello's influence was passed to Michelangelo through Bertoldo, Donatello's pupil.

this time was the painter, Tommaso Masaccio (1401–28), a contemporary of Donatello and with him a progenitor of the art of the early Renaissance in Florence. He was born near Milan and, although living only to the age of about 27, painted a number of important frescoes in the Brancacci Chapel in the church of Santa Maria del Carmine in Florence. These famous works are a pictorial parallel to the sculptural achievement of Donatello and became another source of inspiration for Michelangelo, who made copies of Masaccio's murals while working in the chapel with other students from the Medici School. Perhaps the most famous of these is the *Tribute Money* (overleaf).

A small but significant incident occurred in the Brancacci Chapel which had a permanent effect on Michelangelo. During a visit there, a quarrel broke out with another student, Pietro Torrigiano, which resulted in Michelangelo's nose being broken. The effect lasted for the rest of his life and his face retained the damaged, unattractive appearance which is evident in portraits of him. It may also have been responsible for the fierce reputation that pursued him thereafter.

It appears that Torrigiano, who, it is said, had a quick and jealous temper, harboured envious thoughts because of Michelangelo's increasing closeness to the Medici, though Torrigiano claimed that it was because Michelangelo had made sarcastic remarks at his expense. This may be true since Michelangelo was known for what might be called 'unmeasured language' and is reported as losing many friends in later life as a result. Torrigiano was obliged to flee Florence as a result of the fight and after visiting Spain and the Netherlands went to England where his best-known work is the tomb of Henry VII and Elizabeth of York (Westminster Abbey, London, 1512). Torrigiano was eventually imprisoned and killed in Spain by the Inquisition in 1528

While at the Medici School, other influences of more long-term significance to Michelangelo occurred. The early death of Lorenzo at the age of 44 in 1492 affected the school and Pietro (1471–1503), Lorenzo's son who succeeded him, did not have his father's devotion to the arts or the Academy. As already noted, Savonarola was the prior at the nearby monastery of San Marco, and deeply disturbed by what he saw of the practices in the higher levels of the Roman church and the moral laxity of society in general, preached a series of Lenten

Masaccio (Tommaso di Giovanni di Simone Guidi) 1401–28

Despite his early death, Masaccio was of immense importance to the development of painting, as vital as Donatello was to sculpture and Brunelleschi to architecture. His significance lies in the introduction of a comprehensible expression of natural space, including a coherent linear perspective. He provides a link between Giotto and the High Renaissance style of Raphael and Michelangelo. His frescoes in the Brancacci Chapel in Santa Maria del Carmine represent a milestone in the development of the medium and Michelangelo was greatly influenced by them. There is a comparison to be made between the *Tribute Money* (overleaf) and Michelangelo's *Fall of Man* (page 289 et seq.), in that both contain a time dimension.

sermons in the cathedral of Florence in 1491. In these he launched a excoriating attack on the wicked self-indulgence of the Florentines and the failure of the church leaders to maintain the standards of morality expected of true believers.

Michelangelo, 15 years old, was confronted with a crisis of belief – as indeed were most of the citizens of the city, and it was at this time that his elder brother joined the Dominicans. The city of Florence was shocked into dramatic action. Humanists recanted and became reborn Christians, and what were called the 'vanities', which included the work of painters, were burnt on public bonfires. Members of the great Florentine families took holy orders, the ordinary citizens tried to reform their

OPPOSITE

The Tribute Money by Masaccio

(c.1427)

Fresco mural

Brancacci Chapel, Santa Maria del Carmine, Florence

The importance of this image is that it depicts separate events in time. Christ, in the centre, surrounded by his disciples, is being approached by a tax gatherer, while St. Peter is quietly fishing on the left. St. Peter can be seen again on the right, this time paying the tax man. (See also Michelangelo's Fall of Man, *page 289 et seq.)*

LEFT

Battle of Cascina *(1504–05)*

Charcoal on paper

Uffizi, Florence

A sketch by Michelangelo for an early work which was never completed.

behaviour and bewailed their probable incarceration in Purgatory or Hell unless they swiftly mended their ways. Michelangelo fled briefly to Venice in 1494 after some alarming experiences discussed later. Florence, previously prosperous and self-satisfied, began to reflect on its ways and became a deeply disturbed community.

The Church in Rome, led by Pope Alexander VI (Rodrigo Borgia), of whom more will be said later, was not unreasonably enraged by Savonarola's attack on the Church, and with what should have been a guilty conscience but was probably extreme irritation, demanded Savonarola's presence in Rome, where he was regarded as a 'pestilent heretic'. The pope proclaimed the unlikely intention of making Savonarola a cardinal, while Savonarola, not entirely convinced, was wise enough to find it too difficult to meet His Holiness. But the notorious Borgia pope was not to be thwarted and eventually, in 1498, having excommunicated Savonarola, succeeded in having him, with two other priests from San Marco, hanged and the bodies burnt in the Piazza della Signoria, Florence, where Michelangelo's *David* would later be placed.

As a result, Botticelli broke with the Medici and his *Calumny of Apelles* (1498) is said to express his detestation of the way Savonarola had been treated.

It is an interesting sideline of history that as Prior of San Marco, and before the pope was able to catch up with him, Savonarola had enjoyed considerable influence in Florence, which he used to notable effect. After the expulsion of Pietro de' Medici in 1494 he lent his support to the election of a popular republican government and, under his persuasion Florence became the first and only republic so far to elect Jesus Christ as King. This did not last long.

While at the Medici School, it will be remembered that Michelangelo had also come into direct contact with some of the great Humanist philosophers in the Medici court and had, in his teens, already begun to absorb the Platonist and Neo-Platonist philosophies. The death of Lorenzo was followed, in the same year as Pietro's expulsion, by that of two great philosophers of the Medici court, Angelo Poliziano and Pico della Mirandola, both younger than Lorenzo. The loss to Michelangelo of Poliziano was particularly important since, as already noted, he had been a mentor and philosophical guide to the young student.

Girolamo Savonarola (1452–98)

Born in Ferrara, Savonarola became a Dominican monk at Bologna in 1474, and after an uninspired start eventually became a highly effective and inspiring preacher. In 1482 he was sent to Florence and in the following year preached the Lenten sermons in the church of San Lorenzo to little effect and a small congregation. He was moved to a number of locations from that date and returned to Florence in 1490. In the following year he was appointed Prior of San Marco and was invited to preach in the cathedral.

This was the beginning of his rise to a powerful role in the life of Florence, when he become a serious problem to Lorenzo de' Medici who demanded more respect as head of state than Savonarola was prepared to give. Savonarola claimed that his election as prior was due to God rather than Lorenzo. He rejected the demands of the senior citizens and accurately predicted the imminent deaths of Lorenzo, the pope and the king of Naples. Prophecy tends to impress and Savonarola became something of a celebrity. In 1492 Lorenzo and Pope Innocent VIII died and the populace turned anxiously to Savonarola for guidance.

The new pope was Alexander VI, Rodrigo Borgia, which did little to increase public confidence and again the population turned to Savonarola.

Savonarola's influence increased rapidly and he was appointed vicar-general of the Dominican order in Tuscany (1493) when his preaching turned to the matter of moral reform within the church. He was the guiding spirit in the return of Florence to a republic; his preaching also demanded a return to high moral values and the rejection of vice and self-indulgence.

This was a difficult time politically. Pietro de' Medici had replaced Lorenzo and his incompetence, much too all-embracing to be detailed here, resulted in Charles VIII of France entering Florence in 1494 with demands that the republic's officials could not accept; with Savonarola's backing, they obliged Charles to withdraw within a week, though Pietro was expelled. The people turned to Savonarola whom they perceived as their saviour and, amazingly, Savonarola replaced the Medici as ruler. His first action, unique in history, was to relieve the starving populace, reduce taxes, and exhort all men to place their trust in the Lord. Like the Medici, Savonarola became dictator of Florence without holding office.

His efforts were directed towards the return of Florence to spiritual matters and the annual carnival of 1497 was celebrated by the 'bonfire of the vanities' in the Piazza della Signoria. Although this suggests that he was opposed to learning and the arts, this is not so, and he saved the famous Medici library when it was threatened with sale to pay debts.

However, his biggest test was still to come. Pope Alexander VI was neither pleased by what Savonarola had said about him nor Savonarola's effective activities in Florence. He therefore invited him to Rome to accept a cardinal's hat. Savonarola politely replied that he was unable to leave Florence. Following a sordid and duplicitous negotiation, however, Savonarola and two of his priests were executed and burnt in the Piazza della Signoria on a site which today is marked with a plaque.

Sandro Botticelli (Alessandro di Mariano dei Filipepi) 1444–1510

There are a number of confusing accounts and stories of Botticelli's early life and even the name by which he is known has different suggested origins. His real name was Filipepi, but it is supposed that his elder brother's nickname, Botticelli ('little barrel'), had been passed on to him.

His father was a poor tanner, but Sandro was sent to be trained as a goldsmith. However, he showed a greater aptitude for drawing and painting and was apprenticed to the notable painter Fra Filippo Lippi in 1458 or 59 and remained with him until 1467.

Like many of his Florentine contemporaries, Botticelli soon came to the notice of the powerful Medici family and benefited from their patronage when he was attached to the house of Lorenzo the Magnificent.

The quality of his painting was so delicately attractive that he quickly earned a reputation for excellence; many of his works have come to reflect one major aspect of the Renaissance in that he was influenced, as were many others, by the preaching of Savonarola (page 63), when such pagan works as the *Primavera* and the *Birth of Venus* gave way to religious works such as the *Mourning over the Body of Christ* (shown opposite).

For many writers Botticelli epitomizes the earlier stages of Renaissance painting. His earlier work was focused on classical themes from earlier times and the philosophies of Platonism and Humanism were important to him. At the same time he also contributed to the life of the Church and was commissioned around 1482 by Sixtus IV to paint an Old Testament scene on the lower walls of the Sistine Chapel in the Vatican. He was also responsible, in the late 1490s, for illustrations for Dante's *Inferno.*

Whether he was painting classical mythology or providing religious messages in paint the quality of his craftsmanship remains his greatest attraction.

This period was one of great significance for Michelangelo and helped consolidate his views. The effect of Savonarola's attack on the practices of the Church and the attachment to Platonist philosophy he had acquired from the Medici Academy was to strengthen Michelangelo's faith while he absorbed the wisdom and values of classical philosophy. Students of Michelangelo are in general agreement that this Christian Platonism remained the keystone of his belief during his adult life, a fact which is of central importance to his work and which will be considered further.

After only a short stay in Venice, Michelangelo moved to Bologna as the guest of the Aldrovandi family, where he continued his study of the Italian writers of the previous century, Dante, Boccaccio and Petrarch. As a result, he developed an interest in literature, began to write poetry, and became a recognized authority on Dante. This signals his move at this time towards wider aspects of Italian culture, a growing intellectual curiosity, and the extension of his creative range.

At this time, Michelangelo's work was focused almost exclusively on sculpture – which naturally pleased him. He began an intense study of the human body that was

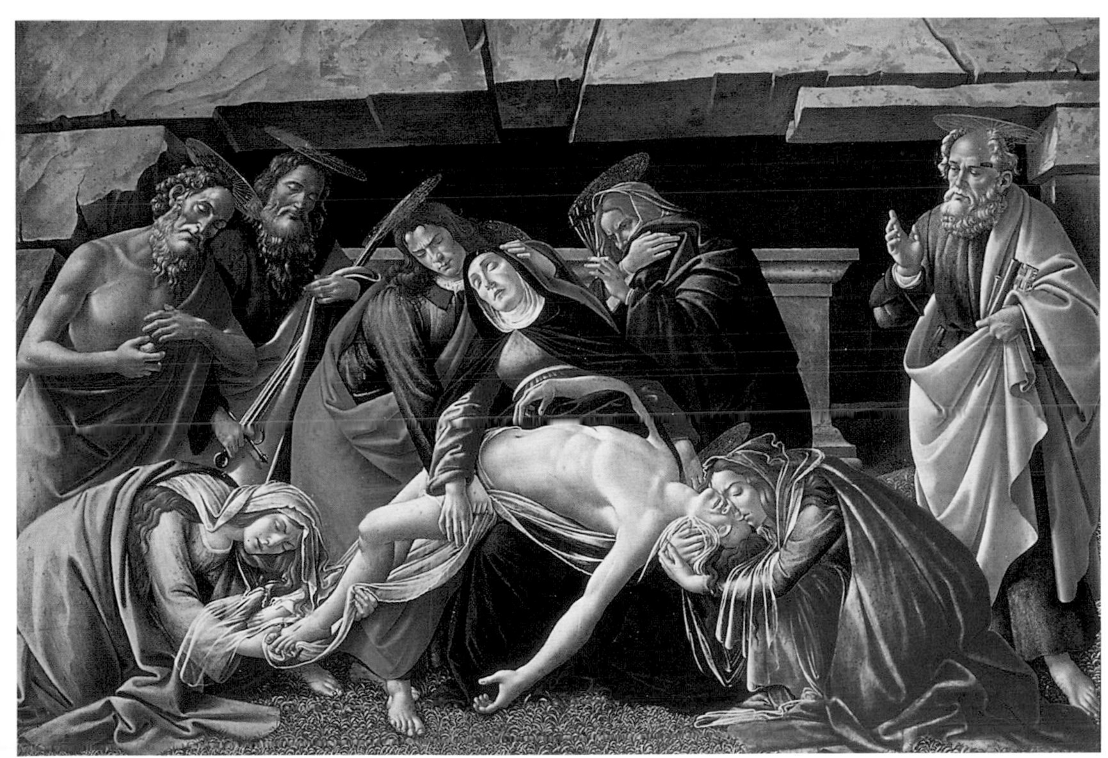

The Mourning over the Body of Christ by Botticelli *(1495)*

Portrait of Dante Alighieri (1265–1321)

Engraved by Stephane Pannemaker (1847–1930) after a work by Gustave Doré (1832–83) for the frontispiece of The Vision of Hell, *published by Cassell, 1903.*

Dante was one of the earlier figures of the pre-Renaissance period whose work had considerable later influence and was much admired and studied by Michelangelo. Born in Florence, he was exiled in 1302. His most celebrated work, the Divine Comedy *(1300–21), a complex poetical analysis of the imagined afterlife, was not published until 1472, only three years before Michelangelo was born. Dante wrote many works of poetry and his interest in such figures as Cicero, Virgil and Constantine preceded the awakening of classicism in the Renaissance.*

later to manifest itself in his uniquely personal expression of emotion in the human form. With the help of the Prior of Santo Spirito, who obtained them from a nearby hospital, he began to dissect human bodies, and this provided him, as an artist, with unprecedented information with regard to anatomy. (It should be said that Leonardo da Vinci also undertook dissections after he had acquired the bodies of hanged felons. However, he was more interested in how the human body worked than as a means of artistic expression.)

FIRST ROMAN PERIOD

Michelangelo returned to Florence in 1495 at the age of 20. However, he was offered no commissions of sufficient importance and having been deceived into participating in the creation of a spurious antique was recommended to visit Rome for the first time in the following year, where, he was told, his talents would be appreciated. There are other versions of this story which involve the figure of a sleeping Cupid, carved by Michelangelo, which so closely resembled an ancient work that it was suggested that he discolour it to make it look older still. In retrospect this was ill-advised, but for his own amusement he agreed and it was eventually sold by a dealer (how he obtained it is not recorded) to a Cardinal Riario in Rome, who realized it was a fake. The cardinal decided to confront Michelangelo, but invited him to Rome once he had seen his work.

Michelangelo arrived on 25 June 1496, thus avoiding the Savonarola debacle. He remained there for about 5 years, after which time he returned to Florence in the summer of 1501. He was greeted in Rome by Cardinal Giovanni Riario who clearly forgave Michelangelo his deception and invited him to look at his collection of statues and offer an opinion. The letter that Michelangelo wrote to his friend Lorenzo de' Medici, though addressed to Sandro Botticelli, is worth reading, since it says a great deal by implication:

11 July 1496. Magnificent Lorenzo. This is to inform you how, that on Saturday last we arrived safely, and without loss of time proceeded to visit the Cardinal of San Giorgio, to whom I presented your letter. He appeared to be glad to see me and immediately expressed a wish that I should go to see certain figures which occupied me all that day, so that on that day I delivered no other of your letters. Afterwards on Sunday the Cardinal came to the new

OPPOSITE
An example of Michelangelo's handwriting
British Museum, London

house and inquired for me. I went to him and he asked what I thought of the things which I had seen; regarding these I said what I felt and I certainly think that there are many beautiful things. The Cardinal then asked me if I was disposed to make something beautiful, I answered that I could not do such fine things, but that he should see what I could do. We have purchased a piece of marble to make a figure, lifesize, and on Monday I shall begin to work. On Monday last I presented your other letters of recommendation to Rucellai, who offered me what money I might want, also those to Cavalcante. I then delivered the letter to Baldassare and demanded the Cupid from him, and said that I would repay him his money; he replied very roughly that he would rather break it in a hundred pieces, that he had bought it and it was his, and that he had letters, that he had satisfied him who sent it, and that he never expected to have to return it, and he complained much of your having spoken ill of him. Some of our Florentines here have attempted to make up matters between us but without success ...
May God keep you from evil. Michelangelo in Rome.

Michelangelo had been treated with respect by a great figure of the church, despite the fraud, and this could only have been because of the reputation he had already achieved in Florence. It was also evident that he was able to have contact with such a figure through a Medici – a family at that time disgraced in Florence. It should be noted, incidentally, that the letter was addressed to Sandro Botticelli, the painter living in Florence, to avoid it being opened by enemies of the Medici. The attempt to get the Cupid back from the dealer, Baldassare, is an interesting indication of some straight talking on both sides. 'May God keep you from evil' is perhaps a stronger sign of affection than 'Best regards'!

The life-sized figure for which Michelangelo had purchased the marble was his *Bacchus* (page 72), which for unknown reasons he did not start for a year. It is interesting to note that both Bacchus and Cupid are pre-Christian subjects and that the works were for a cardinal of the Church of Rome, indicating that the interest in pagan mythology was still strong.

At this point it is necessary to return briefly to Florence, where Michelangelo's family was experiencing financial difficulties. His father was deeply in debt and his brothers were of no great assistance. As already stated, Michelangelo's elder brother, Leonardo, physically ill, had become a Dominican monk and had removed himself from the family. Michelangelo's favourite younger brother, Buonarroto, only two years his junior, had become a cloth merchant, established in business through Michelangelo's generosity, and was having a relatively successful career both in commerce and public service. He became a captain of the Guelph party in 1519, *gonfaloniere* of his company in 1521, and died of the plague in 1528. Giovan Simone was the fourth son, who joined his family in business but was wasteful and lazy, caused Michelangelo much heartache, and died in 1548. Sigismund, the fifth son, was a soldier with a quiet personality who died in 1555.

Michelangelo survived them all, sacrificed much, and though often repaid with ingratitude continued to be an affectionate brother. He was conscious of his role as senior son and did not shirk the responsibility; but concern for his family was a constant part of his life, nagging away in the background, and a worry from which he could never be free. The effect of all this was that from time to time he himself experienced monetary difficulties, even though he was so highly regarded and rewarded.

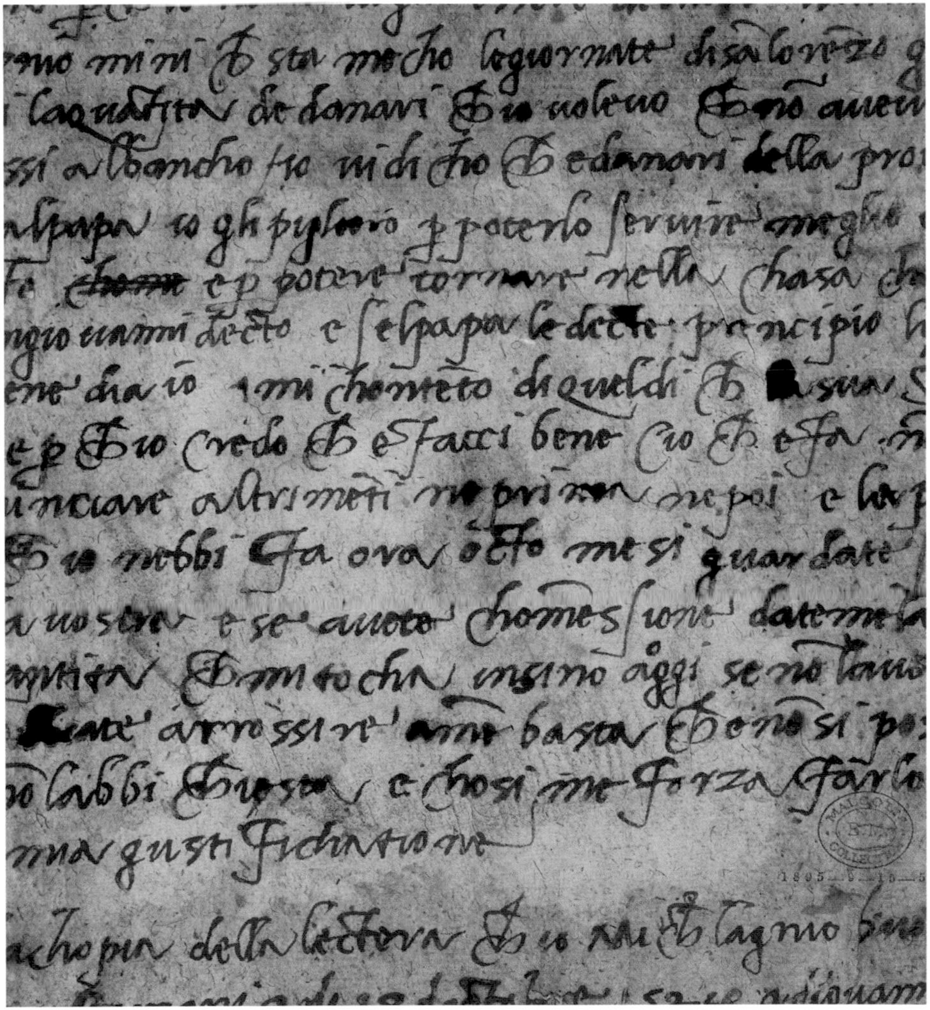

RIGHT
Pietà *(detail) 1497–98*
Marble, 5ft 8½ in (174cm) in height
St. Peter's, Rome

This work is discussed and illustrated more fully on pages 191 et seq., but it is significant that it is the only work that Michelangelo actually signed, the signature appearing on the band crossing the Madonna's breast. The Pietà is a remarkable achievement for one so young and Michelangelo was obviously satisfied with his work.

OPPOSITE
Map of Florence, by Stefano Bonsignori *(1584)*
Engraving

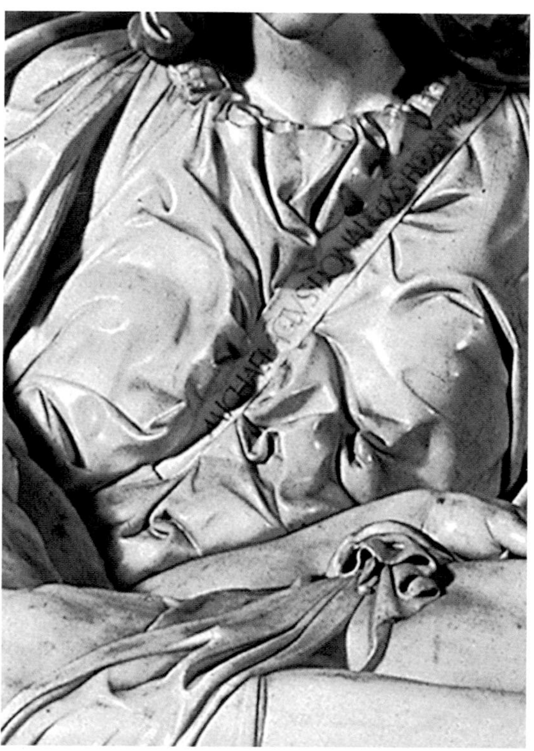

In Rome, the cardinal, whose real interest lay solely in the collection of ancient sculpture, did not purchase any of Michelangelo's work and the *Bacchus* was eventually commissioned by a Signor Iacopo Galli, a Roman collector of some discernment.

In a letter to his father in August 1497, Michelangelo refers to a commission which Pietro de' Medici was intending but which never materialized. Michelangelo decided to use the marble for a work of his own choice, but this, too, appears to have been delayed while he finished his *Bacchus* and the most important and significant work that he completed in Rome during his first visit, the *Pietà* for St. Peter's, commissioned in 1497 when he was 22 years of age. For such a young man the sensitivity of this work is astonishing and was more than indicative of his extraordinary abilities.

Michelangelo was 26 when he returned to Florence in 1501 and had already achieved considerable fame. Before he left Rome, he had received a letter from his father, the contents of which are interesting. It is too long to include it in its entirety, but two extracts are worth quoting:

Buonarroto tells me that you live with great economy or rather penury. Economy is a good thing, but penurious

RIGHT
Bacchus *(c.1497)*
Marble, 72½in (184cm) in height
Museo Nazionale del Bargello, Florence

In Greek mythology Dionysus (Bacchus) was originally a fertility god, but in later traditions became the god of wine, when he was associated with wild and orgiastic rites (evidence of the wild excesses of the bacchanalia can be seen in this sculpture). However, the modelling is rather softer than that of the Pietà *(191 et seq.), produced around the same time.*

OPPOSITE
Angel with Candelabrum
(c. 1495–96)
Basilica di San Domenico, Bologna

Part of the tomb of St. Dominic with the two saints, Petronius and Proculus.

habits are bad, and displeasing to God and to people of this world, besides they will injure you in soul and body. While you are yet young, you may bear the inconvenience for a time, but when the strength of youth is gone, maladies and infirmities will declare themselves the consequences of poor living and of penurious habits.

A caring father's message, perhaps; but who was responsible for his son's poverty? It continues:

Buonarroto tells me that you have that youth with you, that is Piero di Giannotto; he tells me that he is a good youth and loves you and is faithful. I recommend him to you, and act towards him as he does to you.

What does this mean? Does Michelangelo have an assistant? It does not sound like one. Dare we think lover? And what does 'love' mean in this context?

FIRST CREATIVE PERIOD

It should be said that Michelangelo was happy and busy in Rome and it was only as a result of strong appeals from his father that he was persuaded to return to Florence. His fame and reputation as a devout Christian and dedicated republican had preceded him and he was soon in demand in his native Tuscany, where he received commissions from the Florentine administration. His first contract, however, was with the cardinal archbishop of Siena, Francesco Piccolomini, for a number of statues for Siena cathedral which, accompanied by a blatant insult, stipulated that they should be better executed than those that he had made in Rome, failing which they should be done again. The contract called for 15 statues between 4ft and 4 ft 6 in (1.2 and 1.4m) in height and were destined for the Piccolomini altar in the cathedral. But, as usual, only some of them were completed (page 189).

The first important Florentine commission, from the cathedral of Florence, was for the heroic figure of the Biblical *David* (known as 'the Giant'), which was completed in 1504 and set up in the Piazza della Signoria in a commanding position in front of the Palazzo Pubblico. It marked the beginning of Michelangelo's first great creative period and public recognition of both his artistic ability and his Florentine citizenship. The sculpture remained in the piazza until 1873 when it was relocated in the Academmia gallery and replaced by a copy. The pedestal for the statue was designed by Pollaiuolo and Antonio da San Gallo: Michelangelo was not regarded as an architect at that time.

***St. Proculus** (1495)*
Marble
Basilica of San Domenico, Bologna

Michelangelo was about 20 when he completed this work and this detail shows something of his forceful nature, the quality of terribilità *which became attached to his character later on. The tomb was commissioned by Francesco Aldrovandi.*

While occupied with the *David* and the Piccolomini contract, Michelangelo was also working on a number of other contracts, most of which are lost; but a statue of St. Matthew and a relief of the Virgin and Child survive. Between 1501 and his return to Rome, commissions for 37 statues and reliefs of different sizes are recorded.

This quantity of work produced over such a short period of time seems to confirm the popular belief that Michelangelo was a solitary worker, disdaining assistants and beavering away quietly in his workshop. This is part of the Michelangelo myth. In fact, there is clear evidence that he used assistants, and this is confirmed in letters and other documents; but it is also clear that he was difficult to please, could be irascible, and probably had no regular assistants working for him. On the other hand, the evidence that he worked mainly on his own is offered by the unfinished work he left behind. It is also important to remember that he was a young man of less than 30 years of age and possessed of a great deal of physical energy.

One work that was completed was a picture for his friend, Angelo Doni, known as the Doni Tondo. It is unusual in that it is in tempera, the only existing example of Michelangelo's use of the method. The subject is the Holy Family, and the group is surrounded by an early example of Michelangelo's familiar nude youths, probably inspired by a painter whom Michelangelo admired, Luca Signorelli, whose similar studies clearly appealed to him.

After the *David*, Michelangelo received a state commission for a monumental painting to be a companion piece to a work by Leonardo da Vinci, the *Battle of Anghiari*, already being prepared by Leonardo on a wall in the great hall of the Municipal Council. It is an indication of the respect and admiration that Michelangelo already commanded that he should have been set in direct competition with the great master of the day, 23 years his senior, even though Michelangelo was already known as a man of passionate energy and wild spirit, soon to be identified as *furia* or *terribilità*.

Michelangelo began in October 1504 and had barely finished the cartoon for the painting when his time in Florence was interrupted by a call from Pope Julius II (Giuliano della Rovere), who was to become one of his most important and difficult clients. This was his first papal commission and a call he would have been unwise to refuse. (One only has to recall the power, both spiritual and temporal, that popes wielded during the Renaissance, which has been a source of wonderment, dismay – even disbelief – to later generations.) It was also a sculptural commission and therefore a positive attraction from Michelangelo's point of view.

Leonardo finished his cartoon by 1505, intending to use the method he had invented for the *Last Supper* in Milan, the history of which is well known. The method was a failure, with the result that, although regarded with

St. Matthew *(detail) c.1503–05*
Marble, 8ft 10¾in (2.7m) in height
Galleria dell' Accademia, Florence

(See also pages 200–201)

Study for the Battle of Anghiari by Leonardo da Vinci *(1504–05)*
Pen and ink, 6 x 6⅛in (14.7 x 15.5cm)
Galleria dell' Accademia, Venice

This drawing shows the schematic character of Leonardo's intention, rather than the study of the figures and their grouping that typifies Michelangelo's preparatory drawing for the Battle of Cascina *(page 61).*

wonder it has been the subject of constant restoration ever since. Unfinished and in a ruinous condition, the *Last Supper* was painted over by Vasari who commented that it was then 'a muddle of blots'. Michelangelo completed neither the cartoon nor the painting.

SECOND ROMAN VISIT

Michelangelo arrived in Rome early in 1505 at the age of 30. Julius II had a major commission for him, one which, like most of Michelangelo's large works, was never completed. Julius was planning a funerary monument, a sepulchre for himself to be placed in St. Peter's in Rome after his death. Hower, it was still not finished after 40 years of altercations and at least six separate design schemes. What was finished was eventually placed in San Pietro in Vincoli, the most admired single work for the tomb being the noble and awesome figure of *Moses*.

THE CHURCH IN THE RENAISSANCE

As noted, Julius II's tomb was Michelangelo's first major commission for a pope, so a few observations on the role of the Church of Rome during the Renaissance would be relevant at this point, together with an understanding of the importance of religion in the lives of every citizen at that time, which was all-encompassing, dogmatic, and altogether differently regarded than it is today.

As well as moral authority, the Church in Renaissance Italy had much greater secular power and political influence than would be conceivable today. The entire population was inextricably involved: all were nominal believers, and most practised their faith. The Roman Church was ruled by a pope who was as near to an absolute monarch of the whole of Italy as is possible, and the priesthood ruled the laity with an iron hand. It was not far removed from overall government of the country until unification occurred in the 19th century. The pope's dread power of excommunication could to some degree replace a standing army – although popes in the Renaissance usually had an army and the pope was himself, in some instances, a very effective and ruthless military commander.

As well as wielding spiritual and temporal power the Church was also the wealthiest single entity in Italy, its riches derived from the commercial influence it exerted over large areas of the land. It could afford to realize its aspirations and fund its requirements better than any other power in the land. Another source of Church income should be mentioned, since it had a damaging effect on later developments. This was the sale of indulgences – grants by the pope of the remission of the temporal punishment in Purgatory still due for sins after absolution.

It should be remembered that not only did Rome bring civilization to Europe, but when, in the fourth century, the Roman Empire under Constantine became Christian, it also spread Christianity, first officially and subsequently with exclusive legality across all its territories, including northern Europe.

By the 14th century, during the late medieval period immediately preceding the Renaissance, Christianity had established itself in all aspects of everyday life as the accepted arbiter of conduct, spiritual, social and intellectual, defended locally by the priesthood and supported politically by the hierarchy in Rome. Locally, the clergy monitored the faithful, from small communities to large cities, and the pope was unassailably in charge. The churches and cathedrals that were at the centre of life were in character far removed from the architecture that had gone before and very different from the temples and public buildings that had preceded them. They were a potent and highly visible reminder to the population of medieval Europe of the new Christianity that had replaced the paganism of Roman classicism.

However, the medieval architectural style was itself replaced in the Renaissance by a return to classical architectural detailing, by implication creating a major new Christian ethos basically different from that which had gone before. The visually dramatic change which occurred over the 14th to 16th centuries indicates the importance of architectural style as a statement of cultural change, though perhaps not as evident in painting and sculpture.

Michelangelo, later in his life, and at the centre of this stage of artistic and architectural renewal in Italy, can have been expected to have contributed to these important times.

THE JULIAN COMMISSIONS

After Michelangelo's absence, when he had been selecting marble at the Carrara mines for the Julian tomb

Milan Cathedral *(late-14th century)*

There was an important but not very unified programme of building in Italy during the late 14th century, which included the Doge's Palace in Venice, the church of St. Petronius in Bologna and the duomo (cathedral) in Milan. Of these, Milan's duomo holds the most dominant architectural role in the development of Italian architecture of the time and carries to this day elements of Renaissance character added in a long process of completion in the 18th century and ending with the spire.

Started in 1386 by Gian Galeazzo Visconti, his personal ambition and the growth of power and the prosperity of the city are represented in the richness of one of the greatest of European churches.

RIGHT
Pavia Cathedral, built after consultation with Bramante
(c. 1492)

Donato Bramante (1444–1514) was consulted in 1488 on the planning of the interior of the cathedral and a large wooden model was made; the building that resulted, though still incomplete, does seem to have incorporated Bramante's ideas. It should be noted that the cathedral was designed with the Hagia Sofia in Constantinople in mind and Bramante was also inspired by it when he designed St. Peter's in Rome.

OPPOSITE
Pope Julius II

From a painting by Raphael (Raffaello Sanzio) in the Pitti Palace, Florence.

through the winter of 1505–06, he returned to Rome where he waited, with restrained enthusiasm and some impatience, in his workshop close to St. Peter's. The design of the massive monument had been approved but it was so large that there was no suitable location within the existing church to accommodate it. After considering possible suggestions from San Gallo and Bramante, Julius decided that St. Peter's should be demolished and a new church built on a larger scale – a remarkably rational decision for a powerful, egotistical man and one that had highly significant effects. Julius asked several architects to prepare designs and selected Donato Bramante's; to his credit, Michelangelo approved the design, despite his private opinion of Bramante's character and behaviour.

At first, Julius was enthusiastic and frequently visited Michelangelo's workshop, even to the extent of having a covered way constructed to facilitate their meeting. However, this unlikely friendship soon disintegrated for reasons that are not clear (different observers offer different reasons). Michelangelo naturally thought that Julius had been listening to Bramante's lies; Bramante was thought to be jealous of Michelangelo's close association with the pope.

Whatever the reason, Julius had certainly changed his mind, and work on the tomb was halted. Not surprisingly, Michelangelo was furious, immediately confronted him, and found that Julius now wanted him to paint the ceiling of the Sistine Chapel (1473–81), built in the Vatican by Pope Sixtus IV and already containing paintings by other notable artists. Michelangelo was further infuriated because he regarded himself as a sculptor and had based his expectations in Rome around the continuance of work on the tomb. He complained bitterly, with the result that he was refused further access to the pope, was summarily dismissed and, most insultingly, was refused payment for work already done. Greatly disillusioned and in some fear for his life, Michelangelo returned to Florence in 1506.

Soon after Michelangelo's departure, Julius, regretting what he had done, sent couriers after him to beg him to return; but Michelangelo, who had managed a rare turn of speed on his horse, had arrived in Florentine territory before he could be overtaken and, no longer under Roman jurisdiction and despite the authority of the pope, refused to return. It is said that Michelangelo had left behind instructions for the sale of all his furniture in

Julius II (Giuliano della Rovere) 1443–1513, Pope, 1503–13

Of all Michelangelo's patrons, Pope Julius II must surely have been the most demanding. He was a friend and admirer of Michelangelo's work, a slave-driver (perhaps because he heavily involved himself in the work) and was as difficult a person as Michelangelo himself.

Giuliano's uncle, Francesco della Rovere, the general of the Franciscan Order, had Giuliano educated by the order and, after he became pope in 1471 as Sixtus IV, made Giuliano cardinal priest of the Church of San Pietro in Vincoli in the Vatican (in which the unfinished tomb of Julius by Michelangelo was eventually placed).

Under the next pope, Innocent VIII, Giuliano received further favours, but on the election of Alexander VI, Rodrigo Borgia, the Spanish pope, he fled first to Ostia and then to France. After the short pontificate of Pius III, he was elected pope in 1503 and governed the Papal States with efficiency and energy as well as leading the papal armies in conflict. He was, by Renaissance standards, a great pope; but those who had hoped for reform since Savonarola's denunciations were bitterly disillusioned, although his death in 1513 was only a short while before the Lutheran Theses (1517) and the beginning of the Reformation.

He became a generous patron of art and literature and in 1506 laid the foundation stone for the new St. Peter's – a symbolic moment of considerable significance. He also began the famous collection of statuary in the Belvedere which included the antique masterpieces, the Apollo Belvedere and Laocoön. He employed, not only Michelangelo, but also other artists, including Raphael and Bramante, and was what could be described as a singular driving force where the arts were concerned.

Rome, indicating that he had no intention of returning. He wrote to the pope telling him that he would never return, that he did not deserve such treatment for his good and faithful service, or to be turned out like a sad fellow, and that since His Holiness was not disposed to pay any further attention to the monument he was freed from obligation – neither would he bind himself to anything else.

This was dangerous in the extreme, bearing in mind the possibility of excommunication. Julius, however, never one to let the grass grow under his feet, was already involved in another, greater project – the rebuilding of St. Peter's. As noted above, he had selected Bramante to prepare a new design for a replacement of the old basilica at the same time that he had asked Michelangelo to undertake the Sistine ceiling. Work began immediately and the first stone was laid the day after Michelangelo left Rome.

This did nothing to alleviate the deep enmity that already existed between Bramante and Michelangelo. Michelangelo believed that he could thank Bramante for being asked to decorate the Sistine Chapel, when he knew full well that it was Michelangelo's passionate wish to continue with the sculpture; in short, he believed that Bramante had set him up. It has to be admitted that Bramante, although he was a brilliant architect, was not universally popular, while Michelangelo was known to be something of a firebrand; it is no surprise that the battle did not end here.

Michelangelo, despite the aggressive tone of his earlier letter, was eventually persuaded by Julius to return. Julius, having recognized that Michelangelo could not easily be bullied, now treated him with a little more respect and even flattery. He agreed to the back payments and promised Michelangelo a new commission, in itself an extraordinary indication of the regard, despite his actions, which the pope actually had for him.

When Michelangelo arrived back in Rome he was given a new contract for a colossal bronze statue of the pope to be placed in St. Petronius' Church in Bologna (part of the new Papal State) which, when completed, was erected on 21 February 1508 over the church porch. (This work was destroyed three years later in a revolution by the Bolognese against Julius; it was broken up, then its fragments were destroyed in a

Sketch for the tomb of Pope Julius II *(1505–45)*
Pen and ink on paper

This was one of many sketches by Michelangelo of his proposals for the troublesome and ultimately uncompleted tomb of Julius II. It is far from the original design and does not clearly indicate who the central figure was to have been. One might have imagined that the pope would have taken the central position but the sketch suggests that it could be the figure of Moses who eventually took the central role as will be indicated in later illustrations.

The Church of Santa Maria delle Grazie, Milan *(c.1492)*

Leonardo da Vinci went to Milan in 1482 to work for the Sforzas, probably met Bramante there soon after his arrival, and both men worked for the duke (Il Moro) until 1499. Leonardo painted his Last Supper *in the refectory of the monastery of Santa Maria delle Grazie at the same time during the 1490s as Bramante was remodelling the eastern part of the church shown in the illustration.*

furnace.) At this point, a section of a letter sent to Michelangelo by his friend, Rosselli, the painter, makes interesting reading:

Dear as a brother, I have to inform you that on Saturday evening the Pope being at supper, I showed him some designs which Bramante and I had to do together, after supper I showed them. He sent for Bramante and said to him 'Sangallo starts tomorrow for Florence, and will bring back with him Michelangelo.' Bramante replied to the Pope and said: 'Holy Father he will not come, for I am intimate with Michelangelo, and he told me that he would not undertake the Chapel, although you insisted upon giving him this charge, but that he would only attend to the monument and not to painting,' and he went on further to say 'Holy Father, I believe that he has not the capacity, for he has not done much of the figure, especially when the figures are high up and foreshortened, which is quite another thing from painting on the ground.'

And so the letter continues. If this had happened as described, there can be no doubt that Michelangelo was right in believing that he had an enemy in Rome.

Early in March 1508 Michelangelo, having completed

The Tempietto, Rome, by Bramante *(c.1502)*

This small building, located in the courtyard of the Franciscan convent of San Pietro in Montorio is, despite its size, perhaps the most notable of Bramante's architectural works. It is thought that it may have been erected by Ferdinand and Isabella of Spain in honour of St. Peter. The importance of the tempietto *is that it is the earliest example of a Doric style temple, confirming Bramante's importance as a classically-inspired architect and stylistic leader.*

the sculptural commission, left Bologna and returned to Florence; but hardly had he settled and started work on unfinished commissions than he was again summoned by Pope Julius. Despite what he had said in his previous response, Michelangelo immediately obeyed and returned to Rome.

Julius II eventually persuaded a reluctant Michelangelo, still in some fear of assassination but anticipating an opportunity to renew his work on the Julian tomb, to undertake the painting of the Sistine ceiling. This fresco, together with the end wall of the same chapel, constitutes the main painting task undertaken by Michelangelo and is an achievement of monumental proportions. Taking four years to complete and damaging his health in the process, it remains not only one of Michelangelo's most important works, but also one of the greatest pictorial religious masterpieces in the history of art. The result was the only work in his life that he completed entirely in accordance with his own conception and design, both in general and in particular, and was a unique concession that he had forced from Julius. After preliminary discussions, Julius gave him a free hand. A single visit to the chapel will

Leo X (Giovanni de' Medici), 1475–1521
Pope, 1513–21

Born late in the same year as Michelangelo, Giovanni was the second son of Lorenzo the Magnificent. His life was spent as a member of the Roman Church and he received the tonsure at the age of seven, was made a cardinal deacon at the age of 13 and studied canon law for two years at Pisa. When he was 16 he was formally admitted to the Sacred College and settled in Rome. In the same year (1492) Lorenzo died and Giovanni was recalled to Florence where he lived during the Savonarola period, the pontificate of Alexander VI and the invasion of Charles VIII of France until the expulsion of the Medici in 1494.

As pope, he excommunicated Martin Luther and bestowed upon Henry VIII of England the title Defender of the Faith. He was a noted patron of learning and of the arts.

establish, for any visitor who looks heavenward, the dimensions of Michelangelo's achievement.

Begun in May 1508, the ceiling was publicly unveiled to great acclaim on the last day of October 1512. Michelangelo, exhausted and with his health impaired, but emotionally rejuvenated, hoped to return to sculpture and the Julian tomb, although the pope was not anxious that he should. When Julius suddenly died of a fever four months after the ceiling had been completed, his executors drew up a new contract for a reduced-scale tomb monument, extended the time for completion from five to seven years, and increased the fee.

Michelangelo began work with renewed energy and enthusiasm and completed three figures in two years, the most important being the massive statue of *Moses* (pages 202 et seq.), regarded by most art historians as his greatest single figure sculpture. The other two figures were of slaves and he later completed two more figures, those of *Rachel* and *Leah* (page 207).

OPPOSITE
Portrait of Leo X, Cardinal Luigi de' Rossi and Giulio de' Medici, by Raphael *(1518)*
Oil on panel
Uffizi, Florence

In the portrait, Leo X sits with his magnifying glass examining an illuminated manuscript as evidence of his devotion to learning. He was described by a visiting Venetian as 'fat and ugly', a description which, if accurate, has been modified by Raphael. He is accompanied on his right by Giulio de' Medici, later to become Pope Clement VII.

OPPOSITE

The Sistine Chapel, Rome *(a section of the ceiling) 1508–12*

Fresco

The Sistine Chapel contains some of the most important paintings by Michelangelo and together they make a statement of his religious philosophy. The ceiling considers the creation and the progress of mankind, while the Last Judgment *on the altar wall examines the fate of human life after death and the dispensing of God's justice.*

Even though Michelangelo was loath to accept the commission when it was offered, it has come to be regarded as one of the most awesome statements of Christian belief.

THE MEDICI YEARS

Julius II was succeeded by Leo X, who was Giovanni de' Medici, the second son of Lorenzo the Magnificent. He had been a cardinal deacon in secret since the age of 12 or 13 and had been made a full cardinal at the age of 16. This seems astonishing, but such grotesque nepotism was commonplace. As a result of the change of papal families from the Della Rovere Pope Julius II to the rival Medici Leo X, the contract for the Julian tomb was again reduced in 1516 and Michelangelo did little work on the project for the next three years, spending some months in the Carrara quarries selecting marble for a new and exciting commission.

Michelangelo had received a commission from Pope Leo X for the façade and interior of the burial chapel for the Medici family church of San Lorenzo, Florence. Not only was it a return to sculpture, it was also Michelangelo's first architectural commission, since the contract included the architectural context in which the memorial sculptures would be housed. The chapel itself had been designed by Brunelleschi, a contemporary of Donatello and Masaccio and the most significant representative of early Italian Renaissance architecture. His most famous work was the dome of Florence cathedral, the first of its kind.

The new 1516 contract for the Julian tomb was annulled by Leo X in 1520. Michelangelo was outraged by the insult (*vituperio grandissimo*) even though he was now in Florence working on the Medici chapel contract which he had signed in the same year.

The death of Leo X on 1 December 1521 began a new episode of Medici/Della Rovere family rivalry through the elevation of another Della Rovere to the papacy as Adrian VI in 1522. This resulted in a demand that Michelangelo return to work on the Della Rovere/Julius II tomb and he was warned that failure to complete the contract would lead to a demand for repayment of what remuneration he had already received. Before this new work could be started, however, Adrian VI died on 24 September 1523 and was succeeded by Clement VII, who was a Medici. He was elevated on 19 November 1523 and died on 25 September 1534. Michelangelo was, of course, instructed by Clement to return to Florence and continue work on the completion of the Medici San Lorenzo chapel.

However, the following period of 12 years was one of highly successful production which lasted until just

Clement VII (Giulio de' Medici), 1478–1534
Pope, 1523–34
An important figure in Michelangelo's life, Clement VII was a nephew of Lorenzo the Magnificent and the son of Giuliano de' Medici who was assassinated in the Pazzi Plot. In a typical example of high-level nepotism he was created an archbishop by his cousin Pope Leo X even though he was illegitimate. However, a special dispensation was granted and a formal declaration was made that his parents had been secretly married and that he was therefore legitimate! He was made a cardinal in 1513 and during Leo's pontificate papal policy was effectively in his hands. He became pope in 1523. As a Medici and an Italian prince his interests and activities were largely political and too intricate to examine here, although the incipient Reformation should perhaps have been his main concern. As a Florentine and a Medici his interest lay in Florence and much of Michelangelo's sculptural work during his pontificate was in that city.

before the death of Clement VII. Michelangelo returned to Rome in 1534 to complete a new contract for the Julian tomb, which had been signed in 1532.

In Florence, during the pontificates of Leo X and Clement VII, Michelangelo became an architect. He was, of course, already familiar with the classical architectural forms (he had used them on the Sistine ceiling a few years earlier), but had completed no actual commissions. San Lorenzo, the Medici family church in Florence, offered him three important opportunities. Although his great architectural predecessor in Florence, Brunelleschi, had completed the interior in 1470, the façade was still unworked, although Brunelleschi had made a design for it. Leo X, after the banished Medici had been returned to Florence in 1515, decided to complete it and invited new designs from a number of architects. Michelangelo, although not among the first 'contestants', was given the commission in December 1516 to create a wooden model for the façade and in January 1518 his design received Leo's approval. In anticipation of the project, new quarries were excavated at Carrara and Michelangelo spent two years building a road and supervising the extraction and transport of the marble to Florence.

The blocks of marble used in columns, cornices and other achitectural features is different from that used for sculpture and Michelangelo had no experience of producing the working plans and measurements necessary. This became his first real architectural task and was performed at the new quarries while the marble was being cut. It appears to have been a decisive moment for him in that his interest in architectural proportion and detailing must also have been totally engaged at this point.

A further problem presented itself to Michelangelo while he was at the Carrara quarries. Pope Leo X may have had a vested interest in wanting to use marble from some abandoned quarries at Serravezza. These were summarily reopened, but having been abandoned for some years there were no workers and no proper roads. Michelangelo's opinion on the subject was ignored and he was instructed to move production to Serravezza. Moreover, he was unjustly blamed for breaking the Cararra contract, and when he protested the pope accused him of favouring Carrara marble over that of Serravezza.

Michelangelo, as experience had taught him, adapted himself to the circumstances by purchasing a site in Florence on which to build a house and workshops. He realized that he would need a large number of assistants and labourers in the new architectural venture he was contemplating, as had been necessary for the tomb of Julius II. He was, however, embroiled in a tangled web of instructions and counter-instructions and a letter to a Roman friend expresses his feelings of frustration at the time:

I would have you understand that such solicitations are to me so many stabs, for I die of vexation for not being able to do that which I would do but for my evil fortune.

Michelangelo's intention was to build a Roman classical façade which would have included, if the original contract had been realized, 18 life-sized statues, much in the style of the medieval cathedrals of Tuscany. The work was to be carried out within eight years and the sculptures executed by Michelangelo personally. The project was unrealisticallly ambitious and was therefore not completed, although the architectural model is preserved in the Casa Buonarotti museum (page 96). The design for the façade was abandoned in 1520 for reasons

Medici Dynasty

The history of the Medici is based in Florence and begins with their domination of the city from 1434 until, after the death of Lorenzo in 1492, they were expelled in 1494 and the Florentine Republic, led by Piero Soderini, was formed. They returned after the failure of the Republic in 1512 and eventually became titular rulers of Florence under Lorenzo, Duke of Urbino, grandson of Lorenzo the Magnificent. It should be noted that it is the duke rather than the Magnificent who is the Lorenzo portrayed by Michelangelo in the New Sacristy in San Lorenzo.

A second view of the Tuscan countryside, which features in the background of many Italian paintings and is instantly recognizable as such. Michelangelo, however, was no landscape painter, despite growing up in Tuscany. However, he did make several excursions to the Carrara quarries, looking for suitable blocks of marble for his sculpture.

not yet established, although Michelangelo certainly found the manager of the Carrara quarry antagonistic and unhelpful. The whole sordid episode was a source of great vexation to Michelangelo and he considered that he had been treated with 'ignominy'.

On 6 April 1520 Raphael died and Michelangelo must have been greatly saddened by the event. Raphael was known to have thanked God that he had lived at a time when he could study Michelangelo's works and Michelangelo reciprocated his admiration for Raphael. However, it is important to remember that the undermining of their relationship had been very much a part of Bramante's agenda.

In 1521 Michelangelo was working on the statue of Christ (page 208) which his friend Metello Varg had commissioned a few years earlier. He had begun it in Rome but the marble had a defect and for a time he abandoned the project along with the marble. Back in Florence he started on a new block, but was obliged to get an assistant to help him who made a poor attempt and was replaced by another who nearly completed it satisfactorily. Being a figure of Christ it is inevitable that it should receive strong criticism both then and later:

This statue considered as a work of expression and of religious art, is without a parallel in its irreverence. It is impossible to do otherwise than to shrink with pained feeling from a figure of the Saviour represented without covering of any kind ...

This is one of the earlier examples of the negative effect Michelangelo's nude figures had on the minds of many observers, and although it was common practice for artists to use nudity during the Renaissance, Michelangelo's treatment seems to have caused the most offence.

Pope Leo X died on 1 December 1521 and was succeeded by Adrian VI who died within a year. Clement VII, the second Medici pope, was elected on 18 November 1523 and quickly became one of Michelangelo's most important patrons. On 25 November, only a few days after Clement became pope, Michelangelo wrote to a friend as follows:

You have heard how a Medici is made pope, at which I think all the world rejoices and whence I think that here many things will be done for art.

Michelangelo was right in his estimatation of Clement and much of these effects came his way. However, even though Clement was a devoted patron of the arts, he was also a man possessed of ruthless self-interest.

Michelangelo was compensated for the failure of the façade contract with a commission to design the tombs in San Lorenzo for the recent princes of the Medici family. The New Sacristy, on a wing of the transept opposite the Old Sacristy that was intended for earlier members of the family, seemed a reasonable location. Though the Old and New Sacristies were identical in plan and both designed by Brunelleschi, the alterations to the New Sacristy made by Michelangelo produced a very different result, as may be seen (page 210 et seq.). This was Michelangelo's first architectural interior and it was completed under his instructions, even though he moved to Rome in 1534 before the work was finished.

The second major architectural project was the Laurentian Library (page 99), in the grounds of San Lorenzo. Clement VII had moved the famous Medici library, founded in the 15th century, from the family palazzo to the cloisters to make it available to the public, planning to have a new building especially designed for it. Michelangelo was contracted and produced the dramatic design that exists today although this, too, was

OPPOSITE

The Cloisters of San Lorenzo, Florence

Michelangelo was under considerable pressure from successive popes, once his genius had been recognized, and each had a different agenda. Two Medici popes, Leo X and Clement VII wished him to work in Florence in the environs of San Lorenzo, particularly on the Medici tombs in the New Sacristy. Other popes, notably Julius II wanted him in Rome. The struggle continued until Michelangelo finally settled in Rome in 1534.

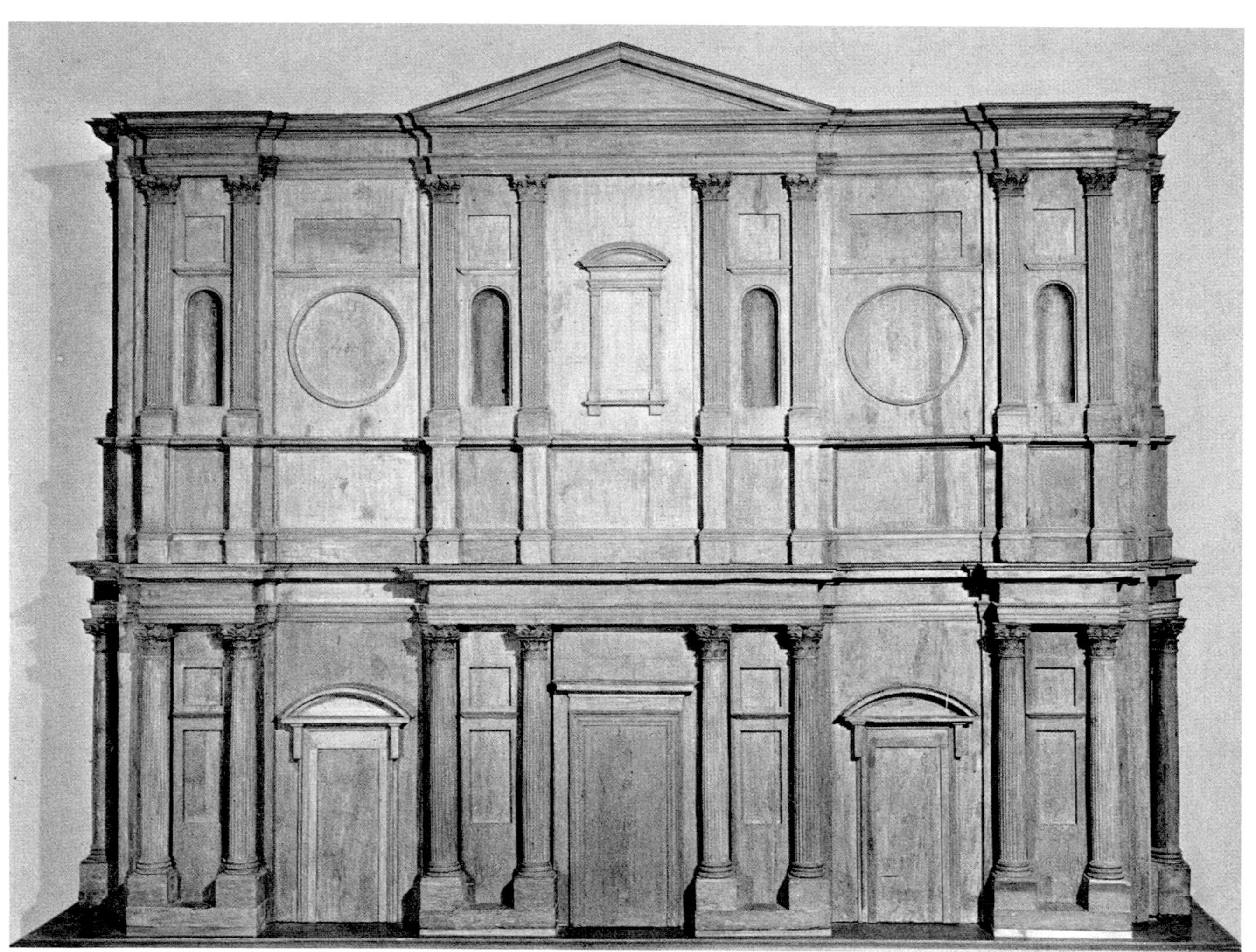

not finished in his lifetime. Work began in 1525 but it was not completed by the time Michelangelo finally moved to Rome.

Clement VII was the illegitimate son of Giuliano de' Medici, killed in the Pazzi plot, and nephew of Lorenzo the Magnificent and his important papacy saw some difficult times. A war between Charles V (Germany) and Francis I (France) resulted, in 1527, in the Sack of Rome and the imprisonment of Clement, who had taken the French side. Florence took the opportunity that the upheavel provided to declare itself a republic and to expel the Medici. In a typical opportunist intrigue characteristic of the times, Clement became reconciled with Charles V and was once again established in the papal chair, determined to return his Medici family to power in Florence with the help of Charles' forces.

Michelangelo became involved in the resistance of the new Florentine republic and was made engineer-in-chief in charge of fortification. The appointment was worded as follows:

The Signory of Ten for war grant to Michelangelo Buonarroti, appointed as Director and Provider over the fortifications, thirty florins of gold as his payment for twenty days, commencing from the sixth of the current month, on which day it was decided to proceed as follows with a provision of one gold florin per day, according to the tenor of his conduct.

Yet another assumed talent by his peers – Michelangelo was also a military engineer!

At the same time, somewhat bizarrely, he was nominally working for Clement in San Lorenzo even though the contract was in abeyance. This is Vasari's version, but seems somewhat improbable since Michelangelo was on the side of the republic and working for it. If it had succeeded, then the Medici would not have returned to power, the Sacristy would not have been completed, and Michelangelo would not have been paid for whatever work he had done.

During this time the new Florentine republic suffered greatly from famine and infections. There was an outbreak of plague in Florence and to Michelangelo's great distress, Buonarroto, his youngest and favourite brother died in his arms.

The position of the republic was hopeless as a result of the inevitable and familiar intrigue and double-dealing and Michelangelo, like other citizens, realized that the overwhelming strength of the imperial forces made defeat inevitable. He escaped to Venice, which he had

OPPOSITE

San Lorenzo, Florence

(Model of the façade)

Casa Buonarroti, Florence

OPPOSITE

Laurentian Library, San Lorenzo
(detail of the vestibule staircase)
1524–34

In 1524 the Medici Pope Clement VII commissioned Michelangelo to prepare plans for a new library within the cloisters of San Lorenzo to house the books and manuscripts belonging to the family. Although the work began in 1524, it was suspended two years later, resumed again in 1530 and again suspended in 1534. It was left in this state until 1550 when the project was taken over by Bartolommeo Ammanati (1511–92).

apparently previously visited on a diplomatic mission of some secrecy. With a number of others he was summoned to return and when he failed to do so was banished. It is reported that he left with 3,000 ducats in gold stitched into his clothes – a weighty but valuable insurance policy.

After the defeat of the new republic and the harsh retribution exacted by Clement which would repay examination (but is too distracting and distressing to undertake here) as an example of the 'political' behaviour of Renaissance popes, Michelangelo was pardoned and returned to Florence to resume work for Clement on the San Lorenzo Sacristy. As noted above, he was also offered the new Medici library (Biblioteca Laurenziana), for which he made designs and on which he commenced work.

Michelangelo had attempted to extricate himself from the problem of the Julian tomb, but a new and further reduced contract had been drawn up in 1532. Michelangelo returned to Rome on 23 September 1534, and the death of Clement VII two days later brought his work on the Sacristy to a halt. Only a few days later he returned to Florence, where he remained until December 1534 before returning again to Rome in the expectation of finishing his Julian contract. His father had died earlier in 1534 in his 90th year as 30 years later Michelangelo would himself. Michelangelo remained in Rome after this last important connection with Florence had been severed.

The decision was then taken to relocate the Julian tomb in San Pietro in Vincoli rather than St. Peter's, which Michelangelo would soon be commissioned to redesign by Paul III, who had become pope following Clement's death.

THE LAST YEARS IN ROME

Michelangelo, aged 60, remained in Rome for almost 30 years and died there on 18 Feb 1564. (Shakespeare was born about a month after Michelangelo's death and Galileo late in 1564.) During this last long period of his life he had worked at sculpture, painting and, towards the end, architecture, producing in each of these disciplines works of consummate mastery despite the deaths of many friends and relatives, increasing emotional isolation and irritability, and the inevitable decline of old age.

Michelangelo had hoped to commence the new contract for the Julian tomb immediately on arrival in

Rome but, characteristically, Pope Clement had other ideas. He had already been considering the repainting of the end wall of the Sistine Chapel since the paintings by Perugino and others were in poor condition and seemed out of sympathy in their simple informality compared with the power and grandeur of Michelangelo's ceiling.

Clement died, as noted above, in 1534 and Michelangelo's programme was yet again disrupted by the death of a pope. Clement's successor was Paul III, a member of the important Farnese family of Rome. After some delay and the preparation and subsequent approval of cartoons by the new pope, Michelangelo began the painting of the end wall above the altar in the Sistine Chapel.

A colossal project, the *Last Judgment* (page 320 et seq.) was a single painting covering an area of over 2,250sq ft (210m²). It was begun in 1536 and finished a little less than six years later in October 1541. Although it did not make the same rigorous physical demands on Michelangelo as the ceiling, it was nevertheless a daunting task for a man of his age and temperament. His wish, of course, had been to continue the sculptures for the Julian tomb; but once he had agreed the contract Michelangelo rose enthusiastically to the challenge. The eventual result is what is arguably the most powerful single expression of the Christian message in Western art. The same single visit to view the ceiling, mentioned earlier, will also confirm the overwhelming effect of the *Last Judgment.* Together, the two vast and unique works by one man make the Sistine Chapel an absorbing and chastening experience. Whatever modern views may be held regarding the truth of the Christian message, there is no doubt that Michelangelo was a fervent believer and an effective proselytizer of his faith.

It might have been expected, after this period of intense pressure, that Michelangelo would have been allowed a little tranquillity in his life. But much had changed in the six years he had worked on the *Last Judgment.* He still wished to return to the sculptures for the Julian tomb, but Paul III, as was not uncommon with popes, had an altogether different agenda from his predecessor. On 1 September 1535 he appointed Michelangelo Chief Architect, Sculptor and Painter of the Apostolic Palace for which he gained the honours and privileges due to the high office.

He had entrusted Michelangelo with the two most important architectural projects in Rome soon after he had begun the *Last Judgment* in April 1535.

In December 1537, in a significant ceremony on the Capitol, Michelangelo was awarded Roman citizenship and a month later began work on the design and reconstruction of the buildings on the Capitoline Hill to be centred around the equestrian bronze statue of the Roman Emperor Marcus Aurelius, which the pope intended to move from another location in Rome.

In 1546 Michelangelo was appointed to the office of chief architect with responsibility for St. Peter's. He accepted the office, but insisted that he would not accept payment, and remained responsible for St. Peter's until his death.

Contemplate, for a moment, Michelangelo's situation: he had just started work on a six-year contract to make one of the largest single-image paintings in Western art; he had also been given the largest public image-creating contract in Renaissance architecture in reminding Rome of its past and creating a new centre for the present city – the Campidoglio, the top of the Capitoline Hill – and he had also been given full control of the redesign of the proposed new mother church of the Christian religion – the Cathedral Church of St. Peter – the largest building programme then in progress in the whole of Europe. There really was not much else he could have been given. It is not difficult to recognize that his reputation was, in an unusually true sense of the word, unique: it was thought that there was nothing he could not do – maybe even walk on water.

There was also one small further contract which does not always receive attention. Paul III had had a new chapel constructed in the Vatican, the Capella Paolina, by the architect Antonio da San Gallo the Younger, and wanted two frescoes for it. Although Michelangelo had not given up hope of returning to the tomb of Julius, he undertook these frescoes, the Conversion of St. Paul and the Crucifixion of St. Peter (page 106 and 107), and completed them in 1550 at the age of 75, the last of his significant paintings.

As a man, Paul III had many facets to his personality. Although a nepotist and of questionable morality in many ways, he could also be seen as a temperate man with deeply held religious views. He was a reformer by nature, an admirer of the Jesuits and the Society of Jesus, and reconstituted the Council of Trent, establishing the Counter-Reformation. An enthusiastic patron of the arts, he was a strong supporter of Michelangelo and very much in sympathy with his aims. Michelangelo was aware of this and offered to design a church for Ignatius

Paul III (Alessandro Farnese) 1468–1549
Pope, 1534–49

Born into the affluent and noble Farnese family, Alessandro had high expectations of advancement to high office in the church which materialized when he was made a cardinal in 1493 by Pope Alexander VI (Rodrigo Borgia), whose mistresses, coincidentally, included Paul's sister, Giulia Farnese. Elected to succeed Clement VII, his first determination was to reform the church in the face of Lutheran Protestantism.

The Lutheran Reformation, inspired by the Wittenberg Theses, had occurred nearly a generation before Paul III succeeded to the papacy and it was clear that his duty, if not his inclination, was to address the problems of the Church. He was responsible for instituting the Order of Jesuits in 1540 and the Council of Trent in 1545 which set the Counter-Reformation in progress. He also issued the Bull of Excommunication and Deposition against Henry VIII of England in 1538. He revived the Papal Inquisition in 1542 and established the censorship in 1543.

He was a man of lax personal morality and one who indulged in acts of flagrant nepotism, one of the first being to appoint his two grandsons cardinals. He also tried to put the wheels in motion to make Erasmus a cardinal, which not surprisingly did not come to fruition.

However, he was a cultivated Humanist, his passion for the arts was real, and he restored the Roman University in 1534, commissioned Michelangelo to paint the *Last Judgment* in the Sistine Chapel in 1535 and appointed him architect for St. Peter's in 1546 while he was also undertaking great, even grandiose public works in the city, including the redesign of the Capitol (Campidoglio).

Although he appears not to have had the close relationship with Michelangelo that Julius II and Clement VII enjoyed, he nevertheless become one of his most important and generous patrons.

OPPOSITE
The Sistine Chapel, Rome:
The Last Judgment *(Detail of Christ in Judgment) 1535–41*
Fresco

The dominant figure of Christ is shown in the act of judging humanity as it passes from life to death and to that which must come after. It is a powerful expression of Michelangelo's deep religious convictions. One can only imagine the awesome effect it had on believers and unbelievers alike when it was first revealed.

Loyola, the Jesuit founder, to be called Il Gesù. Although this was never fully designed or built, the gesture indicates Michelangelo's understanding of what the pope was trying to achieve. Four years after Michelangelo's death the Gesù was built to a design by Vignola based, it appears, on Michelangelo's intention. The original façade was replaced with a design by Della Porta (who was then also responsible for the dome of St. Peter's), though largely to Michelangelo's design.

However, Michelangelo's major works still remained to be undertaken; the rest of his life was largely directed towards these two architectural projects that would importantly change the face of Rome. He is said to have recognized that architecture would not be as physically taxing as either painting or sculpture.

In St. Matthew's Gospel, Christ is reported as saying: 'Thou art Peter and upon this rock I will build my Church.' St. Peter was reputed to have been among the many victims of the persecution of Christians in Rome during the first century AD, although there is actually no record of his ever been there. His death, rather than being torn apart by wild animals in the Colosseum, was by crucifixion, head-down, in the Circus of Nero, and this is the form in which Michelangelo records the event in his painting in the Pauline Chapel. Whatever the truth of the matter, Rome was the supposed location of the martyrdom of St. Peter and the place where he was buried. The first Christian emperor, Constantine, built a structure to mark the fact, from which the great basilica of St. Peter's arose to be the mother church of Roman Catholicism. For political reasons, Constantine moved the capital of the Roman Empire to Byzantium in 330, renaming it Constantinople; but Rome remained the centre of Western Christianity and later the capital of Italy.

Thus Renaissance Rome, as the former capital of the old Roman Empire, retained more that some of its greatness. It had been the centre of the official religion of the Roman Empire since the time of Constantine and was consequently the centre of Christendom, wherever it was to be found. At the end of his life Michelangelo was thus given the contract to 'modernize' the home of Christianity, the new church of St. Peter at the early stages of its construction, and the token centre of the historical imperial city, the Capitol. A more fitting tribute to his unparalleled creative genius could not have been envisaged.

Capitoline Hill, Rome (Piazza del Campidoglio) *View from the Palazzo del Senatore towards the city*

Michelangelo was working on two major architectural commissions by 1546, the Campidoglio and St. Peter's.

The two palaces of similar design, to the left and right of the piazza, were designed by Michelangelo, as was the pattern of the paving. The Roman statue of the Emperor Marcus Aurelius was positioned here by papal order and Michelangelo also designed the elliptical pedestal for it. He was still working on the project when he died in 1564 and it was finished by others sympathetic to his design.

Platonism and Neo-platonism

These two philosophic terms, in use during the Renaissance, identify the work of the Greek philosopher Plato, who was born in Athens in 428 BC and died there in 348. Plato and Aristotle form the core of the Greek philosophical school and perhaps more than any other in history promoted the belief that the mind of man should be less concerned with the surface experiences of life and more with the unchangeable pattern lying behind them. As Plato put it – from becoming to being. (For a clear statement of the Platonist philosophy the reader is advised to search elsewhere; there is a library of books on the subject, some of which are included in the book list.)

Plato ran a school in a grove near Athens which had been owned by a Greek hero called Academus; the school thus became the Academy, a name still used to indicate a centre of intellectual enquiry and the ancestor of the university which later developed in the Middle Ages and was established in the Renaissance. The school itself lasted for 900 years – longer than any other such institution – and was only closed by Justinian in AD 529 because he felt that its classical traditions threatened Christianity. Despite this, as has been noted, interest in classical culture did not entirely die during the medieval period which followed.

The Academy formed the basis on which education has continued to be taught. Its studies followed the earlier pattern of Pythogorean schools and arithmetic, geometry, astronomy and harmonics formed the basic curriculum which lasted for ten years. The aim of the Academy was to train the mind to think for itself in the presence of reason, the intention being intellectual rather than commercial. It concerned the mind functioning towards the Idea, an eternally existing pattern in which individual things in any class are imperfect copies.

Plato's influence on philosophy is the greatest in history. He is central to philosophic thought and, significantly, was not only a great thinker but his writings also distinguish him as probably the greatest of all philosophic writers. His Dialogues, in the form of conversations with his friend and mentor Socrates, are foundation reading.

Cosimo de' Medici was the originator of a new Platonic Academy in Florence, first conceived at a meeting of the Council of Florence in 1439. He engaged Marsilio Ficino in the study necessary to bring the academy into being and Ficino translated many early Platonist documents. The Academy became an important and enthusiastic centre for philosophic discussion and examination of Platonic philosophy, particularly later, under Lorenzo the Magnificent. It was during this time that Michelangelo became engaged with philosophy and a devoté of Plato. The Florentine Academy contributed largely to the eventual role of the city as the greatest creative intellectual centre of the Italian Renaissance.

Michelangelo represented an uncompromising severity in both his art and his thinking. Art was not experimentation, it was a fundamental sense of beauty not accidently achieved but lodged in the Idea. This was an intellectual concept and Plato was its ultimate inspiration.

San Pietro in Vincoli, Rome
RIGHT
The Conversion of St. Paul
(1542–45)
OPPOSITE
The Crucifixion of St. Peter
(1546–50)
Frescoes, 20ft 6in x 21ft 8in
(6.3 x 6.6m)

These companion frescoes were demanded by Pope Paul III to decorate the new Pauline Chapel and are Michelangelo's last painted works; after finishing them he quickly returned to work on the Julian tomb. Thereafter, his major work was concerned with architectural projects that had been entrusted to him by Paul III – St. Peter's and the Campidoglio.

The frescoes do not have Michelangelo's usual power and intensity. Moreover, he appears to have taken over eight years to complete them when the Sistine Chapel was completed in less than four.

***The Church of Santa Croce, Florence** (mainly designed by Arnolfo di Cambio) 14th century*

Michelangelo was buried in this church and his tomb was designed by his biographer, Georgio Vasari. On the monument there are three figures representing Painting, Sculpture and Architecture – each by a different artist – an appropriate recognition of Michelangelo's astonishing range of talents.

The fact that these major city developments had been awarded to one architect was to give the city of Rome a classical stylistic unity at the high point of the Renaissance, providing a Roman base for its development and adaptation throughout the whole of Europe in the succeeding century through both the Mannerist and Baroque periods.

We may now contemplate for a moment Michelangelo's achievements. Firstly it should be said that to conquer just one discipline would be more than admirable, but to be high master of all three, sculpture, painting and architecture, is unparalleled. His sculptures represent the quintessence of the Renaissance and nothing can approach his *David*, *Moses*, or New Sacristy figures. The paintings in the Sistine Chapel have no peers. The architecture of St. Peter's and the Campidoglio are the true memorials of the Renaissance.

Michelangelo also represents the spirit and character of the Italian Renaissance in a way that is uniquely individual. His was deeply Christian and his faith was expressed in his creative achievement. He was also a Humanist which characterizes the intellectual spirit of the age; he was an historian of earlier Italian literature, particularly of Dante the great pre-Renaissance poet, and he was a poet himself. The remaining areas of Renaissance intellectual activity, the sciences in general, were not his concern and it is important to remind ourselves that his contemporary, Leonardo da Vinci, is of equal interest for any broader study of the period.

Michelangelo died in Rome in 1564, within three weeks of his 90th birthday, worn out but with his passion still intact; he only relinquished his life after a tenacious struggle. His body, in accordance with his wish, was removed secretly by his nephew, Leonardo, and taken to Florence where his funeral took place on 14 July 1564, appropriately in the church of San Lorenzo. His body was interned in Santa Croce in a tomb designed by Giorgio Vasari, his devoted admirer and biographer. Tommaso Cavalieri was with him when he died and at his funeral, but Vittoria Colonna, his closest friend, had sadly died 17 years earlier.

Chapter Two
Michelangelo & His Contemporaries

OPPOSITE

The Last Supper by Leonardo da Vinci *(pre-renovation) 1495–98*
Fresco, approx. 15 x 29ft (4.6 x 8.8m)
Santa Maria delle Grazie, Milan

The inclusion of the Last Supper *is a reminder of Leonardo's gigantic contribution to the Renaissance; indeed, he can be regarded as of comparable stature to Michelangelo. The work is as important as Michelangelo's for the Sistine Chapel but has unfortunately suffered greatly over time. This is due to the fact that Leonardo liked to experiment and in this case got the surface composition of the fresco wrong.*

Even in his lifetime Michelangelo was regarded as *sans pareil* (matchless) and it would be of no value to our study to try to justify or demolish this view. Nevertheless, there may be some advantage in placing him within the context of his society and saying something about his peers. The first observation that occurs is that it was certainly not an age of weaklings languishing in the shadow of a great colossus. At a time of exceptional achievement in the arts, sciences and literature, it is unquestionable that Michelangelo was highly regarded, and not only in his native land.

Some of his contemporaries will appear in other contexts within this book and will be considered at that time; but there are others who, while they do not feature greatly in Michelangelo's story, are of such importance in the complex progress of the Renaissance that the fact that they lived at the same time is significant.

Leonardo da Vinci (1452–1519), 23 years older than Michelangelo, and Raphael (1483–1520), eight years his junior, have a special place in the history of Renaissance art. When Leonardo and Raphael died within a year of each other, Michelangelo had about 45 years of further life to live, but together the three epitomize the High Renaissance, the last stage of a process that had its beginnings in the 14th century.

The 45 years that Michelangelo lived on is significant. It provided a period in the middle of the 16th century when Michelangelo was unchallenged and indeed unchallengeable as the dominant artist of the period. He was the first and only choice when only the best would do, and of course the popes always had the pick of the crop. It explains why Michelangelo was so busy in the later years of his life, when all his rivals had disappeared but his own passionate commitment was still intact. For one who remained intellectually aware and physically fit, a lot could be achieved in 45 years.

Leonardo was closer in character to Michelangelo than Raphael, but all three were in contact at some time during their lives and rivalry was clearly evident and acknowledged. Leonardo's mind was on a different wide-ranging plane than either Raphael's or Michelangelo's and he clearly had an intelligence not only unrivalled by his contemporaries but also by most of humanity before or since. On the other hand, he did not have quite the same focus to his life or passionate attachment to the arts which characterized both Raphael and Michelangelo in

OPPOSITE
La Gioconda (Mona Lisa) by Leonardo da Vinci *(1503–07)*
Oil on panel, 30¼ x 20⅞in (77 x 53cm)
Louvre, Paris

Perhaps the most celebrated portrait of the Renaissance and a further reminder of Leonardo's importance. The quiet calm and assurance of both the painting and the sitter is in extreme contrast to the furia *or* terribilità *which characterizes Michelangelo's work. He could never have painted the Mona Lisa and would probably never have wished to.*

their different ways. His curiosity was insatiable, his inventive mind constantly occupied with infinite possibilities. He was the nearest to what could be described as a universal genius that has ever existed. His achievement in the arts represents only a small part of his life and he did not regard himself as an artist, at least not in the particular sense of being either a painter or a sculptor, although he produced work in both disciplines. In Renaissance terms his two most renowned masterpieces, the so-called *La Gioconda* or *Mona Lisa* and the *Last Supper*, in the refectory of Santa Maria delle Grazie in Milan, parallel the Sistine ceiling and *Last Judgment* of Michelangelo. Without these four works the glory of the Renaissance would have been appreciably diminished.

Raphael also made huge contributions to the High Renaissance. His was a different, quieter spirit than either Leonardo or Michelangelo; but in his short life, Raphael achieved much, was adored by a wide circle of friends, was cultured and sophisticated, a pleasure to know and left beind a body of delicate and accomplished work. Leonardo produced some of the most famous paintings in European history and is universally admired for the range of his abilities. Michelangelo is remembered for having created a vast body of work in all three artistic disciplines and is thought of as difficult, bad-tempered and not particularly attractive. Raphael is remembered most for paintings of calm intellectual clarity and technical accomplishment, but it should also be remembered that he was also employed as an architect. His paintings also contributed to the essential body of High Renaissance art and the *School of Athens* (page 131) in the Vatican is a seminal statement of Platonist Christianity.

One unidentified observer may be quoted here:

The equipoise of Raphael is absent from Michelangelo's gigantic energies and deep emotion and human inadequacy – terribilità – a soul torn between Christ and Beauty. Michelangelo was dramatizing a cosmic struggle inside himself, not putting himself into a cosmic struggle.

Although these three masters dominated the Rome-Florence axis there are many other artists and architects who were important in the creation of the artistic climate of the time; although most of them were not directly involved in Michelangelo's life, something must be said about them if a balanced view of the Renaissance is to emerge. They are to be found not only in Rome or

Florence but in the other important city republics or duchies. Leonardo's work in Milan for the Sforza dynasty, and particularly for Ludovico Sforza, known as Il Moro because of his dark colouring, was a major part of his life, and much as Michelangelo was pulled between Florence and Rome, so Leonardo alternated between Milan and Florence. Raphael worked mainly in Rome.

One other great centre of art and culture in Italy should be noted – the powerful oligarchy called the Republic of Venice. In the field of painting, the Bellini family, consisting of the father, Jacopo (1400–70/1), two sons, Gentile (1429–1507) and Giovanni (1430–1516), as well as Jacopo's son-in-law, Andrea Mantegna (c.1431–1506), formed the first stage in the development of art in the Venetian Renaissance and was followed by the masters Giorgione (c.1478–1510), born, it will noticed, not long after Michelangelo, Titian (c.1487–1576), Tintoretto (1518–94), Veronese (c.1528–88) and the architect Andrea Palladio (1508–80). Venice was unique in many respects: in its ambience and location, formed from scattered islands, from its importance as a port and its links with the Orient, in its government by ten families headed by a doge. Frequent public holidays and

organized celebrations were also popular, which resulted in a love of luxury and ornament which is reflected in the work of Venetian artists. There is a sense of pageantry and wealth in the work of the later Venetians which is not seen in Florentine or Roman art and is entirely antipathetic to that produced by Michelangelo. Venetian art presents a quite different aspect of the Italian Renaissance.

One important figure who has already been mentioned is the artist and architect, Donato Bramante (1444–1514). Bramante was first noted as an architect in Milan in 1485 and had been trained as a painter under Fra Bartolommeo.

His relationship with Michelangelo, always stormy and occasionally violently confrontational, was an important part of both their lives and, because he was actually in awe of Michelangelo, Bramante tends to draw the short straw. This is unfortunate and to a degree unfair because he played an influential and creative part in the architecture of Rome during his lifetime. One of the small masterpieces of Renaissance architecture, the circular Tempietto of San Pietro in Montorio, Rome (page 85), built around 1502, is possibly his best finished work; but

his designs for the rebuilding of part of the Vatican and for the new St. Peter's, which Julius II demanded of him, were an important part of the developing modern city. His design for St. Peter's, for which Michelangelo later took responsibility, was preserved and admired by Michelangelo with, however, the addition of his own inevitable 'modifications'.

Another Florentine artist, sculptor and goldsmith is Benvenuto Cellini (1500–71), who will be remembered as a highly individualistic Renaissance figure. His beautifully modelled bronze sculpture of Perseus holding the head of Medusa, placed in the Loggia dei Lanzi in the Piazza della Signoria and still located there, faces Michelangelo's *David*.

Cellini's character was so different from Michelangelo's that he gives a different perpective to the Renaissance. Born in Florence, he was first apprenticed to a goldsmith, then went to Rome at the age of 19 and worked for the papal mint and was once imprisoned after being charged with embezzling papal jewellery. He worked for some time at the court of Francis I of France, returned to Florence in 1545 and wrote his autobiography, which is frank, indiscreet and boastful. He

OPPOSITE
Salt cellar, by Benvenuto Cellini
(1543)
Gold

Cellini was extravert and boastful but had great technical ability as well as a fanciful imagination. He made this saltera *for Francis I of France and for a period worked at the papal mint.*

LEFT
La Belle Jardinière by Raphael
(1507)
Oil on canvas

Raphael, with Michelangelo and Leonardo, form the triumvirate of the greatest masters of the Renaissance. The painting is of the Madonna and Child with St. John the Baptist; the draughtsmanship is very different and reflects an altogether gentler spirit than the other two.

claimed that he was the man responsible for killing Charles, Duke of Bourbon, at the Sack of Rome in 1527. While working for Francis I he made a startling gold salt cellar, topped with reclining provocative nude figures. He had none of the dark majesty of Michelangelo, and was an altogether different contributor to the Renaissance.

Three years younger than Michelangelo, Baldassare Castiglione (1478–1529) was born in Mantua and became a writer and diplomat working in the courts of Milan, Urbino and Mantua. His responsibilities took him across Europe and included a visit to the court of Henry VII in England. From 1524 he was papal *nuncio* to Charles V, the Holy Roman Emperor (Charles I of Spain). He was made bishop of Avila in Spain in 1528 and died there in the following year.

He wrote elegant poems in Latin and Italian which praise Raphael's pleasant character. The work for which he is remembered, however, is *Il Cortegiano* (The Courtier), published in 1528, in which he examines the qualities important in a successful courtier, taking the court of Urbino as an example. It is composed of four books and takes the form of conversations between ladies and gentlemen of the court that took place on successive nights and which provided entertainment on a variety of topics, all concerned with the making of the ideal courtier, whose role, apparently, was to advise his prince on the proper mastery of all the arts of peace and war. It provides an alternative voice to Niccolò Machiavelli's *Prince* (q.v.).

The text was revised before it was published and private copies were made. It became a household name in social etiquette. Vittoria Colonna, Michelangelo's friend, had a copy herself and Michelangelo probably knew of the book through her.

Niccolò Machiavelli (1469–1527) was born in Florence, though little is known of his early life. But Machiavelli has nevertheless made his linguistic mark in the word 'machiavellian', which has come to mean cunning, unscrupulous and scheming – especially when applied to politics in respect of advancing one's career, and came into being through his famous book, *Il Principe* (The Prince). However, his name has acquired more opprobrium than it possibly deserves.

Machiavelli worked for the Florentine Republic and was created chancellor in 1498 (see also Savonarola, page 63), undertaking several missions in Europe on behalf of the city. When the Medici were restored in 1512 he was removed from power, arrested for conspiracy against the Medici, and tortured. Although he was eventually pardoned, his work for the city was effectively over. He withdrew from public life and devoted himself to literature, writing a history of Florence and a number of political-historical essays, poetry, short stories and comedies.

Machiavelli's Prince, like Castiglione's Courtier, has become a representative view of one aspect of Renaissance society. Castiglione explains how a courtier should behave and outlines the activities that will ensure his social superiority. Machiavelli takes a more pragmatic view in *Il Principe*, written in about 1513 after his release from prison but not published in his lifetime. Originally intended for Giuliano de' Medici and subsequently dedicated to Lorenzo de' Medici, who died in 1519, it is intended as a guide for the prince or ruler on how to retain power. He proposes that all means, however complicated, deceitful, underhand, immoral or unprincipled are justified, including murder, and the more subtle the means of achieving power, the more 'correct' the course of action will be.

OPPOSITE

Niccolò Machiavelli by Santi di Tito

Machiavelli wrote a number of interesting studies, including *Discourses on the First Ten Books of Livy* (1515/9), a history of Florence (1525), a number of plays, including one that is still performed – *La Mandragola* (1518), and the only one printed in his lifetime, the *Art of War* (1521), a treatise on military strategy.

Desiderius Erasmus (c.1466–1536) was born in Rotterdam of Dutch parentage, and was one of the great intellectual figures of the Northern Renaissance. A Humanist and a Christian, he was what would now be described as a 'professional' writer. His subjects were so diverse and his intelligence so admired that he is regarded as an intellectual giant. He became involved with Luther's struggle and initially supported him, but he later attacked the subsequent violence of the Reformation. In 1487 he took monastic orders and was ordained a priest in 1492, entering a theological faculty in Paris in 1495.

Erasmus travelled extensively in Europe: from a base in Rotterdam, he visited England twice, first in 1499 and for a longer period of five years in 1509, and was in Italy for three years before his second visit to England. After 1517 he increasingly distanced himself from the Lutheran controversy and moved to Basel in 1521, to Freiburg in 1529 and returned to Basel in 1535. His life is a reminder that the intellectual curiosity that was widespread in Italy, the Humanist Christianity of which Michelangelo was a part, was also to be found in the countries of northern Europe.

Many more contemporaries are of interest, both in the arts and other aspects of society. Some have already been mentioned and/or considered; but there are many more who could justify inclusion in this section. It is indeed difficult to know where to stop.

And we do have another part of the Renaissance to consider. Although we have been concentrating, for our purposes correctly, on the Italian development of the Renaissance, it was also gestating throughout Europe. Figures of great significance were emerging and their influence was being felt (Luther and the Reformation have been mentioned). Philosophers, statesmen, writers and artists of established reputation were close contemporaries of Michelangelo and mention of a few will offer some indication of the lively intellectual and political climate of contemporary Europe. These include the German painter Mathias Grünewald (c.1460–1528); Sebastiano Serlio, a contemporary of Bramante and a Bolognese architect and painter; Thomas Wolsey (1474–1530), Henry VIII of England's first minister; and Sebastian Cabot (c.1475–1557), Italian explorer. There was also Giorgione, the Venetian painter and Pope Leo X, already mentioned.

Near contemporaries include Ludovico Ariosto (b. 1474), Thomas More (1478), Charles VIII of France (1470), Thomas Cromwell (1485), Albrecht Dürer (1471), Isabella d'Este (1474), Vasco da Gama (1469), and Ferdinand Magellan (1480).

All the above are of international interest and importance and the list could be easily increased by casting a slightly wider net, for example to Pietro Aretino (1492–1556), John Calvin (1509–64), Ignatius Loyola (1491–1556), Antonio Correggio (1494–1534), Hans Holbein (1497–1543), Francesco Guicciardini (1483–1540), Parmigianino (1503–40), Rabelais (1494–1553), Titian (1487–1576), William Tyndale (c.1494–1536).

What is indicated by these shortlists is the importance of the period in which Michelangelo lived and worked. It was a period full of illustrious people who are household names to this day. But even so, it is Michelangelo who dominates.

Niccolò Machiavelli (1469–1527)

Machiavelli has an undeserved reputation for which his most famous book, *Il Principe* (The Prince), must take the blame. It seeks to advise those with pretensions to power and advocates unscrupulous, immoral behaviour of any kind in the pursuit of that goal, including murder. Indeed, the word 'machiavellian' is still current to this day to describe a ruthless, unprincipled schemer.

Unfortunately, this belies Machiavelli's actual achievement as a man of many interests and talents. Besides being a writer, he was a politician, administrator and historian. He first rose to prominence after the death of Savonarola in 1498 when he became chancellor, a military advisor and a diplomat in Florence.

When the Medici returned to power in 1512 he was removed from his responsibilities and his subsequent anti-Medici activities resulted in his imprisonment and torture.

He was eventually released and returned to his writing. His *History of Florence* and *Art of War* are two important documents to have emerged from the Renaissance.

Chapter Three

The Italian Renaissance

OPPOSITE

Page of a sketchbook with figures and notes by Michelangelo

Pen and ink on paper

British Museum, London

We have already traced the course of Michelangelo's life to provide the first part of a framework to his work which is, of course, essentially the *raison d'être* of this book. However, it is necessary to place that framework in a larger 'cultural landscape': that of the Italian Renaissance itself.

This is not specifically to learn facts, although they are generally helpful; it is to evoke some feeling for the age in which Michelangelo lived and an understanding of the intellectual base, the living conditions and the culture that supported his work, stimulated his mind, and supplied his values. Since he was such a significant contributor to many of the Renaissance characteristics and accomplishments, the framework will be complex and the connections close but one cannot exist without the other.

In considering the Italian Renaissance, it must be remembered that the term applies to the whole of Europe. It began and matured a little earlier in Italy than in Northern Europe, although in this survey, when the term Renaissance is used, it is referring mainly to its development in Italy.

The Italian Renaissance was an age markedly different from ours. It is not necessary to identify the differences, they are all too obvious, but one example from among a plethora may highlight the fact. We regard communication as a simple immediate activity, forgetting that the horse remained the fastest means of long-distance communication for hundreds of years.

The physical process of living, the social values and religious beliefs held, the simple public services, organizations and structures, personal relationships and the habits of daily life, as we surely realize, were then very different from ours; but we do not necessarily feel or appreciate the actual effects these differences must have produced. Therefore, we will try to engage with the period and sense its moods, excitements and fears. While this is not an automatic process, a sense of imagined participation can be envisaged.

Initially, it is important to recognize that, in our Western civilization, we calculate historical time from the presumed birth of Christ. Although we are aware that this is not actually the case, it implies, without actually saying so, that history – perhaps even civilization itself – began at that moment. We know this to be untrue in terms of the wider history of human development, but we tend to forget this, lack curiosity about what went before, and feel that whatever did happen was of minor importance and probably irrelevant to our culture today. To the people of the 15th and 16th centuries Christ was as far back in time as they could imagine and the Old Testament lay in the realms of mythology. However, a study of the Renaissance will certainly mean a journey back in time before the birth of Christ.

As has already been noted, 'renaissance' means 'rebirth', and for Renaissance Italy the rebirth was that of the civilization of a far-off pre-Christian era in Greece, generally identified as the classical period. It also included its adoption and extension throughout the Roman Empire, into which Christ was born, originating in Italy but at its fullest development covering most of what is now Europe, and was a period that extended into the Christian era for over 400 years.

The name Europe derives from a Greek myth. According to the *Iliad*, Europa, the daughter of Phoenix, charmed Zeus by her beauty. In the guise of a bull he enticed her with his mildness to mount his back, then carried her into the sea, swam to Crete where, by a natural process, she became the mother of Minos who eventually became king of Crete.

Michelangelo

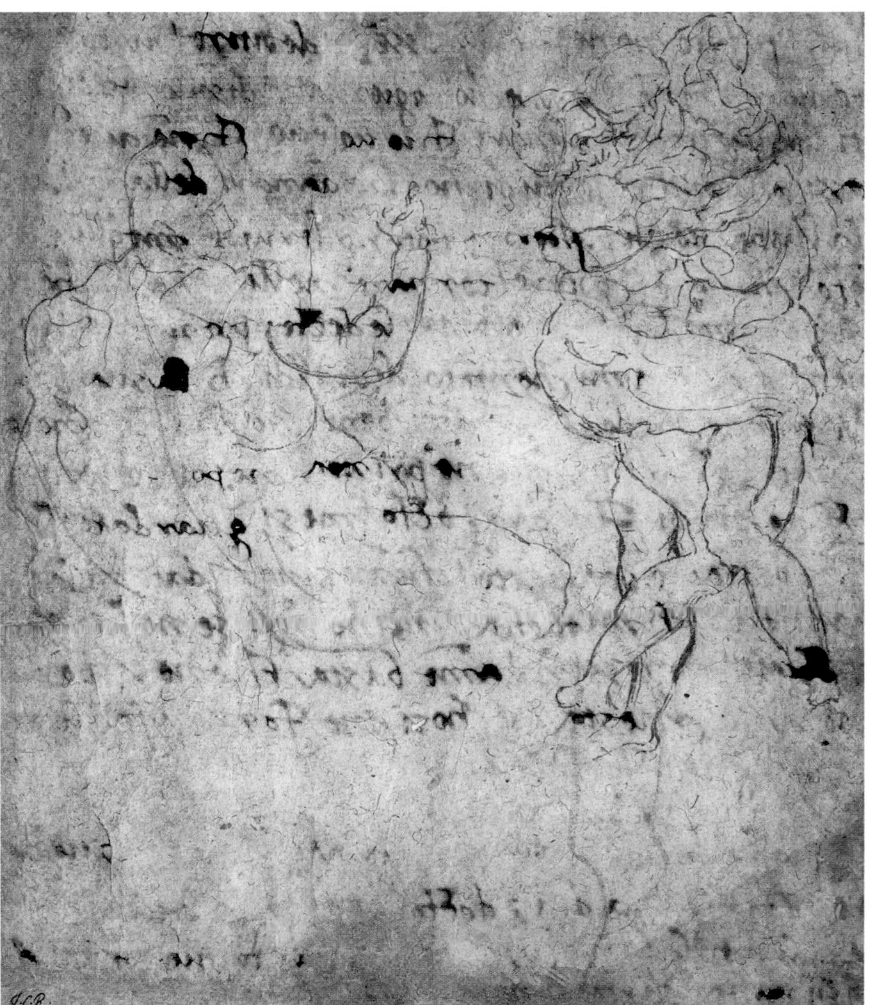

We calculate the classical civilization if we begin, as we do, at 0 with the birth of Christ, and measure the years backwards from this point. What happened during this pre-Christian period is, of course, the greater part of human historical time. Because the Renaissance is therefore essentially concerned with and moulded by what happened before Christ, it is therefore the early civilizations rather than the Christian period that must first be considered and this will include the pre-Christian biblical period in the Near East. The evidence of a familiarity with classical society and Old and New Testament biblical history is part of Renaissance culture and can be seen in the work of all artists of the time, including Michelangelo.

Familiarity often results in assimilation and the people of the Renaissance, as they became increasingly concerned and familiar with the classical philosophers and their culture, succeeded in syncretizing the Platonist philosophy with the established Christian religion. The result was a Platonist Christianity that became acceptable to many Italians and, later, Europeans. Michelangelo was no exception. It is also evident that our contemporary culture can see the whole of the period from earlier classical times to the death of Michelangelo in the Renaissance as unified history, while for Renaissance society the early period was a separate and sometimes unbelievable story.

The most significant of all early societies for Western culture was undoubtedly that which flourished in Greece and reached its peak in the 5th century BC; while it is unquestionably more convenient for Christian societies to see the birth of Christ as a seminal point in history to the extent of calculating time, it inevitably distorts our concept of history before that time. The story of mankind started a long time before the birth of Christ.

Classicism is now identified as embodying the civilizations of both Greece and Rome; however, classicism in Greece comprised a culture of highly developed citizenry and is described as the first democracy, although this is perhaps open to debate due to our present understanding of the word. It was nevertheless a civilization that has come to be viewed as an exemplar, which commands admiration and has served as an inspiration throughout much of subsequent history. The names associated with that civilization are still familiar today.

Early Greek religion was, however, polytheistic, with a pantheon of gods and goddesses who idly observed the doings of ordinary mortals from the lofty heights of Mount Olympus, intervening only when the whim took their fancy. They seemed to be far more absorbed with their own affairs and were regarded with less awe and respect than the gods of subsequent monotheistic religions. Each Greek god was associated with a different concept: for example, there was Ares, the god of war; Hephaestus, the god of fire; Demeter, the corn goddess; Artemis, the goddess of the moon and the hunt; and scores of others which were eventually translated into the Roman pantheon as Mars, Vulcan, Ceres and Diana. The Olympians behaved in much the same way as human beings, but at a more heightened level; they loved, quarrelled, were jealous, vengeful and malicious – but all in the context of immortality and with the power of life and death at their command.

The gods lived a more colourful existence, even consorting with human beings, which provided the Greeks below with unlimited opportunities for fantasy and myths, though moral messages were in short supply. However, it is the earthlings we now admire, and view

OPPOSITE
The Fall of Phaethon
Black chalk on paper
British Museum, London

The transitory nature of the human condition is a popular subject with artists. The Greek myth of Phaethon is most fully elaborated in Ovid's Metamorphoses *and describes how Phaethon, the son of the sun god Helios, persuades his father to allow him to drive the chariot of the sun across the sky. Losing control, he approaches too close to the earth and scorches it, as a result of which Zeus, the chief of the gods, kills Phaethon with a thunderbolt.*

Michelangelo depicts the moment when the chariot and horses are approaching earth. Phaethon, falling head-first, bears a remarkable resemblance to the figure of Adam, though older, in the Sistine Chapel.

the activities of the old gods as interesting, sometimes diverting, fiction.

The Greek myths provided historians, writers, artists and philosophers with an inexhaustible supply of material from which to draw, and the subsequent development of a sophisticated system of arts, philosophies, sciences and jurisdiction eventually influenced the Romans and subsequently the whole of Western society; it was a culture of such excellence that its memory has remained alive and inspirational to this day, even through the revolutionary two millennia of Christian monotheism and spiritual transformation.

Classical Greek society was therefore characterized by great intellectual curiosity concerning such matters as social organization, moral responsibility and the origins of the universe. Greek culture was the unprecedented inspiration and foundation for philosophical discussion, scientific enquiry and observation of the physical world. Pythagoras, Archimedes, Sophocles and Plato are names that echo down the ages and are household words even to this day.

The power of Rome, which transformed it from a city to an empire in 27 BC, during which time it had absorbed

OPPOSITE

The tholos and sanctuary of Delphi, Greece

The tholos is a circular building from which the Delphic Sybil issued her oracular prophesies, and is a direct reminder of Michelangelo's portrayal of her in the Sistine Chapel (pages 304–05).

LEFT

The Parthenon, Athens

This, and the sanctuary opposite, are examples of the classical architecture which, together with Greek philosophy, inspired the Renaissance. The Parthenon is the most famous building of its type to have survived, despite the fact that it was once used to store Turkish explosives which destroyed its central core. Situated on its dramatic eyrie above the city of Athens, it remains the epitome of classical Greek architecture.

much of Greek culture, saw the birth of Christ and the rise of Christianity, facilitated its expansion throughout Europe, and eventually established it as the official religion of the empire. This resulted in two significant developments. Europe became the repository of classical cultural values and subsequently received a monotheistic religious base in Christianity. The seeds of the Renaissance had already been planted.

For about 1,000 years, from the fourth to the 14th centuries, Christianity was the main focus of social, religious and political power and its expansion and organization covered the whole of Europe. While the

OPPOSITE

***The Colosseum, Rome** (AD 70–82)*

This massive structure and the nearby Arch of Constantine (page 133) together represent, as do Delphi and the Parthenon in Greece, the other important but different classical culture that was seminal to the development of the Renaissance. The Colosseum, sometimes called the Flavian amphitheatre, was begun by the Emperor Vespasian and completed by Domitian and is a symbol of the brutality that too often accompanied imperial power, an arena of death for the delectation of the Romans. The Arch of Constantine is a memorial to an emperor's pride, though Constantine eventually became a Christian and is viewed more favourably by history. However, the Arch of Titus (page 136), as a memorial to a tyrant, can in no way be mitigated.

effects of this were uneven, with different parts of Europe providing local expressions of the faith, its centre and hub remained the city of Rome.

When one recalls that Rome, during these earlier formative years, was also the focus of the Roman Empire, it is not surprising that it was the main centre of the conflict that occurred while Christianity was enlarging its influence and eventually its power. The Christian martyrs in the Colosseum would have been surprised if they had known, before suffering a horrible death, that they were reflecting the struggle between Empire and Christianity which, despite ruthless cruelty and apparent defeat, ended with Christianity the victor and the adherence to one deity universal in Western culture.

Art and architecture, in order to express visually the dramatic cultural changes, began to develop a new unfamiliar style and aesthetic throughout Europe. Roman imperial classicism, in both art and architecture, was replaced by what is now called 'medieval' or, as it was interestingly first called during the Renaissance, 'gothic' – pertaining to the Goths of early barbaric Europe. Roman monuments were allowed to decay, the stones of classical buildings were used for churches and other buildings, and classical buildings were modified and used for Christian worship. The old Roman law court (*basilica*) was adopted and adapted for Christian worship and the word acquired a dual meaning, lawgiving becoming part of the Christian ethos by implication. (The greatest basilica was the Constantinian church of St. Peter's in Rome.)

The classical civilization seemed not only to have breathed its last but the achievements of the culture in human terms were also buried by the enthusiasm of the Christian faithful. Of course, as always appears to happen with creative cultures, some classical scholars survived and all evidence of the classical world was not, in fact, destroyed. Classical elements of art and architecture continued to be used and Greek remained a studied language along with Latin, the imperial language of Rome. Both were absorbed into the Christian Church and Latin became the universal language of Catholic worship.

It might then be asked why it was necessary for the classical culture to be reborn. It was polytheistic, anachronistic and antagonistic to monotheism. It had been carried into Europe by the Romans and had saturated society. It could be argued that it was already there.

Time provides the answer. The arrival of Christ and

PIVS·IX·PONT·MAX

the expansion of Christianity changed more than the calendar. The new religion altered the perception of human responsibility so that social and intellectual values were turned into spritual aspirations, which over time affected society and politics, including the arts. A new cultural ethos had arrived.

At the time it was occurring in Italy, the Renaissance was not identified as such – it would probably have been described simply as a Christian society. It is common practice for history to be divided conveniently into what might be called 'cultural parcels', small and large – the Roman Empire, the Holy Roman Empire, the Dark Ages, the Middle Ages or Medieval period, the French Republic, the British Empire. These names, of course, are not usually given by the community itself as it is developing, but only, in the first instance, after the feeling that significant changes have occurred or, later, that an organization with a beginning and an end had been established (as with the Holy Roman Empire) or, finally, by the historical reflections of later societies. Thus the Renaissance came to be named as such only when it was believed possible to see and describe it as a 'parcel', in this case, in the 19th century, at a time when researchers

OPPOSITE
Temple of Poseidon, Paestum, Italy
(c. 450 BC)

This temple, one of three built at Paestum, and Raphael's School of Athens *(overleaf) are two further examples of the Greek ethos, the latter transferred to the Renaissance.*

LEFT
Madonna and Child with St. John
Chalk on paper
British Museum, London

Although the subject is the same as La Belle Jardinière *by Raphael (page 115), Michelangelo's treatment is rather more energetic when compared to the quiet dignity of Raphael's. The drawing of the upper part of the Madonna is suggestive of the Mannerist style which developed following the Renaissance.*

OPPOSITE

The School of Athens by Raphael

(c. 1510–11)

Stanza della Signatura, Vatican, Rome

Fresco

Located within the Vatican, which is the administrative core of Christianity, Raphael's painting depicts great figures from Greek history but also includes some of his contemporaries, including Raphael himself and Donato Bramante, Michelangelo's rival. It thus symbolizes Greek classical culture and its rebirth in the Renaissance. The two central figures of Aristotle and Plato indicate the different aspects of philosophy which are connected through the various Renaissance characters.

could identify the extent of Renaissance culture over Europe. (It is also interesting to recall that it was not until Garibaldi and the Risorgimento in the 19th century that Italy actually and officially became a politically unified country.)

The result is that the Europe of what we call the Renaissance period did not know it was experiencing a period of rebirth. But it was developing a new curiosity and fascination with the classical Greek civilization. And when it is remembered that it was the Roman Empire that eventually overturned that civilization and adopted and absorbed much of its character and, of visual importance, its architecture, there can be little surprise that it was in Italy, the centre of the Roman Empire, where the Renaissance began.

In Renaissance Italy there was thus an important and recognized connection with the earlier societies of both classical Greece and imperial Rome. Renaissance intellectuals were students of the life, philosophy and arts of these civilizations, revered them, and attempted to incorporate them into the culture of their time. Hence the retrospective appropriateness of the term. It was an association which the citizens of Italy recognized. Florence, an important centre of Renaissance culture, has been called 'the Athens of Italy' and Raphael's painting *The School of Athens* – the central figures of Plato and Aristotle surrounded by a gathering of Greek philosophers and followers, even some from the Renaissance – is located in the headquarters of Christian administration, the Vatican.

The situation in the rest of Europe did not parallel that of Italy. Most of Europe had earlier formed into the nations with which we are now familiar. As a country largely composed of small city states with no common overall political ruler but a number of ambitious tyrants, Italy was a natural, if difficult, target for the ambition of rulers from other countries. For much of Michelangelo's life there had been some military action somewhere within its borders. Intrigue, murder, warfare, damage to property and human brutality were common experiences. Although it is not a part of Michelangelo's personal life, and will not be examined here, it is important to remember that the age of the Renaissance, although one of extraordinary achievement, was at the same time a period of brutal, ruthless cruelty and ambitious greed.

The most disturbing element of life in Italy, that one is obliged to record, is that of the hierarchy of the Church itself. It was not free from social corruption and even popes, some might say particularly popes, in view of the political and social power they held, were not without blame. One of Michelangelo's most important patrons, Julius II, was also known as the 'Warrior Pope' because of his aggressive and ruthless military campaigns, and the immoral behaviour of such notorious popes as Alexander VI, Rodrigo Borgia, and his children, Cesare and Lucrezia, is widely reported. Savonarola's complaints during his papacy led Alexander to organize his murder, while first excommunicating him.

Another aspect of the Renaissance requires discussion. The development of Christianity has been considered but the influence on it of classical culture and the way it interlocked with the Renaissance has even greater importance and requires more investigation than we have so far given it.

To recapitulate: by the end of the fourth century AD, the Christian church and culture were established and the period, variously described as the Middle Ages, the Medieval or Gothic Period, lasted about a millennium

OPPOSITE

Study for the Holy Family

Chalk on paper

British Museum, London

LEFT

The Arch of Constantine, Rome

(AD 312)

Built to honour Constantine, the arch is one of the finest in existence and in a good state of repair. Some of the reliefs, including those showing Constantine's victories over Maxentius, are Constantinian, but the majority were removed from other locations.

until the 14th century, during which time it was reflected in the visual arts by an essentially pious society which gave to the age a positive visual, individual identity. The great churches and cathedrals, built throughout Europe, became the centres of local communities and established in the minds of the population a belief in the central role of Christ in their lives, while the wall paintings, sculptures and stained-glass windows confirmed the Christian message.

By this time other influences were beginning to emerge, particularly through the intellectual curiosity of scholars and priests as they became increasingly familiar with writings from the earlier classical civilization. It appeared that there was much of interest here that was not in direct conflict with the Christian faith.

This growing interest received a sudden boost in 1453 as the result of the capture of Constantinople by the Turks. Constantinople, the city of Constantine, where he had moved his capital in 330 AD, was also a centre of learning, which included the earliest writings of the Greek philosophers. The capture resulted in the diaspora of students and intellectuals, and many of them gathered up their papers and fled to Italy. Consequently, it has been suggested that the Italian Renaissance was directly triggered by this event and that it was only at this time that the writings of the great classical civilizations were discovered. Although important, is is now recognized as not as significant as it was once supposed and tends to obscure the earlier development of interest in classicism in Italy.

However, it did provide a moment in which the early classical writers became a part of the developing culture in Italy. By the 15th century there was a rapidly expanding interest in the earlier cultures, and these were studied by all intellectuals, especially members of the church from priest to pope. The Greek philosophers came to be revered – almost worshipped – and Plato was so inspirational that his many followers were described as Platonists, Michelangelo, although a devout Christian, later being one of them. A significant point to note is that the 'pagan' pre-Christian ideas were not regarded as a threat to Christianity and were allowed to flourish alongside it.

The studies of these early writers, from both Greece and Rome, had led to a corpus of belief that was essentially based on the human intellect and the way it dealt with the material world. While not directly denying the truth of the Christian message, the Renaissance intellectuals relied more on their confidence in and expectation of human accomplishment – hence the philosophy of Humanism. In fact there were many Christian Humanists, which included popes as well as Michelangelo, who had originally studied the early philosophers while a youth at the Medici School in Florence. It may now seem difficult to believe that Christianity could seamlessly incorporate the philosophy of Plato into the faith, but it was so.

By the beginning of the 15th century the early elements of Renaissance culture could be perceived in Italy. The products of artists and architects of the time were beginning to change character, with classical elements now being incorporated into their work, inspired by Roman sculpture and painting, and new possibilities in architecture were being newly inspired by the ruins of the classical buildings that remained. Not only was the visual culture beginning to change as classicism became a widespread influence, the opportunity for a new social and intellectual order was also presenting itself.

OPPOSITE

The Pantheon, Rome

A temple for the worship of all the gods, the Roman Pantheon was begun in 27 BC and was finished by the Emperor Hadrian. Of all the ancient buildings in Rome the Pantheon is the best preserved and takes the form of a circular temple which was a feature of Roman architecture.

Nowadays, like the Panthéon in Paris, such a building is a place where famous or important people are buried.

SENATVS
POPVLVSQVEROMANVS
DIVOTITODIVIVESPASIANIF
VESPASIANOAVGVSTO

Michelangelo

Usually, dramatic social change is most visually apparent in architecture. The churches and cathedrals which reflected the medieval style were gradually replaced by those containing classical features of Greek and more particularly Roman architecture. During the Renaissance the early basilica of Constantine was replaced by the great classical church of St. Peter as the focal point of the Christian faith. Representations of saints and prophets came to be presented in classical poses and wearing classical dress such as the toga; good evidence of this is provided in Michelangelo's painting, sculpture and architecture. Moreover, the new architectural style of St. Peter's, in each stage or modification of its design, was derived from Greek and Roman models. Fortunately, Rome itself had many examples of the classical style in a good state of repair, and included the Colosseum and the nearby Arch of Constantine, the Arch of Titus, parts of the Forum Romanum, and the Pantheon.

One development of significance in which Michelangelo later participated was to change an important feature of existing church architecture; as classical architectural elements came increasingly to the fore, the great towers and spires of medieval churches were replaced in the Renaissance by the dome as the surmounting feature for some of the more important churches. This began in the 15th century with the famous dome for the Florentine cathedral of Santa Maria del Fiore (1420) by Brunelleschi and culminated in the 16th century with Michelangelo's dome for St. Peter's in Rome.

There is such a striking visual distinction between a spire and a dome that some interesting psychological aspects for each have been offered. It has been claimed that the spire, a symbolic finger pointing to heaven, reflected the aspirations of the early church, which laid particular emphasis on the fate of the soul after death, life on earth being merely a time of preparation: goodness and purity were the criteria.

Christianity during the Renaissance developed a more complex agenda. While the old perceptions remained, theoretically at least, Christianity was also absorbing the new Humanist philosophies based on Platonism and Neo-Platonism. The use of the dome as a Christian element in architecture is based on the belief that the symbolic effect of the sphere and hemisphere is completeness, containment, and by extension human control, the capture of the Platonic Idea, an eternally existing pattern

OPPOSITE

The Arch of Titus, Rome *(AD 81)*

This is a triumphal arch built after the death of Titus. It has a single opening, flanked by composite columns, and was erected at the top of the Sacred Way. An iteresting feature is a carved relief of the emperor located on one side of the opening.

RIGHT
Panorama of Florence, seen from the Forte di Belvedere

In this view, the most noticeable features are the dome and campanile of the cathedral. The dome is by Brunelleschi and the building, begun at the end of the 13th century, was completed in 1462. It is a scene that Michelangelo must have seen every day when he was in Florence and in general effect the city has not changed very much since his time.

of which individual things in any class are imperfect copies. Whether these analyses hold water is open to individual opinion, but it is evidently true that the spire was replaced by the dome and, of course, the elements of classical architecture that accompanied it throughout the Renaissance. Michelangelo's architectural designs all take the classical form.

This survey of Western society, so brief as to be construed as misleading in that a millennium has been reduced to just a few paragraphs, will not satisfy everyone and suggestions for a more extensive study of what could become a passionate interest are provided elsewhere. Such a study will reveal a great deal of fascinating detail which may indicate that a précis can deceive while not necessarily being inaccurate.

The Italian Renaissance was an important part of the curriculum of schools and universities since the expansion of education in the 17th and 18th centuries. It was also the popular subject of books both biographical and fictional. In modern times, however, possibly due to the distractions of two world wars and the speed with which society is now developing, the study of history, as an essential part of basic education, has steadily

diminished in importance. It is now unusual, as it would not have been little over a century ago, to find widespread knowledge of the Renaissance, its nature and its importance. George Eliot's novel, *Romola*, written in the mid-19th century, is an example of the semi-historical novel set in 15th-century Italy which was popular at that time but now rarely read. Sadly, this must now be accepted; but it does make the study of such important historical figures as Michelangelo all that more difficult to communicate.

One of the apparently incidental effects of the Renaissance, but one which can be seen in the present-day cult of celebrity, was the growth in importance of the famous name. Although all the medieval churches and cathedrals were designed by little known anonymous craftsmen (whose names may be researched but do not immediately spring to mind), from the time of the Renaissance a building's chief attribute was the architect who designed it. This also applies to other works of art: it is Donatello's *David*, or Verrocchio's or Michelangelo's, the subject of the work being relegated to secondary importance. This implies that the fame of the artist has a bearing on how we view his work.

It also follows that it is reasonable to characterize the Renaissance by naming names. Here are an evocative few – most of whom will appear again – often more than once. Michelangelo *is* the Renaissance as are, for instance, Leonardo da Vinci, Raphael, Erasmus, Gutenburg, Niccolò Machiavelli, Lorenzo the Magnificent, Botticelli, Christopher Columbus, Elizabeth I of England, Shakespeare, Montaigne, Rabelais, Dürer, Sebastian Cabot, Charles V, Francis Drake and Cesare Borgia.

Because of this emphasis on individualism, it is tempting to present the Renaissance as a single popular event, a game played out over more than two centuries, with fine players each possessing special individual talents but making up a team with the same aim. As a footnote or alternative, the Renaissance could be thought of as a modern film with starring parts and a strong storyline. This would be to emphasize that the cult of individualism began centuries ago and is with us yet.

This is not to suggest that individualism is an invention of the Renaissance or that the medieval period was filled with anonymous or individually undistinguished men and women. The difference lay in a number of factors. Christianity was then a personal matter between believers and their God, and good conduct was thought to find its reward in heaven rather than on earth. It was not necessary to parade one's righteousness – indeed this was regarded as a sin of pride. Life was not lived as communally; one knew one's neighbours but kept largely to oneself. Communication was difficult outside small groups. Methods of distributing information were tedious; there was no printing. Life was sectionalized in a way that led to the acceptance of local authority and the political culture did not accommodate individualism on a large scale so this was largely concealed. However, it definitely existed.

It could be said that the earlier civilizations that preceded it evolved and mutated into the Renaissance and that, in its turn, the Renaissance withered as a result of providing energy for the Baroque age that followed. As all ages must, it had to end. Michelangelo was uniquely representative of his times, since his long life meant that while he was a significant contributor to the character of the High Renaissance, he was sowing the seeds of Mannerism and the Baroque. Some writers have gone even further and believe that the true roots of Baroque lie in Michelangelo's individualist force penetrating further into the 17th century than is usually recognized.

The Renaissance, as already identified, began to emerge in Italy earlier than in other countries in Europe, but the process was essentially a European phenomenon. The rest of the multicultural world knew little and cared less about Europe, except when it impinged on their consciousness, which was rare but occasional. It is both reasonable and possible, therefore, to concentrate in the first instance on its development in Italy.

The early history of Italy has been referred to and briefly outlined above, but there are aspects of it that require further discussion. Every antecedent event has an effect that is carried to its successor. Sometimes this is unobtrusive, sometimes cataclysmic; sometimes it happens slowly, at other times dramatically fast. Some effects are culturally important while others are insignificant. It is important to try to distinguish between these effects and to analyze them correctly.

The lower leg of Italy, including the nearby island of Sicily, constituted the single Kingdom of Naples and is largely excluded from our concern, since Michelangelo had no connections there. It is sufficient to note that it made no great contribution to the development of the Renaissance although it played a part in the constant friction that existed in Italy and participated in its internecine wars.

The central section of Italy, a wide band across the leg of the country, comprised the Papal States from 1500 and were directly under the control of the pontiff. They stretched from Terracina on the western coast to the borders of Venetian territory to the north end of the Aegean sea. They included Rome and some other important towns and cities, from Bologna and the Byzantine city of Ravenna to Urbino, Perugia, and Orvieto further south.

North of the Papal States, on the western side, were the republics of Siena and Florence and to the north the remaining Italian territory was composed of small and large duchies and republics, including the powerful dukedom of Milan, and the most important and largest of these, the republic of Venice, whose territory included Istria and Dalmatia, which is now part of Croatia and was once the Roman province of Illyricum.

As will be recognized from the map on page 154, an appreciable percentage of physical Italy was not under major territorial threat, such as the Kingdom of Naples. This was not true of the northern republics and duchies which were obliged to create alliances for their protection from near neighbours or northern European powers, since the greatest political threat came from north of Italy in the shape of the Holy Roman Emperor in Germany and from the well-established kingdom bordering the north, France, while other European states active in the game of acquisition included England and Spain. The only physical protection that nature provided was the range of mountains that formed the northern border of Italy – the Alps. It might also be remembered that Italy has a long and varied coastline vulnerable to attack from west, east and south, but also valuable for international communication and trade being at the centre of the Mediterranean, one of the most important trading seas in the Renaissance.

The structure and influence of the city states, both duchies and republics, the power and character of the Church, the commercial activities that had made Italy one of the richest countries in Europe and taken her inhabitants from poverty to riches, fame to notoriety, are important elements of the Renaissance. It should also be remembered that the city states, whether republics or under the rule of petty, self-appointed tyrants or rulers, who liked to identify themselves as dukes whenever possible, were inimical to each other and costly to run. The danger of attack and the necessity of defence were a constant drain on both commercial and human resources. In fact, during the whole of the Renaissance period internecine conflict was endemic. There was no peace throughout the land at any time, and this biblical allusion obliges us to include the Christian Church itself, since self-interest was a feature of the entire population. Even armed conflict under the generalship of popes might be regarded with some suspicion until one remembers that Christianity is described as a militant faith.

There was one other source of conflict that has been mentioned which was not itself directly inspired by the Church or by commercial greed or fear. Two ancient factions existed in Italy, the Guelph and Ghibelline, the former claiming allegiance to the pope, the latter to the Holy Roman Emperor. Over time, and when there was no longer a distinction between church or empire, local communities in the Renaissance still traditionally regarded themselves as either Guelph or Ghibelline; whenever frictions occurred they remained faithful to these factions, long after the reasons for their existence had ceased.

Florence, Michelangelo's native city, was by tradition and history a republican state of the Guelph faction, although for some of its history it was under the domination of a single family, the most notable of which, as we have seen, was the Medici. Florence was the centre of much of Michelangelo's work and it provides a good example of the kind of complicated society to be found throughout Renaissance Italy.

In the earlier days of most city states, certain families had been growing in influence, and as their wealth from commerce (principally wool and banking) increased, so did their ambitions for political control. Rivalries between families led initially to intrigue, murder and subsequently alliances between families, which ranged from murderous antagonisms to close commitments. Followers of such families were also rivals, but could swiftly change sides; one day fighting alongside each other, the next day against. This is not an exaggeration and it would certainly have been unusual for a day to pass without the sound of mayhem and the smell of death present in the streets.

Florentine palaces of the Renaissance
OPPOSITE LEFT
Palazzo Rucellai (1453)
OPPOSITE RIGHT
Palazzo Pitti (1458–66)
LEFT
Palazzo Medici-Riccardi (1444)

The great families of Florence built their great palazzi as commercial bases in addition to country houses. They were close to being defensive castles, the main living space being the first floor or piano nobile. *All the palazzi illustrated are of this order, apart from the Pitti, which is located on an estate away from the centre of Florence and is fronted by the famous Boboli gardens. It is the largest palace in Italy with the exception of the Vatican.*

Palazzo Guadagni, Florence
(1504–06)
Designed by Cronaca

The Certosa di Pavia, Milan

Begun in 1396 in the gothic style, the Certosa was later reorganized with more sytematic geometrical proportions. The west front (1491) was designed by Amadeo (1447–1502) and is the most elaborate marble façade of the 15th century, especially in terms of its intricate sculptural detail.

RIGHT

Villa Capra (La Rotonda), Vicenza

(Begun in 1567)

One of Andrea Palladio's many famous villas distributed throughout the Veneto, the design of the Villa Capra is one that has been more or less replicated in England in Lord Burlington's Chiswick House and Colin Campbell's Mereworth Castle.

OPPOSITE

The Ca' de Mosto, Venice

This partly submerged and somewhat dilapidated house fronting a Venetian canal is a reminder of Venice's location on a group of islands. It is also a reminder that Venetian sea trade was a major part of the Italian Renaissance economy.

OPPOSITE LEFT

Santo Spirito, Florence *(1436–)*

The maturing of Brunelleschi's style in a plan which he himself described as fulfilling his intentions.

OPPOSITE RIGHT

San Lorenzo, Florence *(1421–)*

This famous church, also designed by Brunelleschi, is a basilica in structure and is believed to be the first Renaissance example in which such classical features as Corinthian columns were used.

LEFT

The Porta dell' Arsenale, Venice *(1460)*

Gothic styles of building survived in Venice to the middle of the 15th century. This was the first structure based on antiquity, on the Roman arch at Pola.

The Basilica, Vicenza, by Andrea Palladio (1549)

Although a contemporary of Michelangelo, Palladio (1518–80) has not figured largely in this survey since architecturally he represents the later stages of the Renaissance and his life and work did not engage with Michelangelo's. Nevertheless, he is undoubtedly one of the greatest architects of the period and should be included here. Palladio's contribution to the original medieval structure, completed in 1444, was to add the external classical clothing to the noble medieval hall. The competition for the work was won by Palladio in 1549 but the building was not finished until 1614 after his death.

Villa Medicea Cafaggiolo
Designed in 1451 by Bartolommeo Michelozzo (1396–1472)

It was a brutal and unprincipled society, where loyalty could be bought and assassination was commonplace. The Pazzi conspiracy (page 54) is a good example and involved the Medici and Pazzi families, both powerful in Florence at a time when it was nominally a republic.

The importance of other Italian city states, such as Milan or Venice, was considerable and the story of each makes a fascinating study; but as our primary concern is with Michelangelo's life and he had little or no significant contact with other cities, other than those that have already been included, their history does not concern us except where relevant.

Unlike most other European countries, Italy during the Renaissance can be regarded as a disunified mix of small organizations; it may be thought that the inhabitants had no sense of the larger country, but it is certain that they were aware of the unity of France, Spain and England and knew of the physical extent of their own land. They knew, in general terms, what national loyalty meant. They had also experienced invasion and recognized the power of the military machine. Therefore, it would not be an entirely true interpretation of the situation to think of Italy as a number of small communities either ingratiating themselves with one another or with daggers drawn. The politicians or statesmen had international connections and their representatives travelled abroad. Machiavelli, for instance, had undertaken many missions in Europe on behalf of the Florentine republic.

Several other elements combined to bring a sense of commonality. The Roman Empire had been part of Italy's history, the head of the Church and its centre was in Rome, and it attracted visitors from all European countries at a time that there was no restriction of movement throughout the continent: more importantly, the Italians still had a common language in Latin. (This is slightly misleading because by the 15th century there was such a variety of dialects that almost all areas and even small communities had their own language; however, Latin, the classical tongue of the Romans, still connected them.)

Florentine Tuscany had perhaps the widest spread of a single dialect, but Venice was different and was sprawled across the area north of the Venetian islands. Thus the Italians had a version of Latin as their basic tongue and any one community could generally be understood by the other. From this, with the Tuscan dialect predominating, a written language developed and became Italian rather than Latin, even though the association is close. What is sufficiently clear, however, is that a sense of national identity had been created centuries before it became a political actuality.

Chapter Four

The Art of Michelangelo

RIGHT
The Sistine Chapel, Vatican, Rome
(1508–12)

It is important to realize that the whole ceiling was recently restored and this must be taken into account when looking at later photographic reproductions of the whole or part of the painting. As can be imagined, strong views for and against restoration were expressed before the work was allowed to go ahead, but nevertheless it did. It is therefore important to identify which images show it in its restored state and which do not. It should also be noted, however, that the Sistine ceiling has from time to time been subjected to damage and decay during its 500-year history and has already had partial, less obvious restoration.

This section is concerned with Michelangelo's specific contribution to Renaissance art. It has already been established that his work covers the three main disciplines – painting, sculpture and architecture, each of which have special and different qualities and characteristics which will be considered separately and chronologically. Individual works will be discussed with illustrations and where comparison with works by other artists is made these will also be illustrated.

In the late 19th century the painter Maurice Denis commented that 'before it is a horse, a nude, or some sort of anecdote, [a painting] is essentially a flat surface covered with colours assembled in a certain order'. The materials used for a painting are a suitable surface, the colours to cover it, and the adhesive to permanently attach the two together. Traditional surfaces vary with the method, size, location, permanence and subject demanded and range from paper, board, canvas, plaster and any other flat surface that the artist deems appropriate; there are no absolute rules in this matter. The essential requisite is that the surface be covered with colour. Neither of these requirements are intrinsically

RIGHT and OPPOSITE
Architectural sketches
Pen and ink
British Museum, London

The two sketches reproduced indicate Michelangelo's connection with architectural design, particularly later in his life. There are a large number of such detail studies which clearly reveal his awareness of classical architectural devices.

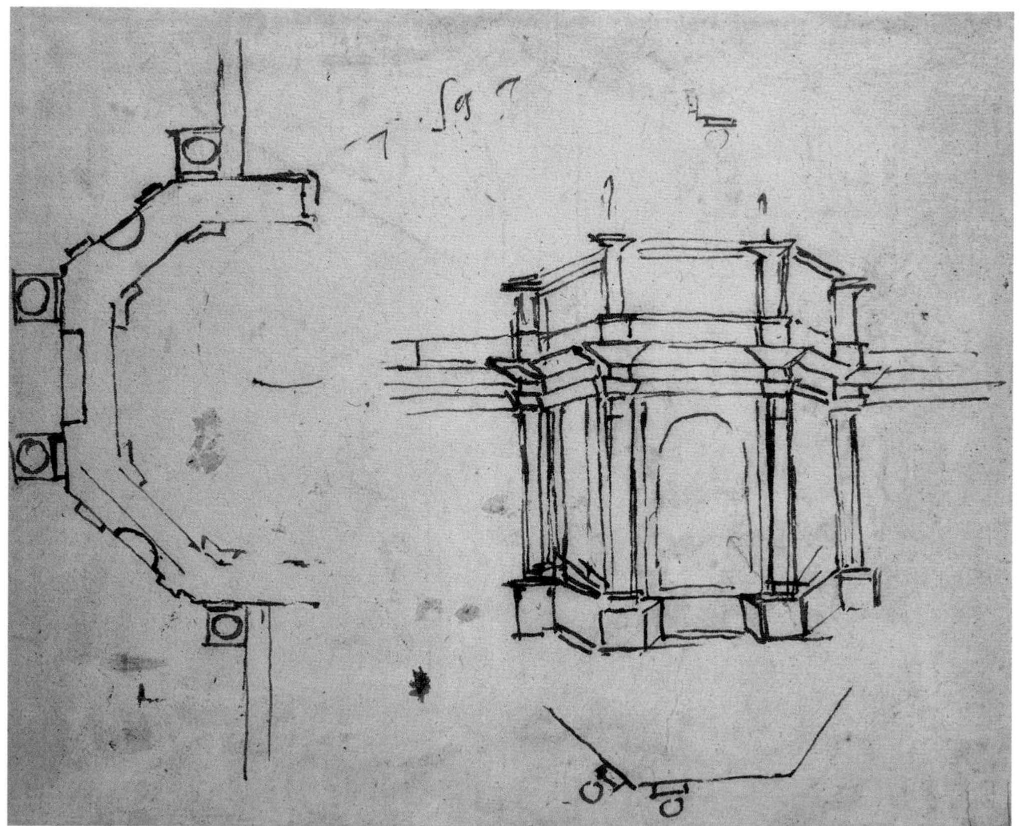

anything to do with the image made by the artist. Insofar as one material is preferred to another, in order that the artist may achieve the effect required, they are aesthetically insignificant.

Experimentation and experience over the centuries has led to a number of different 'methods', each appropriate to certain requirements and, again, more or less attractive to the particular artist. The form that the painting takes and its surface character will be determined by the material that causes the colour to adhere effectively (basically from the same sources in all methods, however different), and without distorting the colour in the process. The best known methods used in traditional painting are fresco, tempera, watercolour, gouache and oil. Acrylic is a recent development not available to Michelangelo. Most large-scale murals were traditionally in fresco and this was Michelangelo's method in the Sistine Chapel. He also used tempera and rarely, although no known examples have survived, oil.

The means used to apply the colour to the surface are varied, the most usual being brushes of varying sizes and shapes. Alternatives include cloth, sponges, knives, sprays and sometimes the human hand. Further information on

St. Peter's, Rome *(detail of the dome)*

When Michelangelo was appointed San Gallo's successor in 1546 he started on a radically new project which involved the demolition of the the Raphael/San Gallo south ambulatory. By 1564, his project was all but realized but his designs for the dome were essentially followed after his death.

Michelangelo's dome, built by Giacomo della Porta from 1588–91, has a drum buttressed by paired attached columns continuing up into the external ribs of the dome surface, with further paired columns in the lantern.

methods will be found in discussion of specific paintings and in separate 'boxes'.

Turning now to sculpture: we find that the essential difference between this and a painting is the dimensional aspect. Sculpture occupies a three-dimensional space and offers a range of imagery observable from different viewpoints; as such it actively (physically) involves the viewer and requires his participation in a changing experience; the viewer has to move about to 'experience' volume. This is very different from looking at a painting and Michelangelo's preference for sculpture throughout his long career is well known. Indeed a predeliction for one or the other of the disciplines is the common experience of the artist, and often of the viewer. Michelangelo's greatest sculptures generally formed part of an architectural structure, as in the New Sacristy for San Lorenzo, or the figure of *Moses* intended for the unfinished tomb of Julius II in Rome. His best known sculptured figure, however, is probably the giant, marble, isolated form of *David*, the slayer of Goliath, now in the Accademia, Florence.

From what has already been said it will be realized that marble was the usual medium for Renaissance sculpture and the main source for Michelangelo's work was to be found at the Carrara quarries about 35 miles (60km) north-west of Livorno (Leghorn) and nearly 60 miles (100km) north-west of Florence. The removal of large blocks of stone, already cut to size for each individual work, and their transport to a location in Florence or Rome, was a considerable undertaking in terms of both expense and time, particularly since there were no roads capable of coping with such large cargoes – at least until later in the Renaissance. It is this problem that distinguishes sculpture (particularly public sculpture) from painting, at least to begin with. When the stone has been delivered it has to be carved, finished and polished. It is then delivered, without damaging it, to a particular site and raised securely in place. Physical effort is consequently an inherent part of the method.

The sculptor's struggle with the material he uses is an essential element of the art he produces. Sculpture is a tough discipline and this generally distinguishes it from painting. In Michelangelo's case, as we have already indicated, this is not entirely true – not because his sculpture was undemanding physically but because most of his painting also made severe demands upon him.

RIGHT
The Madonna della Scala *(c.1491)*
Casa Buonarroti, Florence

This follows antique images such as can be seen on Roman sarcophagi of Greek reliefs and is reminiscent of the Pitti Tondo *(page 166) and Donatello's* Madonna del Latte.

OPPOSITE
The Tomb of Pope Julius II (*Detail of* Moses, *1513–16)*
See also page 202 et seq.

San Pietro in Vincoli, Rome

Before considering the third element of Michelangelo's work, his architectural designs, an important comparison between painting and sculpture should be noted – one that is relevant to Michelangelo's declared preference for sculpture. In producing an actual volumetric object, sculpture identifies its own physical limits. It is also, partly in consequence, peculiarly suitable for the representation of the human form in certain contexts. It is not, however, suitable where more subtle inferences, such as the effect of weather on a landscape or the character of an individual in a portrait, need to be expressed; one has only to look at Turner's landscapes and Rembrandt's portraits to recognize this fact.

When one looks at Michelangelo's Sistine paintings it is evident that he was not interested in landscapes. Neither was he inspired by the character of individuals as revealed in portraits. His preoccupation with sculpture came from the realization of its subtlety in revealing human archetypes and expressing emotions common to all mankind. His slave figures are a case in point: the slave himself is anonymous but the concept of slavery that it reveals is eloquent. (See page 236 et seq.)

The third discipline in which Michelangelo also

RIGHT and OPPOSITE detail
The Battle of the Centaurs
(c.1490–92)
Marble, 33 1/8 x 35 3/8in (84 x 90cm)
Casa Buonarroti, Florence

This early work in medium relief (mezzo relievo) *reveals a different aspect of the developing young Michelangelo. Here, a number of athletic male nudes, supposedly engaged in battle, are effectively demonstrating Michelangelo's ability to inject tension into his sculpted figures. It is almost an exhibition piece, made to show his range, even though it is not finished. Much could be read into the movement of the figures and there is already the suggestion of the Baroque. The fight was a result of the rape of Hippodamia by Eurytion the centaur, recounted in Ovid's* Metamorphoses*; but it is in the accomplished energy of Michelangelo's carving that the real significance lies.*

achieved distinction is in his architectural designs in which he incorporated the basic elements of the classical orders. The description 'architectural design' has been used rather than just 'architecture' to describe his work in this area and it is an appropriate moment to understand the nature of the architect's work.

It consists not only in laying stones or bricks, digging foundations and other constructional tasks, but also in providing all the information to enable the builder to construct the building. It may, and perhaps usually does, require the architect's attendance 'on site' more frequently than he might wish, but his work is essentially to produce a design, which includes making aesthetic decisions as to its style.

Architectural 'style', the details of the design by which the period of a building may be identified and which distinguishes a mere building from architecture, is aptly described in Nikolaus Pevsner's opening sentences in the introduction to his book *An Outline of European Architecture*:

A bicycle shed is a building. Lincoln cathedral is a piece of architecture. Nearly everything that encloses space sufficient for human beings to move in is a building; the term architecture applies only to buildings designed with a view to aesthetic appeal.

'Building', 'design' and 'aesthetics' are all included. While the words building and design would be widely understood, aesthetics is a more abstruse term which,

Pitti Tondo *(c. 1504)*
Marble, 33in (84cm) in diameter
Museo Nazionale del Bargello, Florence

The subject of the Madonna and Child was treated a number of times by Michelangelo and two examples are reproduced on these pages. Neither is fully finished but the subtlety of the carving is taken to a further degree in the Pitti Tondo. *The figure of St. John on the left is only sketchily modelled.*

Taddei Tondo (Madonna and Child with St. John) *c.1505–06*
Marble, 46¼ in (117.5 cm) in diameter
Royal Academy, London

It is almost a feature of Michelangelo's career from his earliest days to leave work unfinished, work whose potential is all but realized, making one fervently wish that it had been completed. The Taddei Tondo *is one such example, and is all the more regrettable since the flowing, linear structure of the composition is beginning to convey a sense of extraordinary maternal warmth and affection. The unusual beauty of the Madonna and her expression of love for the two children is almost unique in Michelangelo's oeuvre and one wishes that he had been able to take it*

Continued overleaf

further. The figure of the Christ Child is delicately and sympathetically modelled, while the sturdy energy of John acts as a powerful foil. The expression of such tender sentiments, unusual in the work of Michelangelo, as well as some of the carving, have always been a source of conjecture that Michelangelo was its sole creator or that others had had a hand in it.

The panel was bought in Rome in 1823 by Sir George Beaumont, a founder member of the Royal Academy and a patron of Constable. He is known for his observation that 'a good painting is a brown painting'! He donated the panel to the Royal Academy where is may now be seen.

since it has already been used in regard to both the other visual arts, deserves some further explication. Of all the three arts, architecture is perhaps the most amenable. Aesthetics is the word that encompasses all the elements in a building that are not structural but are intended to give pleasure to the eye and possibly to other senses. Most people are familiar with the saying 'beauty is in the eye of the beholder'; 'aesthetics is in the eye of the beholder' says the same thing. Aesthetics and beauty are one. There is the usual snag: what is beauty? It is, unfortunately, what you believe it to be and can only be considered on a personal case-by-case level.

Examples that may be helpful are to be found everywhere and one happily comes to mind at this point. Renaissance architecture was different from its medieval counterpart (as found in 13th-century cathedrals for instance). It can be identified as an adaptation of the classical style invented and used by the Greek and Roman civilizations before the Christian era. The clear rules and subtle details that were a feature of the classical style were adapted by the architects of the Renaissance to suit their more grandiose and aggressive views of architectural form, and revealed an ability to extend the possibilities of this highly regulated style in matters of proportion and detail to produce a 'classical' result specifically appropriate to the age. The buildings of the medieval and Renaissance periods are very different from one another while serving the same need. The elaborated towers and spires, the highly decorated exteriors and

Doni Tondo *(c.1503–04)*

This is painted in tempera and it is reproduced here so that it can be compared with the previous two, being the only other tondo Michelangelo produced. It is considered in more detail on page 252 et seq.

Model of a river god
Casa Buonarroti, Florence

An example of the facility of Michelangelo's modelling. Most of his work for public display on or in churches and other public buildings follows the general practice of creating carved figures. It was also usual for him to make small models of the subject in clay as a guide to the intended result, but since these were not intended to be permanent most have not survived. The torso illustrated here is an example and it is probable that there never was a head or the parts that are missing. In its present condition it looks more like a classical survivor than a work of the Renaissance.

interiors, embellished with sculpture and other decorative elements of the medieval style, were abandoned and the classical style adopted; the corresponding change of aesthetic demonstrates how different the visual taste of the Renaissance had become.

Architecture is different again from both painting and sculpture in that its initial purpose is practical rather than aesthetic. The construction of a building is a response to a particular need, be it church, castle, house or superstore. What each looks like, to be effective, will support and reflect the purpose for which it will be used and will come essentially from the non-practical elements, those which constitute the aesthetic element of the art percentage. An architect, in consequence, has to accommodate technical as well as artistic elements in which the latter is adjunctive and subordinate to the former, his function extending beyond that of the essentially artistic.

Nevertheless, it is important to note that architectural design is not simply the presentation of decorative drawings indicating what the designer/architect wants the building to look like; it also has to be a practical solution. It must stand up and all the decorative elements

Atlas Slave *(c.1520 23)*
Marble, 9ft (2.77) in height
Galleria dell' Accademia, Florence

The unfinished figure of Atlas (see also pages 244–245) indicates the most essential aspect of carving – releasing the form from its containment within a greater volume. The technique allows no margin of error and mistakes cannot be rectified. In a notable quotation, the architect Frank Lloyd Wright remarked: 'A doctor can bury his mistakes, an architect can only plant vines.' The sculptor has the same problem.

RIGHT
St. Peter's, Rome

Michelangelo had several connections with St. Peter's, which is an amalgam of the work of other artists as well as Michelangelo, whose work included designs for the dome, although it was not built until after his death by Giacomo della Porta. The cathedral also houses one of his earliest works of sculpture and one of which he was the most proud, the exquisite Pietà *of 1498–99 (pages 190 et seq.).*

OPPOSITE
The Laurentian Library, San Lorenzo, Florence
Casa Buonarroti, Florence

One of Michelangelo's drawings of the proposed doorway between the loggia and the reading room of the Laurentian Library.

must stay on. The architect, like the sculptor, must decide on appropriate materials, their weight, the foundations necessary to support the structure, the effect of light both internally and externally, and endless other practical problems. In addition he must see that the work actually rises in the form he has envisaged; in short, he must supervise and employ the skills of others. This makes the architect different from either the painter or sculptor.

As we are primarily concerned with Michelangelo's art, a full study of the technical aspects of his architectural achievements lays beyond the scope of this book. It is sufficient to say that what is necessary for a general understanding of the designs for his architecture will be considered but it is the forms and their artistic inspiration that will remain our first concern.

Michelangelo's major architectural work is mainly confined to the later period of his life, culminating in his intended design for the Capitol and for St. Peter's in Rome, both of which he worked on until he died. Although Michelangelo thought that architecture would be less taxing than the other arts, one suspects that experience taught him otherwise.

Michelangelo's work on the new centre of

DOMINVS
DOMINANTIVM

Christendom, St. Peter's, provided a model for subsequent generations; his design for the dome of the great church, executed after his death, became the identifying image of Roman Catholicism. Its influence on St. Paul's Cathedral in London or the church of Les Invalides in Paris is more than evident.

It is impossible to find another person to compare with Michelangelo in terms of creativity, accomplishment, power and achievement. It is perhaps advisable to recognize that it is becoming less rather than more probable that we shall see his like again.

MICHELANGELO'S SCULPTURE

As noted above, the three-dimensional aspects of sculpture can be achieved by opposing processes – addition or subtraction, i.e. the material can be either built up or cut down. With a malleable material, such as clay or plaster, the sculpture can be built up from nothing or it can be cut out of a solid material such as wood or stone. The process is different for each technique and also suggests a different mental approach or attitude. In both cases it is the sculptor's intention to create a specific volume which may be nearly identical in either technique.

David

A copy of Michelangelo's sculpture in the Piazza della Signoria which stands in place of the original which was removed and placed in the Galleria dell' Accademia in Florence.

THIS PAGE and OPPOSITE, FROM LEFT to RIGHT

David by Verrocchio *(before 1476)*
Bronze
Museo Nazionale del Bargello, Florence

David by Donatello *(1408/09)*
Bronze
Museo Nazionale del Bargello, Florence

David by Michelangelo *(1501–04)*
Marble, 13ft 6in (4.10m) in height, including base but not pedestal
Galleria dell' Accademia, Florence (with copy in the Piazza della Signoria)

David by Bernini *(mid-1600s)*
Marble

The four Davids illustrated here, covering the period from the early

Continued opposite

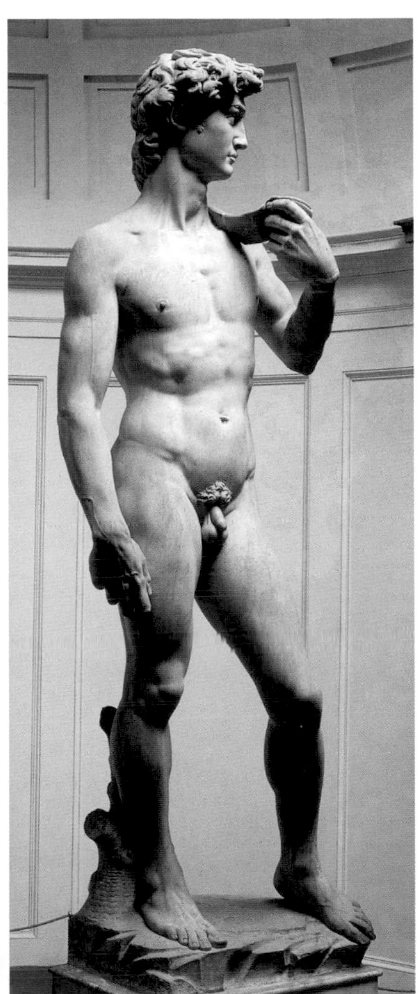

Renaissance to the Baroque, show the development of the idea of David from a callow, slender youth to a fiercely aggressive slayer of Goliath. Strangely, perhaps, it is only Verrocchio's gentle figure which parades the symbolic decapitated head, although Donatello's, looking more elegant than the situation would seem to warrant, has clearly conquered his rival. Michelangelo's David is anticipating action and to this extent he commands the scene, and with an apparently dignified detachment. Bernini's, with a wonderful contrapposto *sweep is in action and the presence of Goliath is indicated just to the right of the viewer. The development of the sense of personal awareness increases across the group and one must admire all the works while retaining a personal preference. This is, presumably, what aesthetic judgment is all about.*

David *(1501–04)*
Marble, 13 ft 6in (4.10m) in height, including base but not pedestal
Accademia, Florence (with copy in the Piazza della Signoria, Florence)

The figure of David illustrates a moment in Old Testament history already so well known that the second protagonist, Goliath, is not included. Michelangelo succeeded in implying the whole story while creating a figure that became emblematic of the city of Florence and its greatest sculptural image of the classical revival. Vasari was later able to say that the figure had 'stolen the thunder of all statues, whether modern or ancient, Greek or Latin'.

So much mythology surrounds the work that it is difficult to consider it solely for its sculptural qualities.

Continued opposite

In the first process, building from nothing, the form is created where there is a void and comes from a notion or intention, clear or vague on the part of the sculptor, who can add or remove pieces at will, and usually does. He has considerable choice: he can add, subtract what he has added and replace it with something else. The form grows as his intention clarifies. In the other technique an almost exactly opposite situation obtains. The limits of the volume are predetermined by the existing size of the wood or stone which is to be transformed into a work of sculpture. This already suggests a limitation. The sculptor can only diminish the volume and mistakes cannot usually be rectified, except, of course, by modifying the original intention.

The most popular sculptural subject is the human form, sometimes with accompanying features such as furniture, animals, decoration, etc. In carving, the loss of a nose may be fatal, while the loss of another part can mean a change of sex! It should also be recognized that due to its weight the scale of a block of stone creates a further limitation, or would have done in the Renaissance. Very large-scale sculpture is almost invariably composed of a combination of building blocks.

A further observation regarding the sculptural process is needed: although the intended result is a carving, the sculptor often makes a model of his intention using clay or another suitable material, usually on a smaller scale, and through this is able to establish exactly what he hopes to achieve. He subsequently uses mechanical means to find the desired scale.

There were models made by Michelangelo for this purpose. Such models may also serve another sculptural method, that of casting, usually in bronze but occasionally in some other metal such as gold or silver. In this process the model, when completed, is encased in a mould from which it is afterwards removed and set aside. A permanent metal sculpture is then achieved by pouring molten metal into the mould. (This, the reader should be warned, is not a technical instruction and he or she should at all costs avoid any attempt to follow it as such.) What it indicates, however, is that a clay model, for example, which is easily and precisely manipulated, can be translated into a bronze version of equal precision which is permanent and not easily damaged. One is reminded, however, that it is not indestructible by what happened to a Michelangelo bronze in Bologna (page 83).

Michelangelo

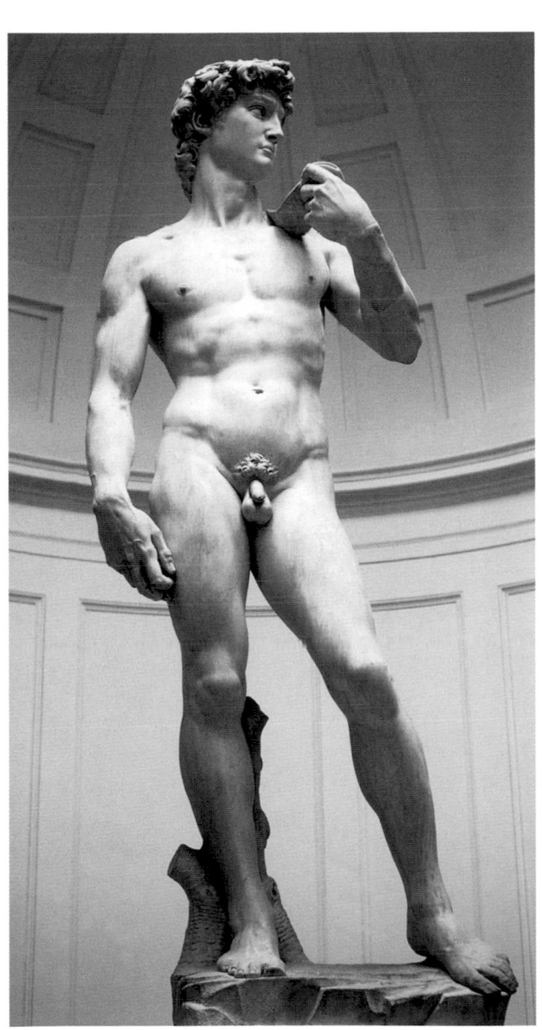

The implications of all these differences should be recognized. The first approach, using modelling, leaves options open throughout the creation of the work. Dramatic changes can be made, new ideas conceived and included; a general rather than specific intent will suffice. But with the second approach, that of the carving, the intention must be crystal clear and the action unerring. The figure or object is imprisoned in the wood or stone and must be released from its incarceration. Most sculptors are practised in both methods, but usually have a preference. It was the case with Michelangelo; there are examples of his modelling but by temperament he was a carver and the story of the Florentine *David*, 'the Giant', is a famous example of his extraordinary ability in this method. It could also be said to reflect the Platonic Idea.

One further form of sculpture should be mentioned: the relief. In effect, this is a three-dimensional pictorial sculpture, sometimes left in the colour of the material from which it is made, sometimes painted, and where the base, though solid, represents the canvas of a painter. The three-dimensional image is constructed or carved so that part of the figures or objects portrayed are

Facsimiles of the statue can also be seen in garden centres, crudely modelled in concrete, which are meant to adorn one's garden. There are other larger-scale versions in public places, modestly dressed, and the image is also used to advertise a number of commercial products.

Michelangelo was working on the original exactly 500 years ago and it has since become an icon. Of exactly what, it is difficult to say with any accuracy. In its broadest sense it has come to represent the quintessential man, in its specific biblical association the small and vulnerable pitted against the strong and brutal. There are many other possible associations but in the end one has to admit that Michelangelo's David *is not just a sculpture in marble but perhaps the greatest image of Western Renaissance*

Continued overleaf

culture to have so far emerged.

The story of the sculpture's creation is romantic enough to set it apart. The great block of marble from which the David was carved had been abandoned 40 years earlier by the sculptor Agostino di Duccio who was, it is believed, also carving a David. What remained was a partially carved and slightly damaged block no one knew what to do with. In September 1501 tit was decided to contract Michelangelo. The block was over 14-ft high and had been rejected by other sculptors as unusable. By April 1504 Michelangelo had completed his task.

Michelangelo's technical ability was not only admired, but the sculpture was also so widely acclaimed and its size so imposing that the Florentines began to see it as an emblem, a symbol of Florence itself. And it was different

Continued opposite

obscured within the base. Some of Michelangelo's very early work was of this order. The early *Madonna della Scala* (page 162), the *Battle of the Centaurs* (page 164), and the *Taddeo Tondo* (page 167) are such examples.

Sculpture, it might also be noted, in both modelling and carving to produce three-dimensional images, has a very long history. Prehistoric man produced female 'Venus' figurines and all subsequent societies created figures of their gods and rulers. By the time of the great classical Greek civilization, sculptures of the human form of the greatest subtlety and accomplishment were created, many of which have survived. The Romans continued this tradition and in the following 1,000 years of developing Christian Europe from the 4th to the 14th centuries, images of Christ, saints, martyrs and church dignitories, kings and nobles, generals and heroes, were used to decorate cathedrals, churches, palaces, houses and a variety of public places.

The earlier civilizations of Greece and Rome had become largely forgotten during the intervening Christian millennium, obscured by religious dogma and imagery. By the 14th century, however, particularly in Italy, classicism again began to stir the imagination of

from earlier Florentine versions. Both Verrocchio and Donatello had sculpted David figures, but they characterized him as a callow, cheerful youth. Michelangelo's David was on an enormous scale for a human figure and shows a young, fully-grown man with unblinking stare, looking towards an even larger foe. Michelangelo's David *is based on classical models (see left), but remains a modern Renaissance man.*

The original intention was that the sculpture should be placed on a buttress of the cathedral. When the figure was finished it was recognized that it was a much too important work to locate in a relatively obscure location and after advice from a number of older artists, including Botticelli, Perugino and Leonardo da Vinci, it was raised on a pedestal

Continued overleaf

especially designed for it in front of the Palazzo Pubblico in the Piazza della Signoria. The site ensured that it received enormous public attention where it assumed the role of cultural ambassador for Florence, a city central to the modern Italian age which, although they did not know it, was to become known as the Renaissance.

Michelangelo had previously sculpted a large figure of Hercules (now lost), which had also been a symbol of Florence, but the quality of the modelling, the assurance of the carving, and the imagination of the design raised his David *to new heights, not only in the realm of his other work, but also of figure sculpture itself. He had already been studying human anatomy and had made dissections of corpses. Vasari claims that he made a crucifix for the church of Santo Spirito*

Continued opposite

philosophers, intellectuals and artists. Italy had retained many works of classical architecture and sculpture, as well as some pictorial works, and a growing interest in classical literature, art and philosophy began to emerge. Copies were made and original work in a 'classical' style began to appear, reflecting modern Italian life; great classical equestrian sculptures of emperors became the models for the statues of the ambitious *condottiere* tyrants, so that by the early 15th century such sculptors as Verrocchio and Donatello had created a different style from that which had been popular in the medieval period and was now in the process of replacing it.

In former medieval times it had been common practice to lodge sculptured figures in niches or spaces within the architectural form or in some other association with it both on the building's exterior and interior. There are a number of reasons for this practice both practical and psychological but perhaps the most important point to remember is that medieval churches were solid structures, brilliantly designed, and with extensive areas of wall space on which to advertise the Christian message and create a sense of awe in a largely illiterate congregation.

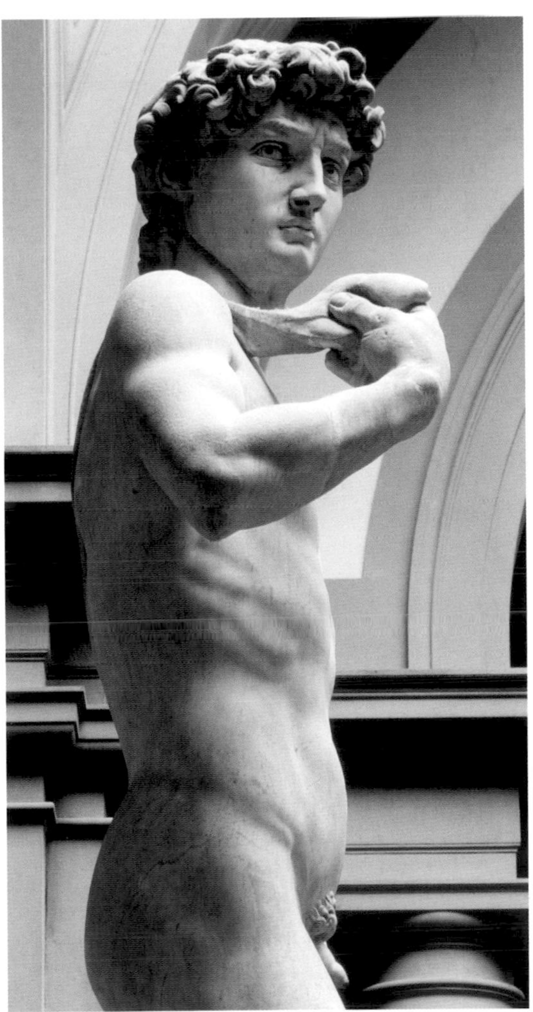

(page 196) as payment for a room in which he carried out these operations.

It is important to recognize the reason for one noticeable aspect of the figure. It appears slightly top-heavy when viewed from below, since its intended location on a buttress of the cathedral would have been well above eye level and the sculpture needed to be foreshortened to allow for this fact. The original sculpture, despite some damage in the 16th century, remained in its original location until 1873 when it was transferred to the Accademia.

The Art of Michelangelo

OPPOSITE and OVERLEAF
***David** (details) 1501–04*

Donatello, by reverting to classical forms, released the sculptured human form, allowing it to stand alone in its own space in the spirit of Renaissance Humanism, which was concerned with the notion that human beings should be able to realize their true potential in life, in contrast with the medieval preoccupation with the health of the soul and life after death.

Michelangelo's admiration for Donatello, encouraged at the Medici School by Bertoldo, Donatello's student and Michelangelo's teacher, resulted in a free and vigorous presentation of single figures, such as *David* or the Slaves for the Julian tomb. Donatello, and his contemporary, Verrocchio, did much to free the human figure where it had previously been imprisoned within the fabric of the great medieval churches. He brought them out into the light of day and introduced a new secularism.

Both Donatello and Michelangelo produced sculptures of *David* and a comparison of the two (with those of other artists) will reveal both the clear influence of Donatello's work on Michelangelo and the different treatment each was given (see pages 176–77).

Since Michelangelo received most of his major commissions from the popes, it is inevitable that his sculptures should have had predominantly Christian or biblical themes, with subjects taken from both the Old and New Testaments. Saints and prophets abound in the painting of the Sistine ceiling but the figures of *David* and *Moses* are among his most celebrated works of sculpture.

One early sculpture of 1498–99, based on a Christian subject, was a Pietà (an image of Jesus in his Mother's arms after He had been taken down from the Cross) of special significance. Placed in St. Peter's and completed when Michelangelo was only 23, it is the only work he signed, his name boldly carved into a band that crosses Mary's breast (page 190). This early work and its important location indicates that Michelangelo, completely of his own effort, had achieved a considerable success in sculpture before even attempting any painting commissions. This sculpture alone indicates the power of his personality, his determination as a creator, and his deep intelligence. Such talent was surprising in a young man who appeared to have sprung from nowhere and who was already attracting a large number of rather puzzled admirers.

Michelangelo's next great public success was the

marble *David* (1501–04), which was placed in Florence's main square, the Piazza della Signoria, in front of the Palazzo Vecchio in one of the most important and central sites in Florence, where it was bound to attract public attention. The large imposing figure, steadily gazing into the middle distance, seemed to the populace to represent the Republic's sturdy defiance of the ambitions of the rest of Italy. With its classically-inspired pose, it also implied the importance of ancient Greece in Italian Renaissance culture.

The figure of David was of symbolic importance to Florence in the greater community of separate city states. Perhaps the youthful David confronting the greater Goliath was seen to represent the youthful Michelangelo, confronting the more mature, acknowledged genius of Leonardo, for it was at this time that Michelangelo and Leonardo were both engaged in a painting for the Council Chamber.

Michelangelo was 26 when he started work on the figure of *David* and he was 29 when he finished it. With its base it stands over 13-ft (4-m) high and in general terms is seen as an early example of the rebirth of Greek and Roman models, transmuted to the modern world.

Essentially, it embodied the spirit of the Renaissance in marble. The figure that we now see in the Piazza della Signoria is a copy and the original is now in the Accademia gallery.

When looking at the figure of *David*, one is immediately struck by the assurance of the modelling and the understanding of anatomy that had been acquired by one so young. Michelangelo's sculptures, and the preparatory studies for them, indicate one essential fact about which many stories are told – Michelangelo's total dedication to his craft. He was a solitary at heart, was hard on himself, and never noticed how long he worked; he was lost in his art and resentful of interruptions. This relentless pursuit of an ideal that would satisfy him is a central feature of his character and is at its most evident in the modelling of *David*.

Almost all public sculpture, by virtue of its cost, is pre-commissioned, and all Michelangelo's major sculptural works were the result of papal requests for personal or family memorials. Pope Julius II commissioned a tomb for himself, intended for St. Peter's, so that he would be remembered when he was dead, while the sculptures for the New Sacristy in San Lorenzo, Florence were for the

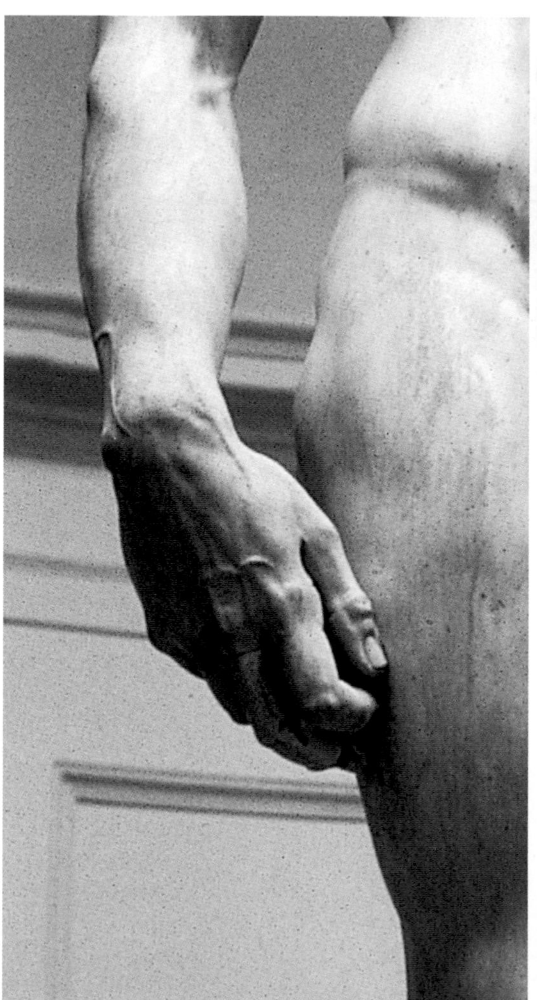

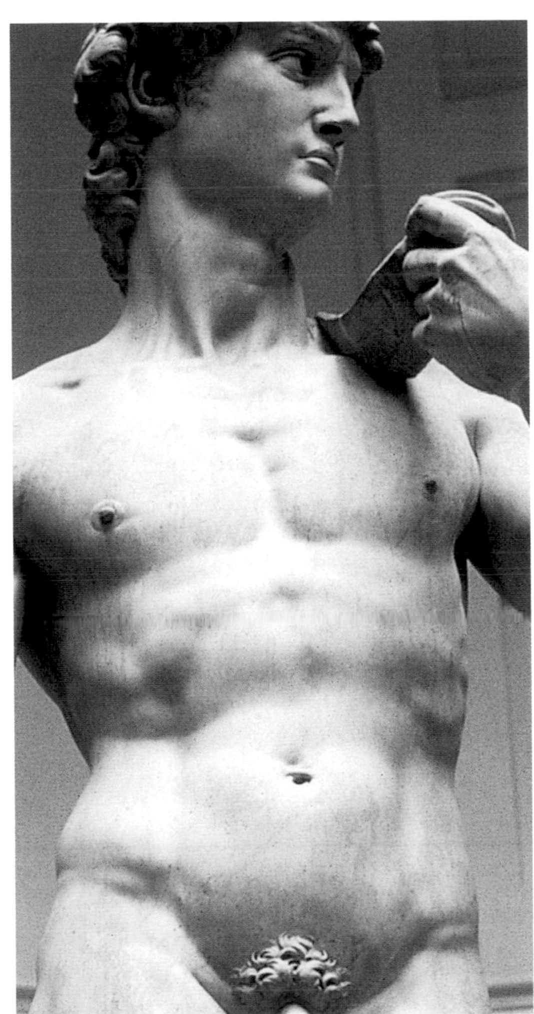

RIGHT
St. Gregory *(detail) 1495*
Church of San Domenico, Bologna

OPPOSITE RIGHT
St. Peter *(1501–04)*
Marble
Duomo, Siena

OPPOSITE LEFT
St. Paul *(1501–04)*
Marble
Duomo, Siena

The niche figures of the two saints, part of the Piccolomini commission for a tomb in Siena cathedral which Michelangelo did not complete, are early works which do not appear to have captured his interest and the lack of passion – even resentment – which he appears to have brought to the work is evident. Although the carving is accomplished and reflects the individual personalities, they are ritualistic figures which, unlike most of Michelangelo's work, do not deeply engage the spirit.

Medici family (see pages 202 and 210). Each of these were to have symbolic figures set within an architectural framework. However, neither of the tombs was completed, but fortunately a number of figures of great sculptural significance did emerge.

If one were to attempt a brief survey of Michelangelo's career as a sculptor, one would have to say that it was one of long periods of frustration and inaction punctuated by periods of intense creative activity, all determined by the whims and caprices of others. His contemporary biographers, Vasari and Condivi, describe how, though he longed to be allowed to get on with his work, he was constantly frustrated, by the popes in particular. He thought he deserved better treatment, and he was right. One gets an overwhelming sense of a man driven almost beyond endurance; since sculpture was his greatest love, this is where it is revealed and, even more than the magnificent Sistine Chapel paintings, testifies to the passionate intensity of his commitment.

A number of individual sculptures for private patrons and not intended for specific locations were undertaken by Michelangelo and these are considered in detail in the captions which are inserted in the chronological sequence of his sculpture.

OPPOSITE and LEFT
***Pietà** (1498–99)*
Marble, 69in (175cm) in height
St. Peter's, Rome

The fact that this work was commissioned in 1497 by a French cardinal, Jean de Villiers de la Groslaye, for the most important church in Christendom when Michelangelo was only 22 years old, clearly indicates how extraordinarily well regarded he already was. That the work is so highly accomplished is also an indication of Michelangelo's precocious genius, a fact of which he was well aware and which is indicated by the bold positioning of his name on the carved ribbon crossing the breast of the Madonna. It was the only work signed by Michelangelo, which perhaps suggests that he was satisfied with his work and indicates

Continued overleaf

that even at this early stage he had ample faith in his own abilities.

The work itself is indeed an extraordinary example of Michelangelo's early technical accomplishment. The figure of Christ is carved with such assurance that the full poignancy of His death is revealed, manifested in the relaxed muscular posture itself rather than in symbolic form. The presentation of the Madonna as a young mother, little older than the son she cradles in her arms, is a brilliant solution to the problem that the straightforward treatment of the ageing mother always suggests – the encroachment of reality impinging upon the mystery of the crucifixion.

The hands of Mary are also interestingly treated; one hand, the fingers only visible, cradles the body of Christ, while the other, open and

Continued opposite

pointing, demonstrates a desperate sadness at the death of her son.

The work is still in the church for which it was made, despite its total rebuilding, although it has been moved to a number of different locations during the last 500 years. It is now in the first chapel on the north side of St. Peter's.

OPPOSITE LEFT
Madonna and Child
Pencil and red chalk
Casa Buonarroti, Florence

OPPOSITE RIGHT and THIS PAGE
Madonna and Child
(Bruges Madonna) *c.1501*
Marble

This was probably begun not long after the St. Peter's Pietà *and shows some of the same surface delicacy. Nevertheless, there is evidence of it having been worked on over an extensive period. The Madonna is clearly related to the* Pietà, *the headdress being very similar, while the expression on Mary's face is almost identical. The Child appears more subtly developed and was probably completed nearer 1506.*

It was the Florentine tradition that the Child should be seated on the Madonna's knee but Michelangelo has placed Him between her knees in a pose from antiquity, at the point of freeing himself from the womb. The sculpture was made at about the same time as the marble tondos (page 166–67) and the Christ figure relates closely to these.

Santo Spirito Crucifix (c. 1492)

This smaller than life-size crucifix was made for the Prior of Santo Spirito, Florence, who had helped Michelangelo in his study of the human body by arranging the dissection of corpses for him; the crucifix may have been a gesture of appreciation. The work was discovered in the cloister of Santo Spirito in comparatively recent times and doubts have been expressed by scholars as to its authenticity.
It is an unusually young-looking representation of the crucified Christ and the contropposto *pose Michelangelo has introduced was probably the first example of what became a popular solution for him.*

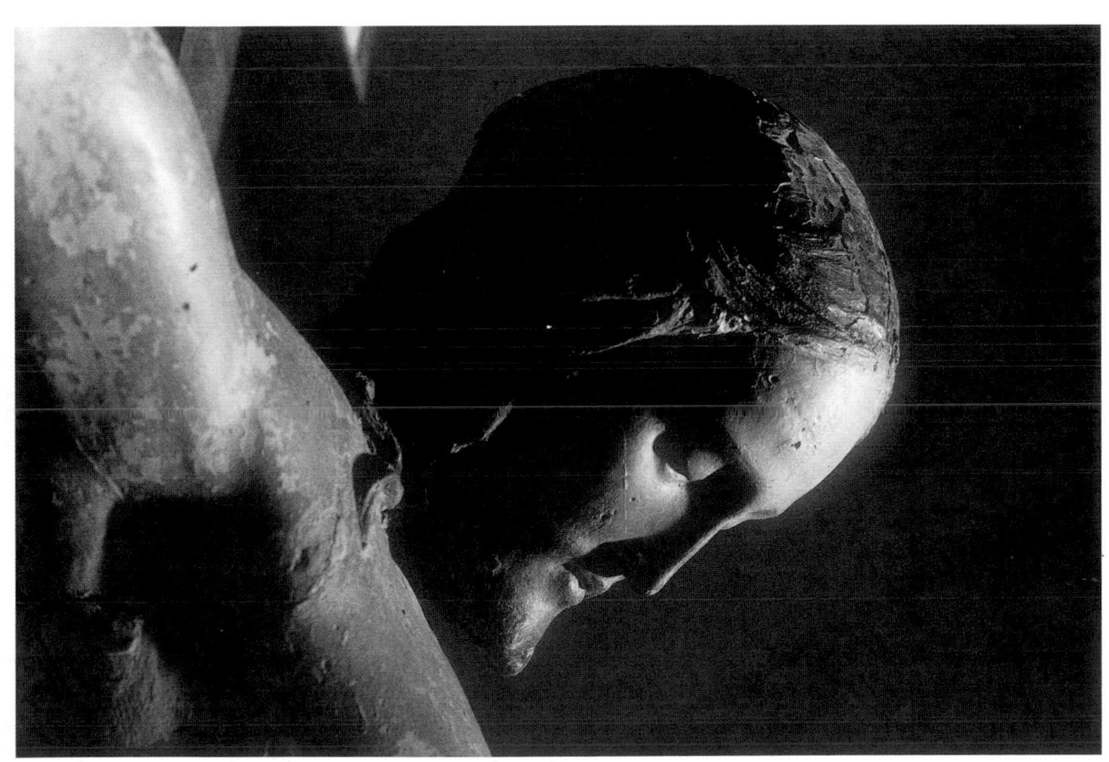

Bacchus *(c.1497)*
Marble, 72½in (184cm) in height
Museo Nazionale del Bargello, Florence

Although held to correspond to a strict classical model, this strangely unMichelangelesque sculpture of Bacchus, the god of wine, is plainly not a work of antiquity. It was bought by Iacopo Galli, a Florentine banker, for the 'antique garden' that he had built for his sculpture collection. Not a unique idea when Michelangelo's youth in the Medici School is recalled. It is believed that the sculpture was originally commissioned by Cardinal Riario but was rejected by him.

Here, the pubescent youth is beautifully modelled and posed to suggest hedonism and voluptuousness. In a drawing of the Galli garden, made in about 1532, Bacchus' right

Continued opposite

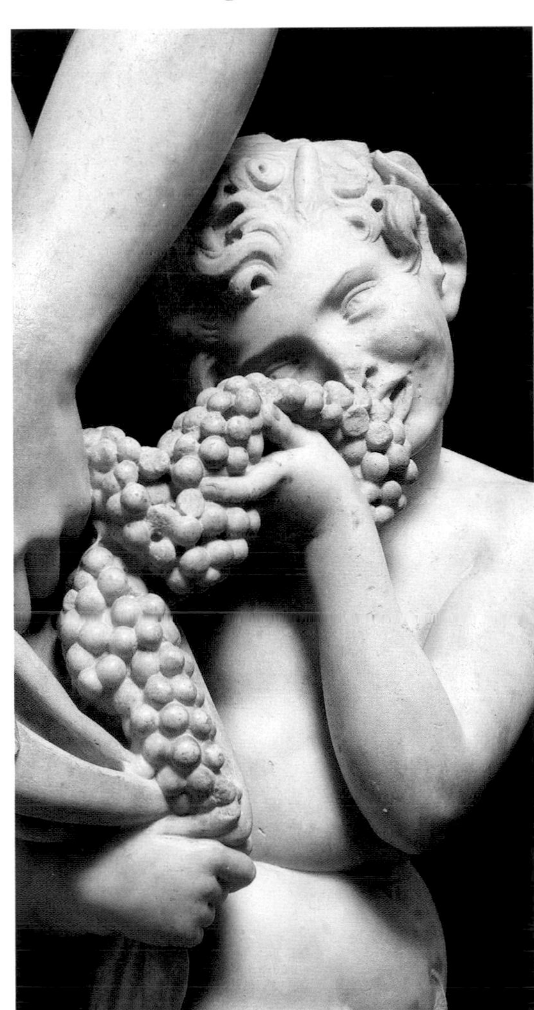

hand and drinking vessel were seen to be missing, as was his penis. However, it is believed that the hand and cup were replaced by 1553, possibly by Michelangelo himself. The headdress of grapes, clearly indicating that the figure is indeed Bacchus, is somewhat less convincing, more formulaic than the St. Peter's Pietà, *carved at about the same time. The subtle modelling and strong emotion of the* Pietà *is also absent.*

It is interesting to note that these two works from early in Michelangelo's career represent his two lifelong preoccupations – the Christian faith and classical themes. Whether or not this is one of his most accomplished early works may be questioned but it certainly indicates that his incorporation of classical sculptural principles had already been absorbed and his technique established.

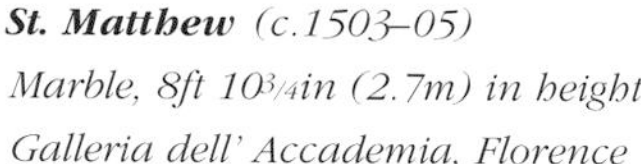

St. Matthew *(c.1503–05)*
Marble, 8ft 10¾in (2.7m) in height
Galleria dell' Accademia, Florence

In April 1503, at the age of 28, Michelangelo received a commission for larger than life-sized sculptures of the Twelve Apostles to be placed in the cathedral of Florence. He was supposed to complete one a year, that is to say the contract was to be completed when he was 40, which reveals both the degree of confidence he inspired and his dedication to hard work. In the event, even he could not sustain the huge workload and the contract was cancelled two years later.

As with most of his work, the date of this sculpture is uncertain but it is most likely that he stopped work on the unfinished figure in March 1505 before he left for Rome. It is his own

Continued opposite

recollection in a letter written 18 years later, in which he also states that it was the only apostle figure he had started.

The most interesting thing about the figure is the extent to which it shows Michelangelo's sculptural technique. The characteristic contropposto *is emerging as the figure is released and the marks of the chisel clearly indicate how he achieved the volumes he required. One of Michelangelo's repeated forms is the straightened arm in tension and the beginning of the carving of it can be examined.*

Tomb of Pope Julius II *(1505–45) (uncompleted)*
Marble, 100in (254cm) in height

Michelangelo spent so much time working on this grandiose scheme that he later declared that he had wasted his youth on it. The contract for the tomb was amended six times, and each time it was reduced. More than 40 marble figures and four large bronze reliefs were planned for the mausoleum's two free-standing storeys and five years were allowed for its completion. In the event, Michelangelo completed only a few of the figures and the story of its progress is outlined in the survey of his life (pages 36 et seq.).

The most important single work he completed was the figure of Moses, *one of four large seated figures intended for the upper storey of the monument.*

Continued on page 204

Continued from page 202

Other sculptures, both finished and unfinished, were Dying Slave, Rebellious Slave, Youthful Slave, Bearded Slave, Victory, Atlas Slave, Awakening Slave, Rachel *and* Leah.

The final structure, as far as it was completed, was placed, not in St. Peter's as originally intended, but in San Pietro in Vincoli. Not all of the work Michelangelo had produced was included; the Slave figures were dispersed and the Victory, *still in his studio when he died, was eventually placed in the Palazzo Vecchio, Florence.* Rachel *(Contemplative Life) and* Leah *(Active Life), together with* Moses *(which was placed in the central bay), were however included.*

The project was an unending concern for Michelangelo since the only possible way to complete the tomb

Continued opposite

was to continually work on it. He had been frustrated again and again by the vacillations of the pope which had resulted in six changes of contract so that the figure of Moses *(left), while it is one of his most powerful sculptures, remains the only work that truly reflects the intention of the complete design. The dominance and grandeur of the powerful Israelite leader seems to relate it to some of the painted figures in the Sistine Chapel, both on the ceiling and end wall. A sense of brooding power and destiny is strongly immanent in the work.*

MARMOREI IVLIO II PONT MAX DIVINA MICH
ANGELI BONAROTI FLORENTINI MANV ROMÆ IN BASILICA S
PETRI AD VINCVLA

FAR LEFT

Rachel (Contemplative Life)

LEFT

Leah (Active Life)

Both 1542–45

The choice of these sisters as figures for the Julian tomb is intended to present opposites and introduces a strange story. According to the Bible, Leah, with 'weak and delicate eyes', whose name means 'cow', contrasts with Rachel, her younger sister who is 'graceful and beautiful' and whose name means 'ewe'. As a result of their father's wedding night deception, Jacob marries them both but loves Rachel more. In recompense, God takes pity on Leah and sends her many children. Rachel remains Jacob's wife and after many vicissitudes becomes the mother of Joseph and Benjamin.

Although finely modelled and reflecting the different characters of the sisters these figures are not the most inspiring of Michelangelo's work and there is evidence of the hand of others in the finish. It might be remembered that these are later works for a difficult project while Michelangelo was also engaged on an architectural programme for Pope Paul III.

OPPOSITE

The Head of Moses *(detail)*

This clearly illustrates a strange element of the work. Moses has horns and they appear to be a natural feature. The subject of the return of Moses to the Israelites with the Ten Commandments is dealt with in Exodus which says his head was qaran, *a word that has fallen out of usage but which is similar to* qalen *(shining) and* qalan *(horns). In a translation by St. Jerome in about* AD *400, it is said of his return that the head of Moses had horns, a translation that would have been familiar to Michelangelo.*

The Risen Christ
(Christ with the Cross) *1518–20*
Marble, 6ft 9in (2.05m) in height
Santa Maria sopra Minerva, Rome

The original marble for this figure, commissioned in 1514, was abandoned in 1516 when a defect was discovered and the block was given to Vasari. The almost-finished figure was sent to Rome in 1521 where it was finished by Pietro Urbano, a pupil of Michelangelo. According to Vasari it represents the Risen Christ but has also been identified as the Man of Sorrows who holds in His hands the instruments of the Passion. The contrapposto *stance appears in much of Michelangelo's work and here the influence of classical statuary is also evident. Its placing in the Dominican church of Santa Maria may have been a wish to reflect Michelangelo's admiration for Savonarola.*

The Medici Chapel (New Sacristy), Church of San Lorenzo, Florence
(1520–34)

The church of San Lorenzo became the family chapel and burial place of the Medici and there were already five tombs there, two of which had been designed by Brunelleschi for the Old Sacristy; Michelangelo became responsible for the chapel while it was still being constructed to Brunelleschi's design. It is not clear how much either contributed to the finished chapel but its basic symmetrical shape by Brunelleschi must have been acceptable to Michelangelo.

The original commission, probably by Cardinal Giulio de' Medici, consisted of six tombs for Lorenzo de' Medici (the Magnificent); Giuliano, his brother; Lorenzo de' Medici, duke of

Continued opposite

Urbino, Lorenzo the Magnificent's grandson; and Giuliano, duke of Nemours, Lorenzo the Magnificent's third son; and popes Leo X and Clement VII, both Medici. Only two of the tombs were completed which has given rise to the widespread misunderstanding that the tombs finished are those of Lorenzo the Magnificent and his brother Giuliano.

Nevertheless, this was an important commission and was still not completed when Michelangelo moved permanently to Rome. The reason for this lies in the papal succession. When Michelangelo was contracted Leo X was pope but died in the following year (1521), and it was not until Cardinal Giulio became Pope Clement VII in 1523 that Michelangelo was able to return to the chapel, both Leo and Clement being Medici popes.

Continued overleaf

Clement was a scheming and demanding man but Michelangelo was able to continue work on the tombs until 1534 when he was recalled to Rome and arrived only two days before Clement died.

During Clement's papacy, while work progressed, Michelangelo's designs became more ambitious and the planned programme became clearly impracticable. It was the lesser part containing the two capitani *that was completed and the loss of the intended tombs of Lorenzo the Magificent and his brother with their attendant sculptures is a considerable diminution of the effect planned for the chapel.*

What was achieved, however, is a powerful legacy of the Renaissance's greatest sculptor at the height of his powers. The four reclining figures offer further examples of the vast emotional

Continued opposite

range that Michelangelo achieves in his sculpture.

The six completed figures and their architectural context should be looked at individually; but it is significant to remember that Michelangelo was essentially a sculptor and saw life with a sculptor's eye, regarding buildings as sculptured living forms. In consequence, instead of a traditional mathematical calculation he saw them as dynamic organisms and altered relationships in their elements according to his emotional response to his overall concept of the structure. If this seems a little obscure or confusing, perhaps it will be helpful to think of a human body and how, without losing the necessary elements of the form, it can express different feelings. He used the classical elements of column and cornice, window and doorway with

Continued overleaf

such variations from the Vitruvian standard as his nature demanded.

His architecture, using the same elements, is as different from, say, Bramante's or Raphael's as is their temperaments. He is quoted as claiming that it was certain that the parts of a building relate to the parts of the human body. With this in mind the examination of the New Sacristy in San Lorenzo becomes more complicated than the mere consideration of the six figures. Interestingly, there is a seventh, a Madonna and Child (see page 211), also in the New Sacristy, together with figures by other sculptors.

It is important to understand that this Madonna and Child, situated on the wall between the two tombs and between two Medici patron saints, although not given the architectural

Continued opposite

context of the tombs, is nevertheless the spiritual centre of the entire composition. The sideways glances of the main figures, Lorenzo and Giuliano, are directed towards the Madonna, thus creating a spiritual unity in the funerary chapel. It could be said that this was the first use of the device used in later centuries.

In the tombs in the New Sacristy Michelangelo has placed the figures of the dukes within an architectural context and recessed them as they might have been in the medieval period. The supporting figures, howevever, are balanced somewhat precariously on a curious coffin-like architectural element from which, with their sculptural support, they seem in imminent danger of slipping. One of the stranger elements of these sculptures are the thin supports for

Continued overleaf

the feet of the figures of Night *and* Day – *uncharacteristic of Michelangelo's work.*

When Michelangelo was commissioned by Cardinal Giulio to undertake the Medici tomb, it would have been for four figures of people he knew well and for two he did not. The duke of Nemours was 37 when he died and was four years younger than Michelangelo, while the duke of Urbino was 17 years younger and died in 1519 at the age of 27. The point is made to explain the assumption that the two completed figures were not, as might have been expected, Lorenzo the Magnificent and his brother killed in the Pazzi plot. It remains a question of interest why Michelangelo chose to sculpt the least-known figures first, or was he was asked to do so by the Cardinal who became Clement VII and one of his important patrons.

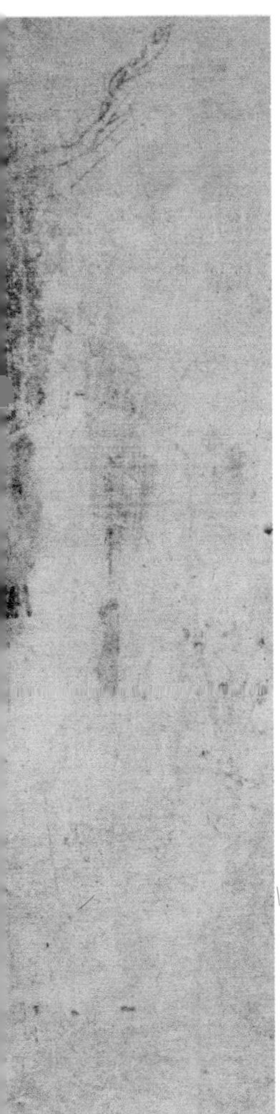

CARTOON

A drawing, design or painting, usually made as a preparation for work in another medium, e.g. fresco or tempera. Michelangelo prepared cartoons for his Sistine Chapel paintings. The drawings are sometimes used full-scale for the purpose of outlining a form to be painted within a composition, using a pointed tool to outline the necessary shapes. In this context it bears no relationship to the modern use of the word.

THESE PAGES and 214–15
These preliminary sketches were executed by Michelangelo in the 16th century and found in the Medici Chapel, Florence during restoration work around 1975.

RIGHT

Tomb of Lorenzo de' Medici, Duke of Urbino, with the suporting figures of Twilight and Dawn

OPPOSITE:

Tomb of Giuliano de' Medici, Duke of Nemours, with the supporting figures of Night and Day

Giuliano, duke of Nemours was the third son of Lorenzo the Magnificent and was 13 years older than Lorenzo, duke of Urbino, the Magnificent's grandson. Since the general presumption was that the Lorenzo represented was the Magnificent it has been supposed that the other figure was Giuliano his brother, which is also why it is Lorenzo who is usually considered first. Neither figures, it might be said, were of great distinction but the duke of Urbino was the father of Catherine de' Medici who married Henry II of France.

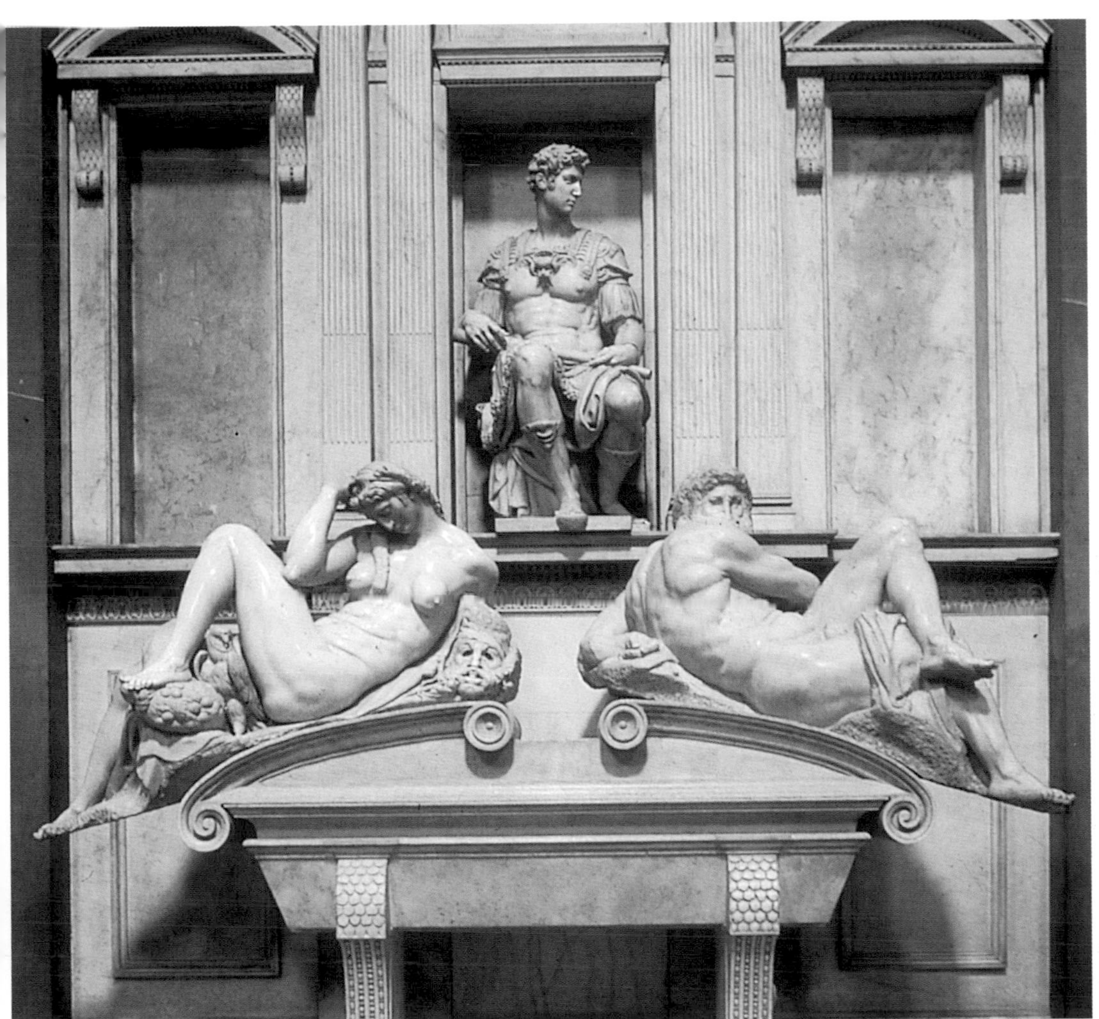

The two figures, as sculpted by Michelangelo, are different in character. The militant armoured figure of Giuliano contrasts with the reflective figure of Lorenzo. The supporting figures enhance that feeling; the tense figures of the female Night and male Day, one face in deep shade and the other like a sun rising, represent change and action while the figures of Twilight and Dawn are extended and relaxed, the figure of Dawn being one of the most sympathetic female figures Michelangelo ever sculpted.

It may be wondered how Michelangelo would have treated the subject of Lorenzo the Magnificent since he was described by a contemporary as having a large and well-formed body but ill-shaped nose, and a massive jaw which deprived his face of beauty. His voice was also harsh, his sight was weak and he had no sense of smell!

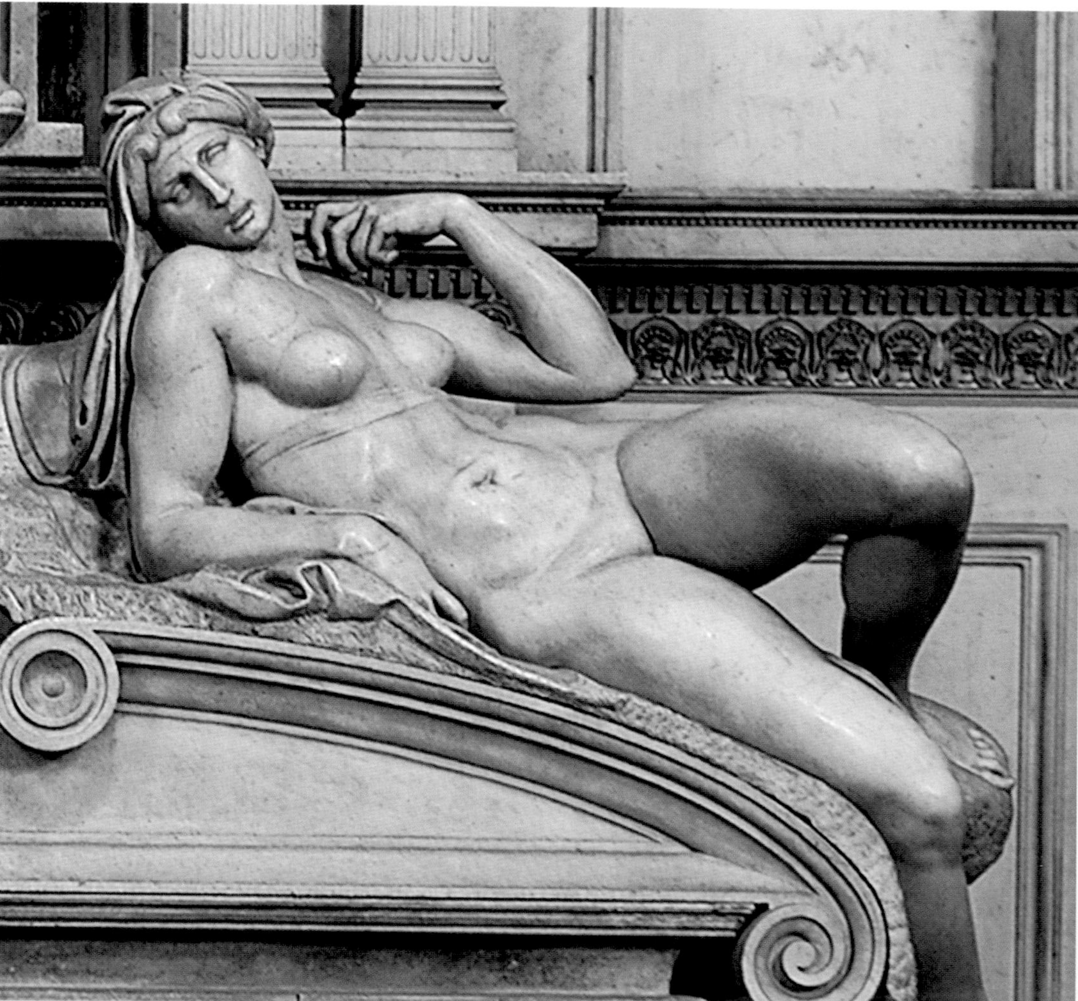

Tomb of Lorenzo de' Medici, Duke of Urbino *(showing detail of Dawn)*

Tomb of Giuliano de' Medici, Duke of Nemours *(showing detail of Night)*

Tomb of Lorenzo de' Medici, Duke of Urbino *(showing detail of Twilight)*

Tomb of Giuliano de' Medici, Duke of Nemours *(showing detail of Day)*

Sketches for the tombs in the New Sacristy, San Lorenzo, Florence

Rondanini Pietà *(1553)*
Marble, 77in (195cm) in height
Castello Sforzesco, Milan

This late and unfinished work is the most moving of all the Pietàs by Michelangelo. His first, in St. Peter's, Rome (pages 190–193), reflects an extraordinarily accomplished young man's presentation, in as perfect a form as is possible, of emotional distress – that of a mother whose child has been brutally and slowly killed and his body returned to her. It is a moving statement well made but the Rondanini Pietà *is very different from its predecessor. Here the body of a bearded, older-looking Christ is supported by the hunched figure of the Madonna who almost appears to be teaching him to walk again; that life is coming back to the dead limbs.*

Continued overleaf

It is known that under the influence of Vittoria Colonna, who had died in 1547, Michelangelo's faith had gone through a change and it seems that he is searching in the stone for the core of the Christianity he had absorbed through her to be 'justified by faith alone'.

The stone used is clearly part of another sculpture of which the disengaged arm and the legs were a part; they do not relate in scale to the upper bodies. In this unfinished state it is a great masterpiece – one which we may be glad Michelangelo did not finish – this time because of his own death. It was reported by Daniele da Volterra that Michelangelo was re-working the Pietà *only six days before he died.*

The particular poignancy of the work lies partly in its unfinished,

Continued opposite

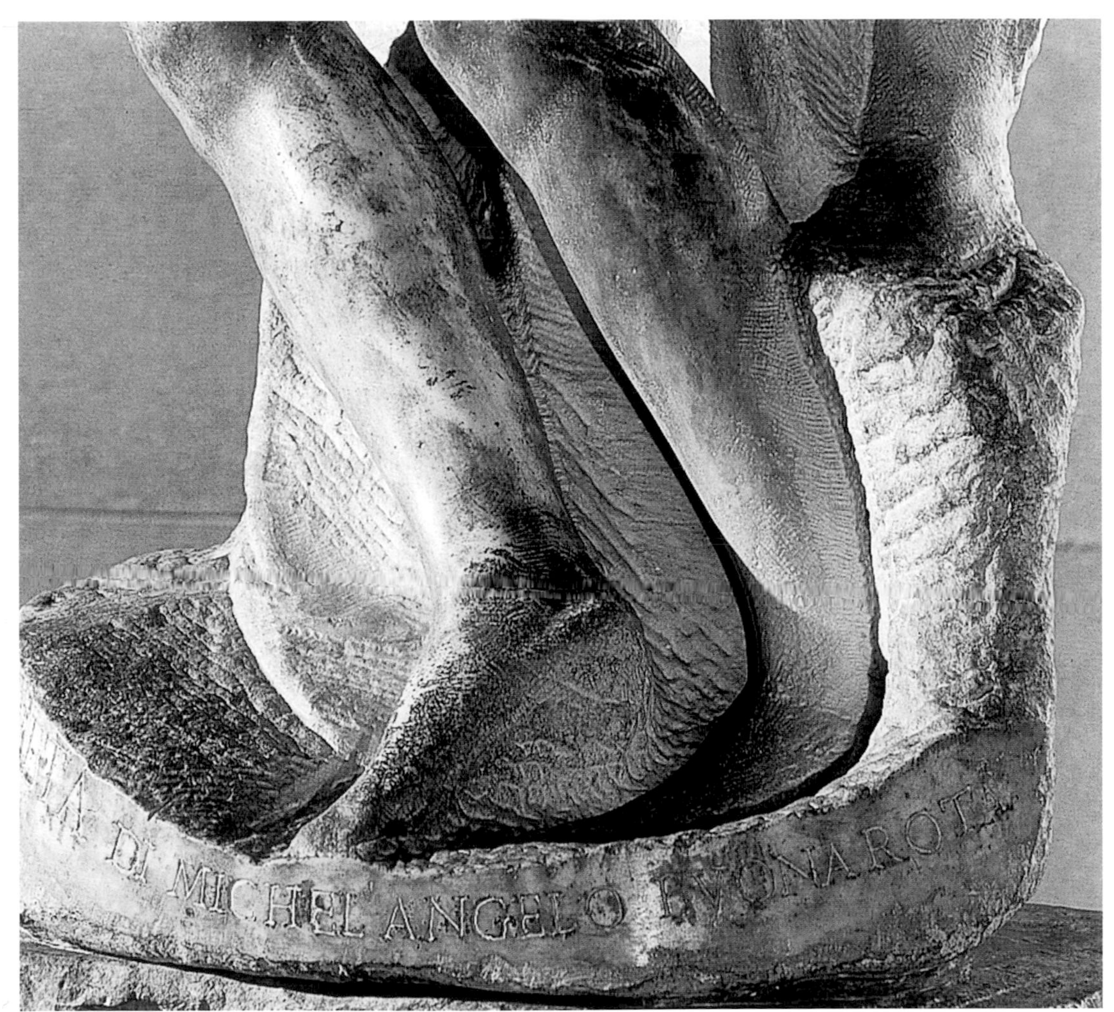

unresolved state. It is evident that Michelangelo was struggling towards a new presentation of the subject, and if we accept that he had a hand at least in all the earlier interpretations it is almost heart-rending to see the sculptural perfection of the early St. Peter's Pietà *gradually disintegrating into the agonized, despairing attack of an old man on marble which had been used before. It is a last response to the Crucifixion – the mother with the dead child, the future at an end.*

Pieta del Duomo *(also known as a Deposition) c.1547–55*
Marble, 92in (234cm) in height
Florence Cathedral

There is always some confusion over the naming of such sculptures – whether they should be referred to as Pietàs (the word pietà *meaning pity), where the body of Christ is already placed in the arms of his Mother, or Depositions, where Christ's body is being removed from the Cross. This is clearly a Deposition in the terms described above, and is a strange and poignant group with somewhat curious attributes. As with the* Taddei Tondo *(page 167), authenticity has been questioned; one must remember that with all great artists there is always a wish to attach as much work to them as possible, usually for commercial*

Continued opposite

reasons, of course. The question in this instance is more open since the group is so strangely constructed. Whoever sculpted it must have known that the scale of the figure of Christ is disproportionate to the two female supporting figures and that the kneeling figure is disproportionately large in the lower half. Although this is placed as a late sculpture by Michelangelo, it is more than likely, if it is his work, that an assistant was involved. Moreover, the usual power and energy present in Michelangelo's carving throughout his life is not in great evidence.

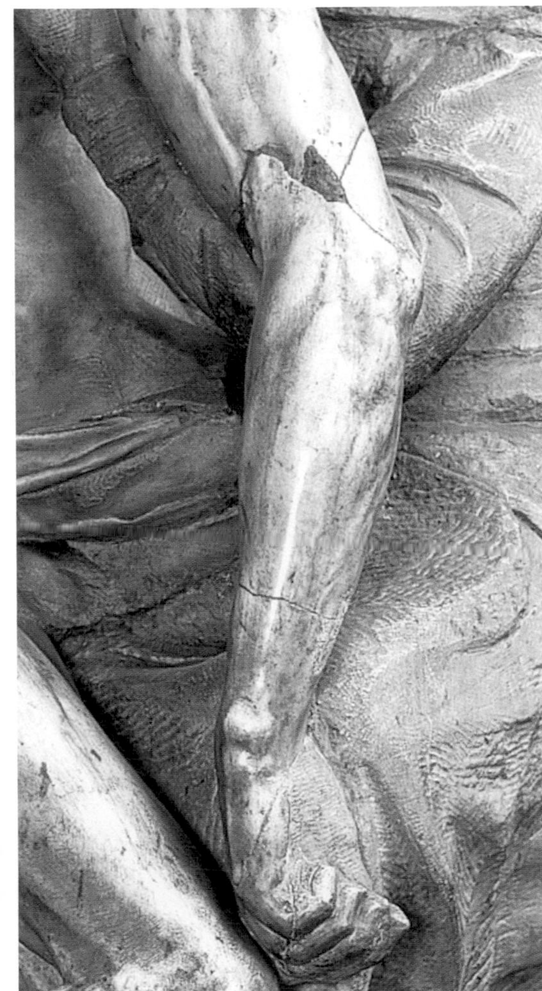

Palestrina Pietà *(c.1556)*
Marble, 81in (206cm) in height
Galleria dell' Accademia, Florence

Again the subject is a Deposition or Entombment rather than a Pietà, although it is generally known as such. It is a late work, like the Rondanini, but is unfinished and one wishes that it had been completed since there is again some doubt concerning its authenticity. The carving is Michelangelesque and the bulking and modelling typically his but it was not recorded until the 17th century when elements of the Baroque were by that time noticeable in the work of a number of accomplished sculptors. This does not deny the possibility that it was by Michelangelo but it certainly raises questions, some technical, some aesthetic. If I had to vote it would be that it is not. But it is included in most reviews of his work and so justifies a place here.

Dying Slave *(c.1513–16)*
Marble, 9ft (2.74m) in height
Louvre, Paris

The most complete and polished of the several Slave figures destined for the tomb of Pope Julius II, the Dying Slave *is an apt choice of subject. For Michelangelo, the task of the sculptor, faced with a block of stone, was to release the figure trapped within. The slave is the epitome of such confinement but in a psychological rather than a physical sense. The subject gave Michelangelo the means to express all the range of emotions that can assail the human spirit, which he explored with almost superhuman detachment. Most of the slave figures are unfinished but each of them, as they are described, show a different aspect of mental suffering. As a group these figures are an enormously impressive creative achievement.*

The Dying Slave, *being the most finished, clearly indicates the intensity of Michelangelo's vision, his so-called* terribilità, *in which the marble seems almost to exude the feelings of the subject, in this instance, the approach of death. Acceptance and hope are equal elements in this gradually fading muscular figure.*

Dying Slave, by Paul Cézanne
(c. late 1800s)

A graphic reminder of Michelangelo's continuing influence on the 'modern' artists of the 19th century.

Rebellious Slave *(1513)*
Marble, 7ft (2.16m) in height
Louvre, Paris

The observations made in respect of the Dying Slave *are appropriate here but the spirit released is different. The* Rebellious Slave *is not resigned to his fate, his body is in turmoil like his spirit and instead of slowly subsiding into death he continues to struggle, looking upwards with a determination and a different kind of hope.*

It is interesting to note the use of a small artificial device. One of the problems with most standing figures is the thinness of the legs which must support a heavy body. The solution adopted by most sculptors, including Michelangelo, is to buttress the lower part with some associated object. A frequent solution used by Michelangelo was to leave an amorphous form attached to the legs.

The differences in the two Slave figures are not inadvertent. The slowly downward-curving shape in the Dying Slave *suggests a slow, subsiding movement, while the* Rebellious Slave *is provided with an upward-stepping feature and a back support for his muscular efforts; he is not giving in.*

Bearded Slave *(c.1520–23)*
Marble, 8ft 8in (2.63m) in height
Galleria dell' Accademia, Florence

The unfinished slave sculptures illustrated on these and the following pages provide an opportunity to examine Michelangelo's method of carving. Firstly they indicate the real sense of discovery that seems to invest all Michelangelo's carved sculpture. There is a strong sense that he is releasing an already existing form which he 'finds' in the block of stone. In each case it is the middle section that he first 'discovers' and works upwards and downwards from this, finishing with the extremities, the last element being the head.

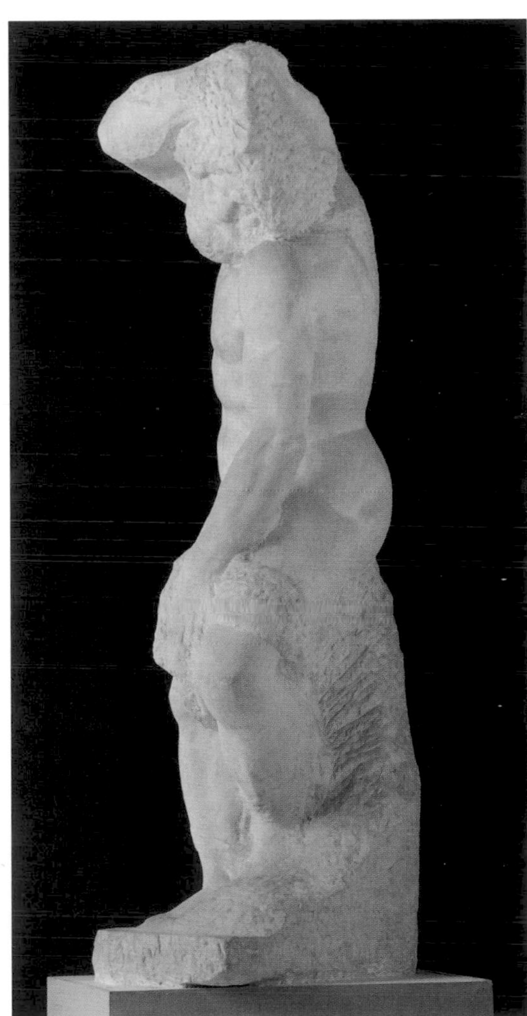

Awakening Slave *(unfinished)*
Marble, 8ft 9in (2.67m) in height
Galleria dell' Accademia, Florence

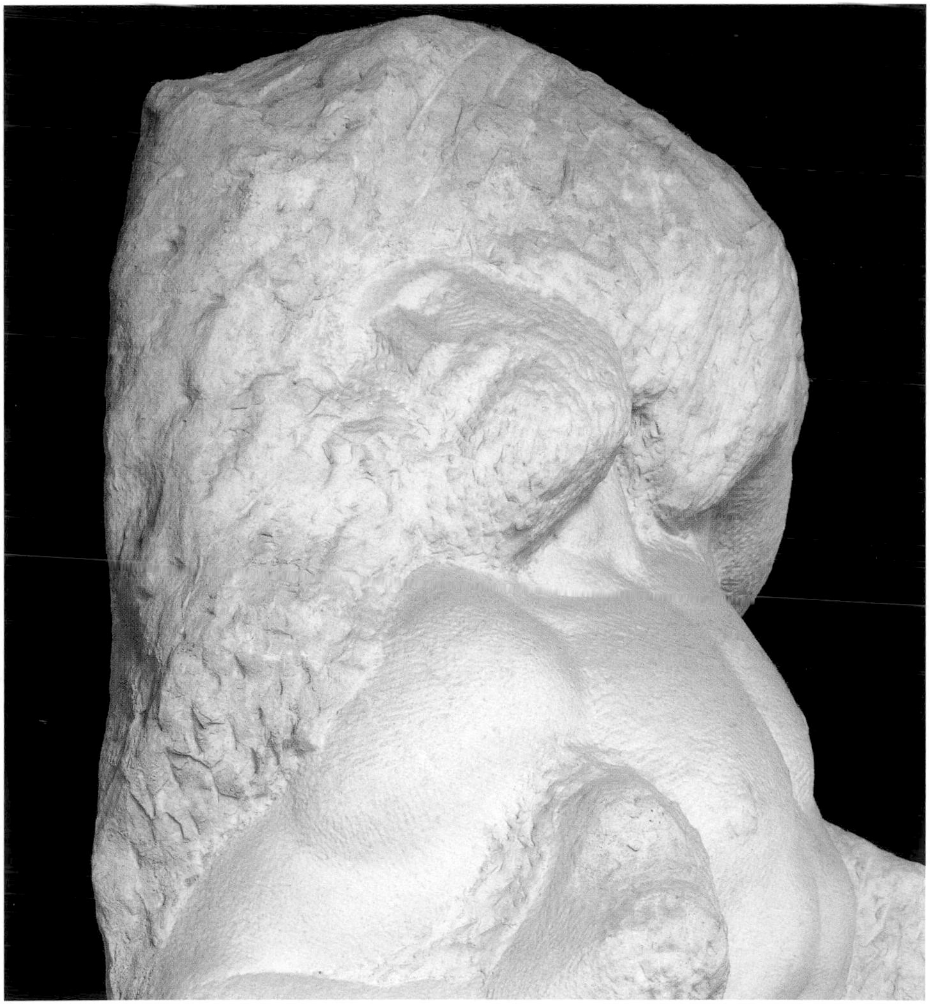

Youthful Slave
Marble, 8ft 5in (2.56m) in height
Galleria dell' Accademia, Florence

Victory *(c. 1519)*
Marble 103½in (263cm)
Palazzo Vecchio, Florence

This is another of the sculptures originally intended for the tomb of Julius II and most likely one of two to be placed on either side of the central door of the tomb. It was suggested on Michelangelo's death that it might be sited over his own tomb but in the event it finished up in the Salone dei Cinquecento in the Palazzo Vecchio, Florence.

This is a remarkable and revealing sculpture. It has been suggested that it is more similar in feeling to the Medici chapel figures which is perhaps not surprising since it is one of the later tomb figures to have been carved.

The aggressive vigorous twisting movement, known as contrapposto, *is more evident here than in any other of Michelangelo's figures and is a clear indication of his potential and later realized influence on the two successor developments of Mannerism and Baroque. This figure has all the features of* contrapposto, *including the balance of weight held on one leg.*

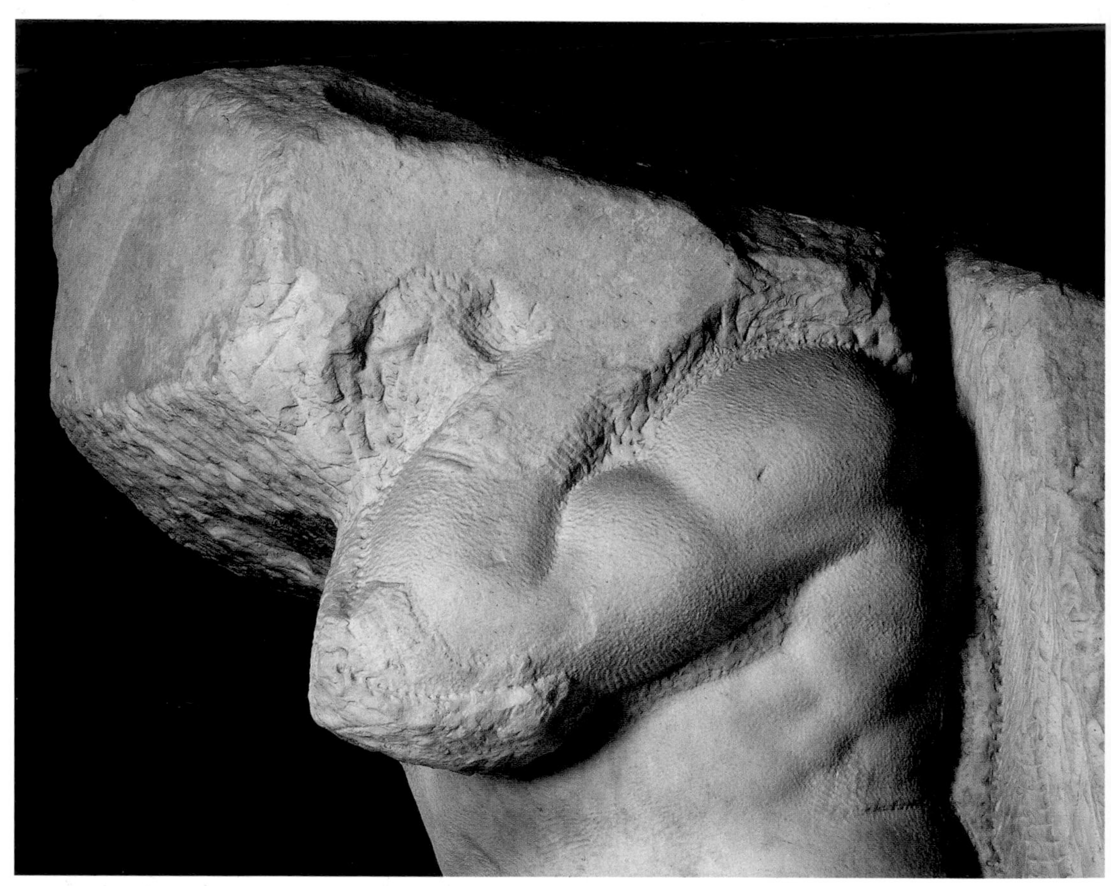

Atlas Slave
Marble, 9ft (2.77m) in height
Galleria dell' Accademia, Florence

Apollo/David *(1525–30)*
Marble

The history of this work is not entirely clear. Vasari claimed that Michelangelo made an Apollo figure in 1530 for the leader of the papal army, Baccio Valori. The same figure was described by Duke Cosimo de' Medici as a David.

It has been suggested that Michelangelo originally began it in 1525 as a David for the Medici tombs but later converted it into an Apollo – hence the dual identification. The not unusual fact that it is unfinished rather adds to the confusion since if it had been finished it would have been assured a clear identity.

Brutus *(c.1540)*
Marble, 29in (74cm) in height
Museo Nazionale del Bargello, Florence

Michelangelo arrived in Rome in 1534 and was made a Roman citizen in December 1537. He was soon to engage on the two most important architectural commissions that Rome could offer, St. Peter's and the Campidoglio. Rome was to be his home for the rest of his life – Florence was the past, Rome the future.

His friend, Donato Giannotti, who published a 'dialogue' which included a discussion with Michelangelo on the subject of the justification of Caesar's assassination, about which Michelangelo was equivocal, commissioned him in about 1536 to make a bust of Brutus. Although uncompleted it follows the

pattern begun in the Roman portrait busts of emperors, senators, and other Roman dignitories of the empire.

It has also been suggested that the inspiration may have been of more modern origin and linked with the murder of the much reviled Alessandro by Lorenzino de' Medici in 1536, who was much praised as a hero for ridding the world of a vile tyrant.

The model for the bust was an antique gemstone believed to be of Brutus but which has subsequently been identified as more likely to be of the Emperor Caracalla.

Even in its unfinished state it is a dramatically imposing bust, the shoulder drapery having being treated with a clean, lively finish, while the aggressive self-confident features of the head in their rougher state seem to emphasize the power of Michelangelo's interpretation.

The Manhattan Cupid *(c.1496–97)*

This sculpture was discovered in 1996 in a damaged condition on a fountain in the foyer of a mansion in New York, occupied by a part of the French Embassy where it had remained unidentified since 1906.

It is now claimed by a number of art historians as the lost Cupid made by Michelangelo for the Renaissance banker Iacopo Galli, and if genuine is the only work of his to have made it to the U.S.A. Discussion is continuing as to its authenticity.

There are a number of features of the damaged work that leave the question open to conjecture, not least in the mind of the author. If it is indeed a lost work by Michelangelo then it is an exceedingly exciting discovery. This will also be the first time that it will have been published as Michelangelo's work.

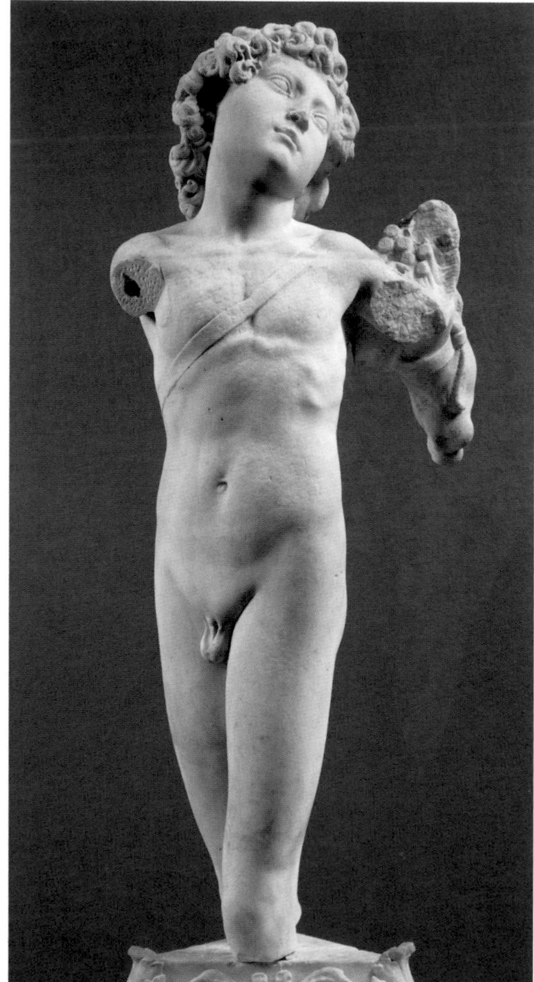

Doni Tondo (The Holy Family)
(c.1503–04)
Tempera on panel, 47½in (120cm) in diameter
Uffizi, Florence

The first known painting by Michelangelo and the only executed in tempera, this work is believed to have been commissioned by Agnole Doni as a form of commemoration of his marriage to Maddalena Strozzi in the winter of 1503, but in the event Doni refused to accept it.

It is another example of Michelangelo's early attachment to a classical linear style which he later used in the Sistine Chapel ceiling. The nude youths in the background of the tondo *are also a foretaste of the* ignudi *on the ceiling. His interest, almost a preoccupation, with the nude male*

Continued on page 254

Michelangelo's Painting

It is one of the more surprising facts, bearing in mind Michelangelo's already stated passion for sculpture, that what is probably his most famous work – the one that he is best remembered for and which is always quoted when he is discussed – is that of the Sistine Chapel in the Vatican. Apart from his design for the painting in the Florentine Council Chamber and the *Doni Tondo* there are no finished paintings before the Sistine ceiling. Indeed, there is little after, except the great *Last Judgment*, also in the Sistine Chapel but painted 20 years later. Two frescoes in the Pauline Chapel in Rome complete his paintings. (See pages 342–345.)

There are two unfinished tempera panels (pages 262–265 which, with reservations, have been attributed to Michelangelo, both of which are located in the National Gallery, London. There are certainly some Michelangelesque qualities to both these works but it is generally accepted that at best they are only partly his work and the hand of assistants is apparent.

Before considering the major works the small *Doni Tondo* should be mentioned since it is an early work and in a different medium from all his other paintings, including the frescoes in the Sistine Chapel. The date of the tondo, the earliest surviving painting, is not certain, but it is generally considered to be around 1503/04 although even later dates have been proposed, 1507 being the latest. It does not fit easily within the corpus of

Tempera

The process of painting, simply described, is the attachment of colour to an appropriate surface. The practice raises a number of questions and problems, one of the most important being the element of attachment which, in general, gives its name to the method. The form in which colour is prepared is common to most methods, that is, as a pigment or powder. The surface in the traditional methods is characteristically flat and one to which colour can be made to adhere. It is usually chosen for its durability and resistance to damage.

The method chosen is partly dependent on the surface or support. The most common methods for traditional painting at this time are either watercolour or oil, which is almost always used for large-scale, 'serious' paintings. Watercolour is more commonly used for sketches and smaller works.

During the Italian Renaissance oil painting, although beginning to be used in northern Europe, was rarely used by Michelangelo, fresco being his choice, as it was for most painters of large murals. Fresco is described on page 258, and since it was the preferred method for the large-scale paintings demanded by Michelangelo's patrons, he used it, though it was not his favourite medium. For the *Doni Tondo*, however, he used tempera and this, like fresco, is not the easiest technical method.

The special quality of tempera is that it uses an emulsion, a mixture of oil and water, to attach the colour. Since oil and water do not naturally mix, other substances such as egg-yolk, milk or dandelions are used to facilitate the process. Artificial emulsions such as gum are not as satisfactory as natural emulsions.

Tempera, despite its oil content, appears to dry with the evaporation of the watery element.

figure in his paintings has led, with other matters, to the suggestion of homosexuality; but this has not been established or dismissed and remains one of the open questions about his life.

The sketchy nature of the open sky and indeterminate groundscape are another typical element in his painting which essentially concentrates on the human form both in painting and in sculpture. The band crossing the middle seems to suggest that the young painter is dividing the picture, the Christian foreground pushing the classical world to the back. Bearing in mind that Michelangelo was still in his 20s, and reconciling Christian and Platonist beliefs, it is an interesting possibility. There is a certain harshness in the delineation of form and colour to be found in this precise tempera technique that is later softened in his frescoes in the Sistine Chapel.

Michelangelo's work and cannot be easily related to the two great works in the Sistine Chapel, but it is clear from the quality of the draughtsmanship that it could not be a very early work. It is painted in tempera on a panel and is about 47½ inches in diameter.

It is unquestionable that Michelangelo was both temperamentally and physically more attuned to sculpture, which makes the unique reputation of the Sistine Chapel paintings unexpected to say the least. As a stone-carver, the act of releasing a preconceived image/form from a block of stone, which demands immense measures of concentration and confidence, would have attracted him far more than the gradual building up of paint in the restrictive way imposed by the fresco method.

Indeed it clearly did so, since his few public paintings were undertaken under considerable pressure at a time when he was also engaged in major large-scale sculptural contracts commissioned by the popes. His powerful temperament, mentioned earlier, his *terribilità* or *furia*, released in the secrecy of his workshop, was also more appropriate to the creation of sculpture than working on scaffolding, lying on his back, and under

OPPOSITE

Doni Tondo

(background detail of naked youths)

LEFT

San Lorenzo, Florence

Drawn on the wall of the crypt where Michelangelo was in hiding, this is said to be a study for the Sistine Chapel.

Fresco Painting

The 19th-century French painter, Ingres, once observed of his predecessors that the greatest masters always had a special predilection for fresco and that fresco painting produced greater inspiration than any other technique. This view is probably still held, particularly by painters with an expansive view of life, since it is also claimed that 'a thrilling tension persists as long as the painter paints'. Moreover, when Michelangelo was required to pictorially cover the vast expanse of the Sistine ceiling, with all its demands, it was the method he naturally chose. It was also the method commonly adopted for all large works during the Renaissance.

Fresco painting takes two forms: *fresco buono* and *fresco secco. Fresco buono* (true fresco) is executed on wet lime plaster, while *fresco secco* (dry fresco) is done on plaster, but with a dry lime surface. For the ceiling and end wall of the Sistine Chapel, Michelangelo used the more demanding *fresco buono.*

A cartoon (see page 217) for each area to be painted is made and traced over the plaster. The surface of the wall is prepared with a base of several layers of moist lime plaster, while lime-resistant colours are prepared with slaked lime.

Only the area that can be painted in a day is given the top coat (the so-called 'day piece') and hair and bristle brushes are used.

As the water evaporates, the lime plaster absorbs carbonic acid gas from the air which together forms a glassy skin of crystalline carbonate of lime. The colours when applied are incorporated into the wet plaster and become fixed as the plaster dries, producing the slightly delicate sheen characteristic of fresco. As the materials dry overnight, the painter has to decide how much he can complete in a day and restrict himself to that amount. There is no margin for reflection, error or alteration, either in line or colour.

It is generally perceived that the Sistine ceiling is the most stupendous example of *fresco buono* ever achieved; it is a 133 x 43-ft (41 x 13-m) rectangle, painted in small areas that had to be finished daily, and matched on subsequent days so that the joins could not be seen. The colours are accurately matched and the forms seamlessly connect.

It is an indication of Michelangelo's emotional strength and determination that after he had finished about one-third of the area, the plaster failed and he had to begin again; such physical and psychological courage is almost unbelievable. A further point should also be made: he did not trust or like the helpers he had been assigned and undertook all the preparatory work himself.

constant interruption from Pope Julius II who, though enthusiastic, was also extremely demanding.

Michelangelo worked on a scaffold nearly 80ft (24m) above ground and all materials had to be carried or hoisted up by a pulley. He was also painting in fresco, one of the most demanding of techniques. It is also said that, after about one third of the ceiling had been painted, the plaster failed and had to be replaced. Michelangelo attributed this to the architect Bramante, who was Master of Works, believing that he had deliberately supplied inferior plaster. It seems unlikely that this was the case but there was certainly no love lost between the two.

With no previous experience of the fresco technique, or even of working on the scale that the Sistine Chapel demanded, Michelangelo succeeded in transferring the sense of power and immediacy present in his sculpture to the flat surface of the Sistine ceiling.

The preparatory process was time-consuming and had to be undertaken daily before painting could begin, which hardly suggests itself as a method in tune with Michelangelo's temperament. In addition, he mistrusted the workers originally supplied and did the preparatory work himself, working with only an assistant to mix the colours for him.

The result may be seen as one very large single work or as a number of scenes from the Bible, each an individual painting, accompanied by supporting figures and painted architectural features. For the purposes of this general survey the ceiling will be considered as a whole while most of the many scenes and figures will be examined in the captions that accompany the illustrations.

The Sistine Chapel in the Vatican was named after the pope who built it in 1473, Sixtus IV. The ceiling of the long rectangular 85-ft (26-m) high chamber, measuring 133-ft long by 43-ft wide (41 x 13m), was coved and had been painted with golden stars on a dark blue background, more as interior decoration than art. The upper part of the side wall contained a range of round-headed windows and below these, above ground level, a number of religious scenes had been painted by notable artists, mainly Florentines, about 30 years earlier when the chapel was built.

The original contract that was offered to Michelangelo was to replace the existing decoration

with representations of the 12 Apostles. He was unhappy with his preliminary drawings but he later wrote that the pope 'gave me a new commission to paint what I wanted, whatever would please me'. He adopted the present design plan and had worked it out by the end of 1508, starting work at the beginning of the following year. By the end of August 1510 he had completed a major part of the work and revealed it. A second section was finished in the following August and from midsummer 1512 he began to contemplate completion, which occurred early in October.

Unusually, the pictorial progression starts from the entrance and works towards the altar, which results in the sequence of the main panels, presuming that one starts to look at them as one enters, going backwards so that the earliest event is the last one you see (they are listed below starting at the entrance). The first and third panels encountered are concerned with Noah and indicate that the sequence ends after the Deluge which, considering the epic nature of the first few, will probably come as something of a surprise. (This will be discussed in the captions to the illustrations.) The nine main history panels are supported by smaller panels and spandrel paintings of prophets and sybils.

The nine history paintings are as follows: the Drunkeness of Noah, the Deluge, the Sacrifice of Noah, the Fall of Man, the Creation of Eve, the Creation of Adam, God Dividing the Earth from the Waters, the Creation of the Sun, Moon and Planets, God Separating the Light from the Darkness. Around these are ranged 12 prophets and sybils (female prophets): Zacharia, Joel and the Delphic Sybil, the Erythrean Sybil and Isaiah, Ezekiel and the Cumaean Sybil, the Persian Sybil and Daniel, Jeremiah and the Libyan Sybil, and Jonah (over the *Last Judgment*).

Further scenes are depicted in the spandrels and a number of nude figures (*ignudi*) are included in the painted architectural details, including the pedestals that surround the panels. (A selected number of the panels and figures will be considered individually where they offer special opportunity to explore Michelangelo's methods. All of them, with some explanation of why they were included – not always easily established – will be considered separately.)

The altar wall in the Sistine Chapel contains the single-image painting of the *Last Judgment* in which Michelangelo has depicted the stages through which the soul passes, from death to judgment and ultimately to Purgatory, Heaven or Hell. The central figure of Christ, attended by His mother Mary, dominates the scene which includes other biblical characters such as St. Peter on Christ's left side holding the keys of heaven.

The original commission was to paint only the upper portion of the wall, the lower part having been already painted by Perugino at the time the building was constructed. Michelangelo felt inhibited by the restriction and by the fact that he had been required to paint a Resurrection, a subject that did not attract him, and he proposed a new plan for the entire wall, a Last Judgment. This was agreed, the existing frescoes were destroyed, two windows were blocked in and the wall replastered. The whole work took nearly six years to complete and remains one of the greatest pictorial achievements of the Renaissance.

OPPOSITE

The Sistine Chapel, Vatican, Rome

(c. 1473)

The chapel, originally built by Pope Sixtus IV, is reputed to have been designed to the proportions of Solomon's temple and was decorated with the work of Tuscan artists. It now contains two of the most famous pictorial works of the Renaissance, both by Michelangelo, that of the ceiling and the Last Judgment *of the altar wall. Michelangelo's solution for the ceiling was a number of scenes from Genesis surrounded by other figures of prophets and sybils and a number of nude youths* (ignudi), *all contained within an architectural structure. Twenty years later a plan to replace the existing painting on the altar wall gave Michelangelo the opportunity to produce the* Last Judgment, *a painting that evoked both awe and controversy.*

RIGHT and OPPOSITE detail
***The Entombment** (before 1500)*
Tempera on panel (unfinished)
63⅔ x 59in (1.6 x 1.5m)
National Gallery, London

This panel and that of the Madonna and Child with St. John on the succeeding pages were bought by the National Gallery in London in 1868 and 1870 respectively, and are usually included in any survey of Michelangelo's work. However, there is some doubt as to the authenticity of both, but there are elements of quality which suggest that Michelangelo's hand may indeed have touched them. The gallery catalogue suggests that the Entombment has a stronger claim than the Madonna and believes that, on balance, it is a strong candidate.

RIGHT and OPPOSITE detail
Madonna and Child with St. John
(before 1500)
Tempera on panel (unfinished),
41½ x 30¼in (1.05 x .077m)
National Gallery, London

THE SISTINE CHAPEL: A PERSONAL MEMORIAL

Pope Sixtus IV was one of a number of popes who desired to leave behind a personal memorial when he died. This was hardly unusual during the Renaissance when popes were more important than kings whose authority extended only to earthly matters. Sixtus therefore had built within the Vatican a memorial chapel named after him and commissioned a number of famous painters to embellish its walls. Sixtus' life is an intriguing and revealing portrait of a not untypical Renaissance pope.

Sixtus IV (Francesco della Rovere), who lived from 1414–81 and was pope from 1471, was a dedicated nepotist, an enthusiastic intriguer and an aggressive military commander. The year following his elevation he sent a fleet to fight the Turks and after a number of unsuccessful forays abroad began to concentrate his attention on Italian politics. He was party to the Pazzi Conspiracy (page 54) against Lorenzo de' Medici, and entered into a fruitless war with Florence which lasted for two years. Following this debacle he incited the Venetians to attack Ferrara, then placed them under an interdict for refusing to desist from a war which he had himself initiated.

The Sistine Chapel Ceiling

The sequence of the subjects of the main panels, from the altar wall to the entrance, begins with the Creation and ends with the Drunkenness of Noah although the visitor sees this one first and may wonder why it has been included. The explanation is that Noah becomes a second Adam following God's decision to submerge the earth because of Adam's sinful descendants.

Here, the panels are placed in a logical order, from Creation to Noah, with their attendant ignudi. *The panels, starting with small ones, are alternately small and large. They are followed by the prophets and sybils and small scenes enclosed within spandrels. The ceiling is painted in fresco.*

LEFT and PREVIOUS PAGES
God Separating the Light from the Darkness

OVERLEAF
The Creation of the Sun, Moon and Planets

A somewhat more praiseworthy aspect of his pontificate was his support of the arts and literature and as a restorer of churches and the builder of new ones. He endowed the first foundling hospital, sought to improve church music and created the Sistine choir. He commissioned many paintings, including some in the Sistine Chapel, and was a founder of the Vatican library which eventually became the most important repository of classical documents. This was only achieved, it should be noted, through crippling taxes and annates (first-year revenues from a see or benefice and paid to the pope), which were increased. Simony (the buying or selling of ecclesiastical privileges, for example pardons or benefices) was rampant.

However, a grand mausoleum or an impressive memorial of the calibre of the Sistine Chapel goes somewhat further to guarantee that one will be remembered by history, even more so than noble or ignoble deeds. Moreover, Sixtus was extremely fortunate that his relative, Pope Julius II, should have decided to employ Michelangelo to repaint the ceiling of Sixtus' memorial chapel about 20 years after it had been completed, and replace the star-spangled ceiling with such a colossal and awe-inspiring masterpiece.

Michelangelo's initial contract was to paint representations of the 12 apostles but, after discussion with Julius and dissatisfaction with his initial designs, he was given a free hand to make his own choice of subject. The result, it must be acknowledged, has assured Sixtus' immortality in a way that he could not have foreseen.

The ceiling is divided into major sections through the use of painted architectural features so that there are nine biblical subjects painted in architecturally-defined rectangles, beginning chronologically from the wall at the opposite end of the chapel from the entrance, a somewhat surprising and unusual decision which rather denies the logic of the *Last Judgment* on the end altar wall. Indeed, it is difficult to understand immediately why the *Drunkenness of Noah* should be the panel to greet one on entry. Nevertheless, the order is reasonable although some parts may need explanation. That the earliest event, *God Separating the Light from the Darkness*, is at the altar end, near the *Last Judgment*, is surprising.

Around the history panels 12 prophets and sybils are

RIGHT

God Dividing the Earth from the Waters *(detail)*

Still surrounded by human forms, God appears as a rather more benificent figure than in the previous panels.

OPPOSITE

Sketches for the Sistine Chapel

Charcoal on paper

Uffizi, Florence

The figure of Eve for the Fall of Man *(page 288).*

placed in the actual spandrels, but seated on painted podiums. In addition there are 19 nude male figures, *ignudi*, placed on the corners of the history panels on architectural painted plinths (there were 20 but one is no longer there in a discernible form). The four corner spandrels and eight intermediary spaces are filled with smaller figures, all more than enough to occupy a painter for a period of four years.

Most of the main rectangular panels are famous as paintings in their own right and perhaps two have a special resonance, the *Creation of Adam* and the *Creation of the Sun, Moon and Planets* (also sometimes called the Creation of the World). It is in these that one is most aware of the overwhelming creative power of Michelangelo's *furia* or *terribilità*, and one can come some way to understanding his grasp of the nature of divinity. In the *Creation of Adam*, the nascent life immanent in Adam is being stirred by the touch of the finger of the Almighty as he and his cohorts soar above the empty planet. Whether or not one implicitly believes the biblical story, one cannot fail to be moved by the power of Michelangelo's vision and his mastery in describing it.

The relaxed and dignified seated figures of Isaiah and

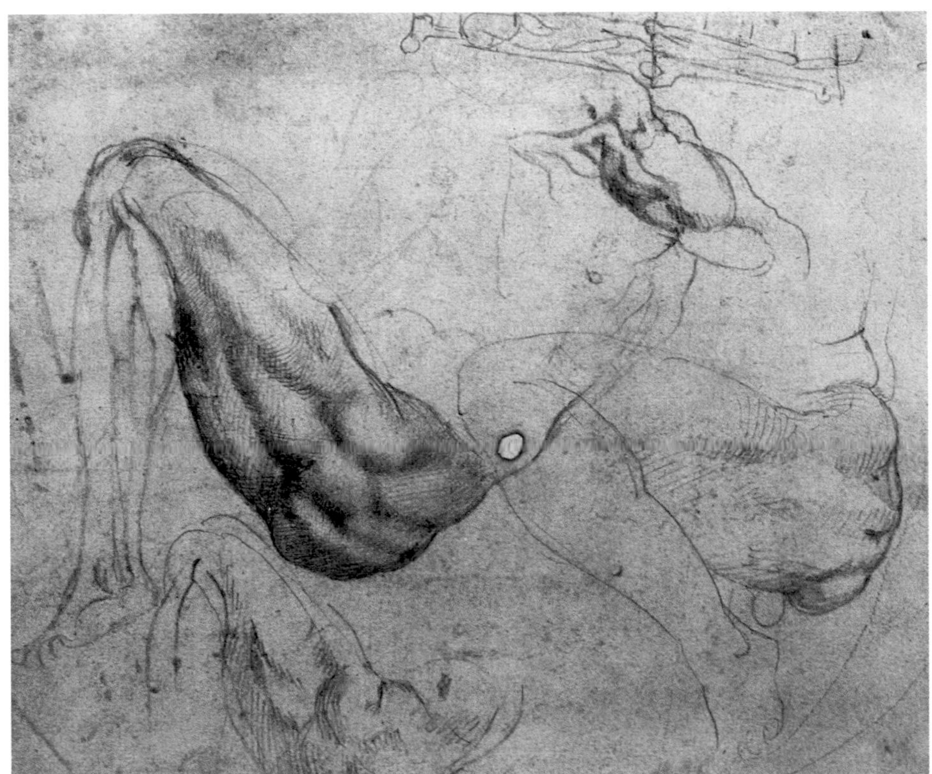

OPPOSITE and LEFT

God Dividing the Earth from the Waters

OVERLEAF

Details of ignudi

the Delphic Sybil contrast sharply with the frenetic postures of the many figures in the *Deluge* and it is the oppositions of emotion and characterization that Michelangelo so effortlessly and effectively conveys that elevates his work so that it becomes the greatest expression of the human condition, making the viewer a participator in God's plans for mankind. No one has gone deeper, seen more, been more aware of the internal struggles going on in the human heart than Michelangelo. He was not happy with his lot; he was never satisfied and was driven by an uncontrollable internal conflict, pulling him this way and that, between spirit and intellect, the divine and the human, Christianity and Humanism.

PREVIOUS PAGES and OPPOSITE
The Creation of Adam (Man)

This is the most powerful image on the ceiling and probably the single most famous depiction of the momentous moment of creation. It shows man, already formed, about to receive the touch of God which will give life to the recumbent form. It is the contrast between the swiftly moving figure of God and the languid pose of Adam that gives the painting its force. The location of the scene, on rocky barren earth, would seem to confirm Michelangelo's usual disregard for landscape. Could the figure accompanying God and looking towards Adam be the future Eve?

LEFT
Study for The Creation of Adam
Red chalk on paper
British Museum, London

OPPOSITE and LEFT (detail)
The Creation of Eve

Eve emerges from the body of Adam and is blessed by a benign Almighty who seems to have lost some of the thrusting power seen in the Adam panel and to have taken on the role and appearance of a prophet.

OVERLEAF
Details of ignudi

One of the notable elements in the ceiling painting are the 19 nude male figures (there were originally 20 but one was destroyed). They are in many different poses, from the energetic to the relaxed, and most of them appear on the following pages. They reveal, if nothing else, Michelangelo's great knowledge of anatomy, and their physicality and beauty add life to the work.

LEFT and OVERLEAF

The Fall of Man

The left-hand side of this scene depicts Eve, having been tempted by the Serpent and accepting an apple from the Tree of Knowledge of Good and Evil. The result is the expulsion of Adam and Eve from the garden of Eden by the archangel, depicted on the right.

This is an example of the presentation of sequential actions involving the passage of time and condensed into one image, another example of which can be seen in Masaccio's Tribute Money *(page 60).*

The landscape of the Creation of Adam *and the* Deluge *is present again but less barren and the action of the figures more lively on the left of the picture before their expulsion. But there is full internal tension on the right of*

Continued overleaf

the picture as they flee from Paradise.

The least convincing figure is the cloaked archangel; small and unstructured, it seems inadequate to the important task in which it is engaged, and one suspects that Michelangelo was not inspired by the necessity of having a clothed figure in the scene. Nevertheless it carries the sweeping flow of the composition from the head of Eve on the left, through her arm and that of the woman/serpent, towards the sword and the head of Adam on the right. It stops with the emotional focus of the work, the fearful and ashamed head of the sinful Eve, which is in sharp contrast to the happy, self-satisfied Eve on the left.

OPPOSITE, LEFT and OVERLEAF
The Sacrifice of Noah

The Deluge

This multi-figure action scene portrays the fear and distress that succeeded the flood. In the foreground the land, much as it is portrayed in the Creation of Adam, is bleak with only a tree to indicate that it had once been cultivated. In the background the Ark can be seen with the hovering dove. Most of the figures are again naked and suggests that there is something of a fixation with nudity since there is no reason to suppose that the survivors would have been unclothed. It reinforces the point made earlier that the human form was of paramount importance to Michelangelo's art. The landscape and other elements are treated so cursorily that it is to the human figures that one must look for the meaning of the scene. It is also strange that there are no animals.

The Deluge

DETAIL OPPOSITE
The figures having reached dry land, it is noticeable that of the original two-by-two procession of animals only a horse (top left) seems to have survived. As it is bridled, it appears to have assisted in the rescue from the flood.

DETAIL LEFT
View of the Ark. The extraordinary structure which Michelangelo has created seems somewhat impractical if it was intended to carry the number of people and animals stated in the Bible. Notice the dove hovering over the roof of the Ark.

OPPOSITE and OVERLEAF
The Drunkenness of Noah

The first panel that one encounters on entering the Sistine Chapel, the Drunkenness of Noah, *leads backwards into the biblical sequence of the Creation ending with* God Separating the Light from the Darkness *in nine major panels that follow the main central line of the vault.*

The story of Noah is of seminal importance and is an appropriate final image in Michelangelo's programme as Noah could be regarded as a second Adam after the destruction of the Deluge.

The importance of the story lies in Ham's disgrace because he has seen his drunken father naked, and the advancement of his brothers by default, leading to the creation of the tribes of Israel.

THE DRUNKENNESS OF NOAH

The first panel nearest to the entrance of the Sistine Chapel is the *Drunkenness of Noah,* from which the sequence moves historically backwards, finishing at the *Last Judgment* wall behind the altar with *God Separating the Light from the Darkness.* The *Drunkenness of Noah* is of basic importance to the whole sequence and, although placed at the entrance end of the chapel, is the final image in Michelangelo's plan.

The story refers to the time after the Deluge when Noah planted a vineyard, sampled the product too enthusiastically, and ended up drunk by the side of his wine vat. Ham, Shem and Japhet were his three sons and when Ham found him inebriated, he called his brothers who, shielding their eyes from the naked figure, covered him with a cloak as depicted in the panel. The figure pointing is Ham who, of course, in finding his father has seen him naked. The disgrace of Ham has the effect of improving the status of his brothers by default, and leads to the creation of the various tribes of Israel.

The use of naked bodies, mainly male, on both the ceiling and on the *Last Judgment* of the end wall, calls for a general comment: Michelangelo used the male nude in both sculpture and painting with no attempt to disguise the genitalia, which was a bold step to take. Most painters, if they did not actually cover these areas, frequently placed the figures so that the genitals were not visible or were hidden by a fortuitous tree-branch or, more conventionally, by a strategically-placed fig leaf. It will also be noticed that Michelangelo does not include pubic hair on females, revealing them as 'clean-shaven'.

While this general subject is being considered, it is interesting to note that none of Michelangelo's male figures are circumcised. Since Genesis XVII suggests that the covenant between God and Abraham included the command that every male child be circumcised, Michelangelo's familiarity with the Old Testament should have made him aware that such characters as David and Noah and his sons would have been submitted to this ritual: presuming that it was not ignorance on Michelangelo's part, it is necessary to look elsewhere for the explanation. There appears to be none, however, but having raised the subject one is obliged to offer an opinion.

Michelangelo used their bodies to reflect on the strength and weaknesses of his characters. The human body was the most potent means by which he could express emotions and a damaged or disfigured one would have been an inadequate vessel to carry his message. He would never have used a fig leaf, which

would have diminished the dignity of the human form.

Thus the repeated use of the nude is more evident in Michelangelo's work than is usual in Renaissance painting, although other painter and sculptor contemporaries did produce undisguised naked figures. Signorelli's influence on Michelangelo has already been noted and his frescoes at Orvieto are closely related to Michelangelo's in character. Much discussion and many inferences have been drawn from this recurring element in Michelangelo's work, that it is an important message from him and not evidence of a hidden agenda. Michelangelo is stating what for him is an essential truth: that the human body, which we all inhabit, is the best means of expressing the human condition, and to cover it is to evince an emotional response to the clothing rather than to the true content of the painting – the human spirit in the human body.

Perhaps this is the moment to discuss another possible reason for Michelangelo's extensive use of the naked male form: that he was a homosexual. It is certainly true that he never married and had no special female friends except, later in life, Vittoria Colonna. It is also true that he wrote love poetry, though it is not clear to which sex it was addressed. His only other close friend was Tomasso Cavalieri, a recognizably beautiful youth from an ancient Italian family. However, there is no direct admission or suggestion in any of Michelangelo's writings, and this includes his letters, of any homosexual inclinations. Therefore, the case is open and one suspects that it will remain so. It might be noted that at the time of the Renaissance and before, homosexuality bore no more of a stigma than it does today. The observer must make his or her own mind up on the matter, but many who are themselves homosexuals believe that he was.

There is one interesting aspect of the subject which the reader may care to digest. The poems were not published in his lifetime and the original text was, it is said, written to a male recipient; but when published after Michelangelo's death they appeared as if addressed to a female.

After this digression we return to Noah, who is old, bent and round-shouldered, unaware of the disgust that his excesses have aroused in his sons, all of whom look awkwardly away. If one imagines the figures clothed, perhaps the importance that Michelangelo attached to the naked body will be understood. In fact, a great deal of the poignancy and power of the story would have been lost; the effect would have been diluted and relegated to little more than a medieval tapestry. This, incidentally, also explains why the question of nudity has been discussed in this context.

ESAIAS

The Prophet Isaiah and the Delphic Sibyl

In the spandrels on the outer edge of the ceiling surrounding the main panels, there are 12 prophets and sibyls, arranged mostly in pairs. The two remaining figures are on the end walls , Jonah *immediately over the Last* Judgment *and* Zacharias *over the entrance.*

The Prophet Isaiah and the Delphic Sibyl *has one of the* Forefathers of Christ *in the triangular space between them. This scheme replaced the original intention to place the apostles in these locations. The exceptions to the general plan are the prophet Isaiah over the entrance – predicting Christ's entry into Jerusalem – and Jonah, the prophet of the Resurrection over the altar. The placing of Jonah here makes the important connection between Resurrection and Judgment.*

RIGHT
The Persian Sibyl

OPPOSITE
The Cumaean Sibyl

The presence of the sibyls in the context of the Sistine Chapel ceiling needs some explanation. Sibyls, in classical antiquity and consequently pre-Christianity, were inspired oracular prophetesses, reputed to have been mistresses or daughters of Apollo or they may have been merely his priestesses. According to different sources, they vary in number between one (Sibylla – hence the name) and ten, the most important being the Delphic, Persian, Cumaean, Erythrean, Samian and Trojan; of these the most celebrated is the Sibyl of Cumae, Greece's earliest colony in Italy, founded in 1050 BC near Naples.

The Delphic Sibyl

One of the most delicately painted of the single figures on the Sistine ceiling, the Delphic Sibyl sits elegantly poised in a painted architectural niche, holding a scroll on which her prophesies have been recorded. This is one of Michelangelo's most sensitive images of a female figure.

Delphi, situated to the north of the gulf of Corinth in Greece, on the slopes of Mount Parnassus, was the site of the famous oracle and the temple of Apollo. It held the omphalos*, or conical stone, said to mark the centre of the world. The method of divination was by possession when a medium, commonly female, was filled by the god or his inspiration and her words were interpreted accordingly. In fact, the god Apollo appears to have been introduced into every myth where prophesy or inspiration is involved.*

The Libyan Sibyl

The Erythrean Sibyl *(restored)*

Before even discussing the pros and cons of restoring famous works of art, one point should be made. Fresco is a difficult medium and one side of the argument for restoration is that paintings do deteriorate and plaster ceilings are subject to cracking as, for example, the illustrations of the Creation of Adam *reveal. The result of doing nothing would possibly end in tragedy when the painting finally disintegrates and is lost forever: on the other hand, however effective it might be, restoring a work means that to a large extent it is no longer the work of the original creator and an attempt to visualize what a painting nearly 500 years old actually looked like, and without the benefit of photography, makes the aesthetic task of judging the work all but impossible.*

Sketch of a sibyl for the Sistine Chapel
Pen and ink on paper
British Museum, London

OPPOSITE

The Prophet Ezekiel

The fierce energy that is invested in the figure of the prophet Ezekiel is in stark contrast to the delicacy of the Delphic Sibyl. Ezekiel, meaning 'God will strengthen', was a Hebrew prophet taken prisoner by Nebuchadnezzar in 597 BC when he was taken into captivity in Babylon along with others of the Jewish community. He appears as a prophet in about 549 BC after a remarkable vision. The Book of Ezekiel is in three parts: Nebuchadnezzar's conquest of Jerusalem and overthrow of Judah; threats to seven surrounding nations; proofs of the delivery of the Hebrew Nation and the rebuilding of Jerusalem, with several messianic prophesies. His particular merit is that he enclosed the soul of prophesy in the body of a community that was non-political and from which the sacred constitution of Judaism developed.

LEFT

The Prophet Isaiah

The Prophet Daniel

In general, the biblical prophets can be regarded as half-mythological, half-historical, and reading the Bible may lead one to make up one's mind which is which; in the end it is a personal opinion. Should one wish to make a judgment on the truth of any of the images of the prophets shown on these pages, there are two criteria by which they should be judged. Firstly, with what one knows of the prophet's life and work, has the artist succeeded in stimulating the imagination to the point of belief in the image? Secondly, does one admire the quality of the workmanship and derive aesthetic satisfaction from the result?

The Prophet Zacharias

RIGHT

The Death of Haman *(small spandrel panel)*

This story can be found in the Old Testament Book of Esther. Because of her beauty the Israelite Esther was chosen by the Persian king Ahasuerus (supposed to be Xerxes I) to be his queen. Haman was a servant of the king and an enemy of Israel and Esther was the adopted daughter of Mordecai, an opponent of Haman. After much intrigue and bad behaviour on the part of Haman, the outcome of the story is that Haman himself was hanged on a gibbet he had intended for Mordecai.

OPPOSITE

Judith Carrying the Head of Holofernes *(small spandrel panel)*

Judith was a rich Israelite widow who saved the town of Bethulia from Nebuchadnezzar's army by seducing the besieging general Holofernes and cutting off his head while he slept. This is an Apocryphal story from the Bible.

ELEAZAR
MATHAN

OPPOSITE LEFT

The Forefathers of Christ: Josias

(detail from pages 304–05)

In addition to the main panel subjects, Michelangelo has included paintings within the spandrels, the almost triangular space between one side of the outer curve of the wall and the ceiling.

OPPOSITE RIGHT

The Forefathers of Christ: Obed

THIS PAGE

Sketches for apostles and prophets

Uffizi, Florence

OPPOSITE

The Last Judgment *(detail) 1535–41*
Fresco, 55 x 43ft 7in (16.8 x 13.3m)
Sistine Chapel, Vatican, Rome

The original commission given to Michelangelo was for only the upper part of the end wall of the Sistine Chapel. The lower part contained paintings by Perugino and after fire damage in 1525 the upper part needed a new work. Michelangelo was inhibited by the idea of a partial work, a Resurrection, and he introduced a new plan for a Last Judgement which was agreed; the existing frescoes were destroyed, two windows were blocked in and the wall was replastered. The painting was made with the help of only one assistant who mixed the colours.

THE LAST JUDGMENT

This work has to be viewed as a single image, divided into layers and with the figure of Jesus immediately below the central spandrel, which confirms Him as the focus of the painting's message. The work is an extraordinary achievement, and although it did not make the same physical demands as the ceiling, it took longer to complete.

Pope Paul III commissioned Michelangelo to paint both end walls of the Sistine Chapel. On the entrance wall the subject was to have been the Fall of the Rebellious Angels (never executed) and on the altar end, the Last Judgment, a proposal that had been agreed earlier by Clement VII after the Sack of Rome in 1527, for which he had to some degree been responsible, and which he intended as a kind of visual reparation.

Michelangelo had already prepared sketches before Clement died in 1534. The usual plan for churches and chapels had been to place a Last Judgment on the entrance wall and it was Clement who proposed this deviation from the norm. It is interesting to contemplate the change of location: to be faced with the importance of the ultimate judgment as one leaves the place of worship is very different from being confronted with its significance during a long service. One wonders if Clement was intending to ram home the message rather more effectively.

The scaffolding was erected in April 1535 but work did not begin until over a year later. Michelangelo was clearly no more reconciled to the second painting in the chapel than he had been to the first and recognized it from the beginning as a completion of the interior and not a separate unconnected work.

The *Last Judgment* may be regarded as the culmination of human existence and for the Christian the moment of truth. As described by Aretino, it represented the end of the saga of the world's beginnings depicted on the ceiling. The intention of the ceiling and end wall was that on entry one arrived at the division of the tribes of Israel and an unknown future, and worked backwards as one advanced down the chapel to the Creation over the altar wall. Here the sequence of the *Last Judgment* begins for the observer – from life to death to life.

When the Sistine Chapel was built, a number of artists had been involved in painting fresco panels; on the end wall two frescoes by Perugino, a Finding of

RIGHT

The Last Judgment

The entire back wall of the Sistine Chapel.

OPPOSITE

Detail of Christ

The central commanding figure of Christ, with the Virgin Mary at his side, is balanced on the left by St. John the Baptist and to the right by St. Peter who holds the keys of Heaven. Christ is surrounded by the righteous who nevertheless look with some concern at the majestic figure whose dominance seems to spread throughout the whole work. If studied carefully it will be seen that there is little satisfaction on the faces of these fortunate few – rather a cautious hope – and a number of hands are held in protective gestures in front of bodies. The figure of St. Bartholomew, holding his own flayed skin, is pictured

Continued opposite

to the right of Christ and it is generally accepted that the face on it is that of Michelangelo himself. Christ is clearly the central image and everything flows from Him. He is one of the few male figures in the painting that was clothed from the beginning. The Virgin Mary has a tender, sweet expression not always to be found in Michelangelo's women.

In this detail, taken from the vastness of the painting, it is possible to work out the main areas of unified painting. The information on fresco painting, supplied on page 258, will have explained that the painting was done in daily sections on wet plaster so that it would dry overnight. Although some paint could be applied using fresco secco *(dry fresco), after the first drying the composition would have been already fixed. Slight changes of colour and joining lines are the clues.*

OPPOSITE

The Last Judgment

(detail of top-left-hand corner)

LEFT

The Last Judgment

Key to the location of the individual details which follow

1 When the lowest level of the painting is examined we are in the area of direst straits and this detail is as disturbing as it gets. It should be recognized that this was the part that would have been nearest to the original viewers and would have offered little comfort to those who had not been behaving as they should. But this is before judgment and reveals a whole graveyard struggling to respond to the call as their bodies are restored to them ready for judgment. The skull-like figure is regarding his re-forming hand with blank astonishment as the buried bodies come slowly to life.

As was explained earlier, the movement through the layers is up on the left and down on the right. What is seen in this section is a further stage in the transformation of individuals who have mostly resumed their human form; but the skeleton indicates that not many have so far succeeded. It can be seen that not only do they return to their bodies but some have also assumed their clothing. The scene, however, remains terrifying and disturbing.

RIGHT

3 This central group immediately below the figure of Christ is a band of angels whose role is is to raise the dead. Judgment day, as described by St. Matthew, is illustrated here: 'He shall send his angels with a great sound of trumpet, and they shall gather his elect from the four winds, from one end of heaven to the other.'

The open Book of the Dead is carried by other angels on the bottom right of the detail.

OPPOSITE

The Last Judgment: studies for a flying angel

Black chalk on paper

British Museum, London

Moses and a Nativity flanked an altarpiece by him, but were destroyed to give Michelangelo access to the full wall. Two lunettes that had been part of Perugino's ceiling painting were also removed. The wall was then prepared with new bricks and the base plaster was laid. The story that Vasari tells claims that Michelangelo's friend Sebastiano del Piombo was given the task of preparing the plaster, but instead of laying a ground for fresco laid one for oil – Piombo's favourite medium – and the wall had to be replastered. Knowing Vasari's unreliability, however, there is doubt as to the truth of this story, but the wall had to be prepared again which prevented Michelangelo from beginning his task until spring 1536.

From that time until late in 1541, Michelangelo, with only one assistant, Francesco degli Amatori, called L'Urbino, worked in relative peace and solitude. Not unnaturally, Pope Paul was both curious and impatient to see the work in progress, but if he succeeded in viewing it, it was not often the case. Vasari reported that Michelangelo fell from the scaffold and hurt his leg so badly that he had to stop work and retire to his house but would not let a doctor near him. Despite this and

4 Moving upward on the left are some of the resurrected, helping each other to rise. The figures are now fully fleshed and showing some of the energy characteristic of Michelangelo's treatment of the human form. Among the figures represented is the heart-warming scene of one angel raising up two deserving mortals by means of rosary beads.

increasing ill health, Michelangelo finished the painting at the end of October 1541. (Vasari states that it was revealed on Christmas Day 1541, but the records confirm the earlier date.) Whenever it was unveiled, Vasari's account of its reception is accurate. He recounts how it was 'revealed to the amazement and admiration of all Rome' and it is clear that it was the subject of universal praise and respect. It is in many ways hardly surprising that it had such a reception: it is, after all, one of the largest paintings ever made and its impact is awe-inspiring to the extent that the first people who saw it, all Christians and mainly clerics, must or should have had cause to give serious reflection as to where their lives were taking them.

As a subject, the Last Judgment was familiar before Michelangelo's masterpiece, but from the Giotto, in the Arena Chapel at Padua to the Fra Bartolommeo in San Marco, Florence, the subject, although treated on many levels as was Michelangelo's, is ritualistic, charming and attractive, without inevitably demanding the involvement of the viewer. Michelangelo has produced a gigantic painting of such power that deep emotion, self-examination and all the feeling that contemplation of the subject can and should evoke in all believers, covers every part of the composition. Awesome and uniquely moving, it is the definitive Last Judgment.

Due to exhaustion, perhaps, this widespread public admiration drew from Michelangelo a wearied response. It is moving, self-deprecating and completely untypical:

I perceive that you suppose me to be just what God wishes that I were. I am a poor man and of little merit, who plods along in the art which God gave me, to lengthen out my life as far as possible.

It is perhaps this quotation that one should remember while bearing the image of the painting in mind; it had drawn so much of Michelangelo's spirit into itself that there was little of him that remained.

It will be recalled that the painting was unveiled to a pope, Paul III, who was in the process of reforming the church, attempting to reduce inequities and abolish the widespread licence that characterized early 16th-century Italy. The *Last Judgment* may have been greeted with overwhelming enthusiasm by the majority of the public, but the inclusion of so many naked figures was at the same time disturbing to many. A temerarious priest commented that it was 'more fit for a place of

5 *The large bare-breasted woman dominating this detail is reminiscent of other female figures by Michelangelo that can be seen in the* Deluge *panel on the Sistine ceiling or in the sculptures of the New Sacristy of San Lorenzo in Florence.*

Her body and head appear masculine rather than feminine, and it is only the presence of somewhat improbable breasts that confirms that she is indeed female. She also seems masculine in her protective attitude towards the rather more delicate female figure on her knees before her.

Although the group has not been placed in any biblical context, it does suggest that there is a close relationship between the two. Like other figures in the painting, the standing figure is looking towards Christ the Judge with an expression of hopeful anticipation.

The central figure in this group has sometimes been identified as St. John the Baptist, but there is no unanimous agreement on this. One element suggested as an identifying factor is the curly animal skin protecting his modesty. Since it does not appear in early, pre-'breeches' copies of the wall this is hardly a convincing argument. The same refutation applies to another suggestion that it is Adam.

As with the previous detail, several of the figures are leaning towards and gazing at Christ the Judge. They are part of the throng of the blessed, healthy and confident, described by Condivi as part of 'a crown and circle around the Son of God'.

The key to the message of the Last Judgment *is the figure of Christ, and deserves close consideration as an entity in itself. The proportionate bulk of the figure, with its massive width though normal height, imparts a uniquely dense, permanent quality to the form. Moreover, the firm handling of the small delicate head, with its stern expression of dedication to the task in hand, is proof of Michelangelo's unique genius. Christ's responsibility for judging humanity is, one feels, in just hands.*

The support of Mary, close by His side and in sharp contrast to Christ's bulky figure, emphasizes, in her self-deprecating posture, the all-powerful nature of Christ.

The lunette at the top right provides a reminder of the last days of Christ's life. A bevy of cheerful and energetic celestial spirits are carrying the column against which Christ was scourged before His crucifixion, while the figure at top right is carrying the rod on which the sponge soaked in vinegar was offered to Christ on the Cross. The whole small section (about 15-ft/4.5-m wide) is a self-contained composition of typical muscular figures engaged in carrying a heavy load. It is difficult to be certain, but the top group is carrying a folded green fabric which may be Christ's shroud.

debauchery than for the pope's chapel'. Michelangelo was furious and, rather more characteristic of him than the above meek quotation, included a portrait of the priest languishing in the depths of Hell. Paul IV later questioned Michelangelo on the matter of the naked figures and as a result a pupil of Michelangelo, Daniele da Volterra, was employed to paint draperies over some of them, in the process earning the nickname *il braghettone*, the breeches maker. Later popes continued to apply breeches, detroying Michelangelo's intention and adding an element of the ridiculous.

Michelangelo had himself justified and explained the use of the nude in this painting, particularly the importance of the human soul stripped of the trappings of this world and standing before the Judge at the end of life, naked as it had been born. Fortunately, a number of copies had been made before the breeches had been added, and while they are inferior and the motive suspect, they are closer to Michelangelo's original intention than the painting that can be seen today.

In this connection it may be recalled that the reforming Council of Trent, which sat between 1545 and 1563, made specific comments concerning immodesty in art and made efforts to curtail it.

The impression of the composition is movement and isolated action – upwards on the left, the meeting with Christ the Judge, and downwards on the right to the bottom corner and onwards into the uttermost pit. Each small group at every stage of the process carries a special message, each dominant figure has a role.

There is a great problem in reducing a painting covering over 3,500sq ft (325m^2) to less than one square foot in a book and still convey an impression of reality; in fact, one must acknowledge that it cannot be done. However, some idea of the quality and intention of the painting can be gained by an examination of the details and individual figures in relation to the whole. The method of achieving this has been to reproduce the whole, with the location of each detail indicated upon it. This way the story can be told. However, the only way to appreciate fully Michelangelo's greatest painting is to visit the chapel and see the masterpiece for oneself.

After they are reunited in Paradise the figures in this detail are embracing and showing every sign of relief and happiness. The figure on the right, taking the weight of the Cross, is Simon of Cyrene who, it will be recalled, was compelled to help Christ carry it when He stumbled on His way to Calvary – a plus mark for Simon.

The two lower figures are St. Catherine of Alexandria and St. Sebastian. Each carry the symbols of their martyrdom; St.Catherine has the section of the wheel to which she was bound, which disintegrated rather than cause her pain, while St. Sebastian carries the arrows that were shot at him by order of the Emperor Diocletian.

10 The central figure in this detail is on the lower right of the painting, on what might be described as the descent side, where the condemned are approaching their ultimate fate. The half-covered face of the damned soul reveals a look of ultimate despair while he is being inexorably drawn towards Charon's boat and the final passage to Hell. All around him are the avenging angels struggling with the rebellious damned. There is such a strong sense of loss and it is so poignantly expressed that this is perhaps the most moving single image in the whole work.

11 The martyrdom of St. Bartholomew by flaying alive is one of the more dramatic stories of the cruel death of this apostle, though other accounts claim that he was beheaded or even hanged. He is also identified with Nathaniel, which figures in the Gospel of St. John. Briefly, it can be said that he was a shadowy figure and Michelangelo has chosen to include him because of the brutality of his death.

Since the head on the skin clearly resembles Michelangelo's, including the broken nose, it may be that Michelangelo himself felt that he was being 'flayed alive' by the demands of popes. However, to make it clear that it is Bartholomew, he gives him the offending knife to hold in his other hand. The discreet placing of the piece of cloth by the 'breeches-maker', Daniele da Volterra, suggests that the cloud on which Bartholomew sits is solid and he looks fiercely towards Christ as if demanding reward for past loyalty.

12 The significant figure in this detail is a bearded St. Peter, holding a key to Heaven in each hand and offering them to Christ as evidence of his loyalty and sorrow for his denial of Him. This is another figure whose modesty was protected by Daniele's loin cloths, rather flamboyantly on this occasion.

Of the surrounding figures, the only one that can be tentatively identified is that of St. Paul, whose bearded head is next to St. Peter's. The gesturing raised hands can be interpreted in a number of different ways – from supplication to the need for protection to extreme anxiety.

13 This is the final scene. It carries the ultimate message of the lowest level and covers the bottom right half of the work. On the left, Charon the ferryman is using his paddle to force the damned to disembark so that he can collect a further batch of condemned souls. His eyes of 'living coal', as described by Dante in the Inferno, *clearly inspired Michelangelo who was something of an authority on the works of the poet.*

At the other end of the ferry the figures are tumbling into the brimstone sea to be welcomed by the snake-entwined Minos, the denizen of Hell, while over his head the glow of its fires can be seen as a reminder to the poor souls of what is yet to come.

Thus completes the cycle, from the upwardly aspiring of the left, through the layers of trial, to the acceptance of

Continued opposite

the blessed to proximity with Christ and, on the right, through the recognition of the essential righteousness of the saints to the descent into the bottomless pit and fires of Hell of the sinners.

A tough message, if it is to be believed, and during the Renaissance most, if not all, did believe it.

Michelangelo's full stop to the message is seen in the face of Minos. It is the face of the pope's master of ceremonies, Biagio da Cesena, who had had the temerity to criticize the painting.

The Crucifixion of St. Peter
Fresco, 20ft 6in x 21ft 8in
(6.3 x 6.6m) 1546–50
Pauline Chapel, Vatican, Rome

This was a remarkable crucifixion due to Peter's insistence that he be crucified upside down in order not to emulate Christ. The result is a strange disposition of figures. The cross, if it is to fit into the hole prepared for it by the rather indistinct form of the man crouched below, would leave little room for Peter's head and the impracticality of the idea is revealed. Moreover, the spatial provision in the painting is unconvincing and the figures to the left and right of the central action seem hardly to relate.

One suspects that Michelangelo only returned now and then to the painting and the concentrated power that appears in almost all of his other work is consequently absent.

OTHER PAINTINGS

Although something of an anticlimax, the following two frescoes in the Capella Paolina were painted after the completion of the *Last Judgment* and were Michelangelo's last works in fresco. They do not carry the same authority as the Sistine works, probably because Michelangelo did not wish to undertake them. After finishing the *Last Judgment* he had hoped to return to sculpture and the Julian tomb and it must be remembered that all his painting was accepted under duress of one kind or another. Moreover, he knew that these were promotional memorials for Paul III, the subjects themselves being more anecdotal than doctrinal, and that he had no alternative but to acquiesce. Given the circumstances, although they are works by a great master, it is not surprising that they seem a little less than inspiring.

Each of them took between three and four years to complete and when compared with the *Last Judgment* are small frescoes (each about 400sq ft/37m² compared with over 3,000sq ft) and still took nearly as long to complete. This suggests that Michelangelo was engaged in something that interested him more, such as architecture or sculpture, and that he returned to the frescoes and worked on them when he could.

The Conversion of St. Paul
(1542–45)
Fresco, 20ft 6in x 21ft 8in
(6.2 x 6.6m)
Pauline Chapel, Vatican, Rome

Of this and the previous painting, the Conversion has the more dramatic appeal. The composition is divided into two: the upper section centres on the dynamic figure of God homing in on a crowd to pin-point the person of Paul and deliver the famous Damascene conversion. The middle section, a vague mountainous landscape, shows Michelangelo's typical lack of interest in physical locations and his inevitable concentration on the human element. Even the horse here is sketchily observed, while the human figures, engaged in unrelated activities, are strongly observed and painted.

RIGHT
Figure study for The Battle of Cascina *(1504)*
Pen, brush, brown and grey ink on paper
British Museum, London

Michelangelo

Michelangelo's Drawings

Distributed among many galleries and private collections throughout the world, and much treasured by their owners, is a large number of drawings in different media and on different surfaces that have been produced by Michelangelo with various intentions in mind. The study of the drawings of any master, or indeed of any artist, well known or otherwise, is a rewarding experience and a necessity if one is to engage fully with the mind and character of the artist. In the case of Michelangelo it is both rewarding and enjoyable and some examples follow this introduction.

As will be apparent, if not earler realized, the range of drawing, from complexity to simplicity, is wide. Some sketches carry only a few guiding lines, while others are delineated with precision and refinement. All define the same purpose: an analytical mind in the process of forming an idea of how to proceed.

It may be how to present a relationship, a scene, a feeling, or an abstraction. On others it may be to personify, by discovering the precise way that an idea can be related to a concept. To offer practical examples: how should Christ appear on the Cross? or how can an energetic act be effectively represented? How does one express different forms of love within a single context?

There is also the question of technical ability to address. Michelangelo is concerned (and it is hoped that this has already been effectively established) with the human form and its manifestation of that humanity in the face of different situations. He is concerned with the structure and movement of the body. To acquire the freedom that knowledge would provide, he undertook many studies of the naked body, and indeed dissections, in order to understand the mechanics of anatomy. From simple movement in linear drawings to elaborated muscular expression, Michelangelo acquired a facility of expression which is evident in all his drawings, from folds in fabrics to facial features.

The drawing on the opposite and succeeding pages, and others that appear throughout the book, many of which have a close relationship, and which a keen observer will identify with the works of sculpture and painting included in this book, have not been placed in any calculated order of subject or date and may be enjoyed purely for themselves.

OPPOSITE

Study of three male figures

(after Raphael)

Red chalk on paper

Private collection

LEFT

Study of the Holy Family

Red chalk on paper

British Museum, London

RIGHT
Figure studies
Red chalk on paper
British Museum, London

FAR FIGHT
Study of drapery
Pen and ink on paper
British Museum, London

Kneeling man
Pencil on paper
British Museum, London

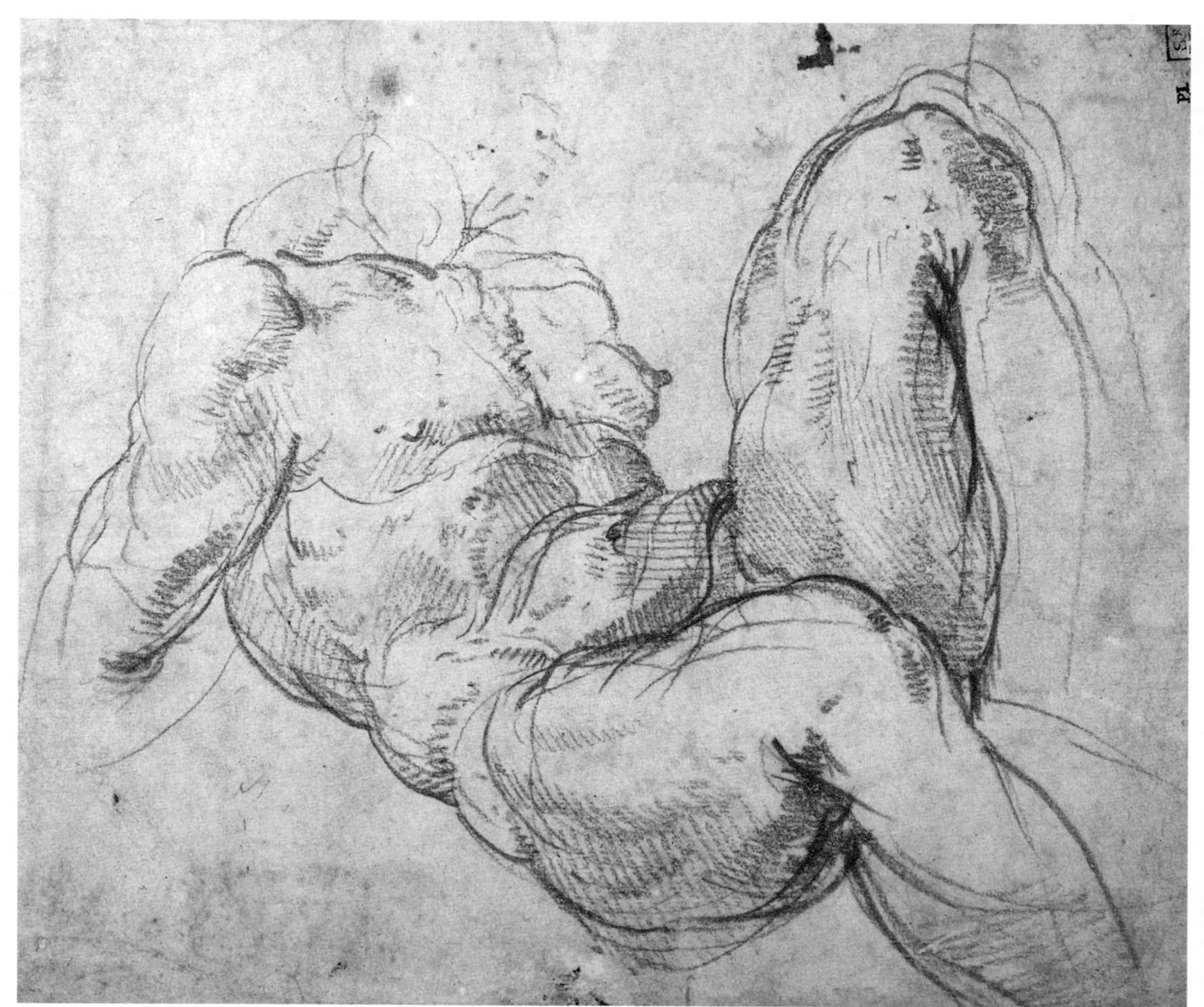

OPPOSITE
Study of a nude
Red chalk on paper
British Museum, London

LEFT
Ideal head
Red chalk on paper
Ashmolean Museum, Oxford

OPPOSITE

Study for The Creation on Adam

Chalk on paper

British Museum, London

LEFT

Figure studies for a man

Pen and ink on paper

British Museum, London

PAGE 356

LEFT

Cleopatra

Red chalk on paper

Uffizi, Florence

RIGHT

Figure study of male nude stretching upwards

Red chalk on paper

British Museum, London

PAGE 357

Study of arms and hands

Black chalk on paper

British Museum, London

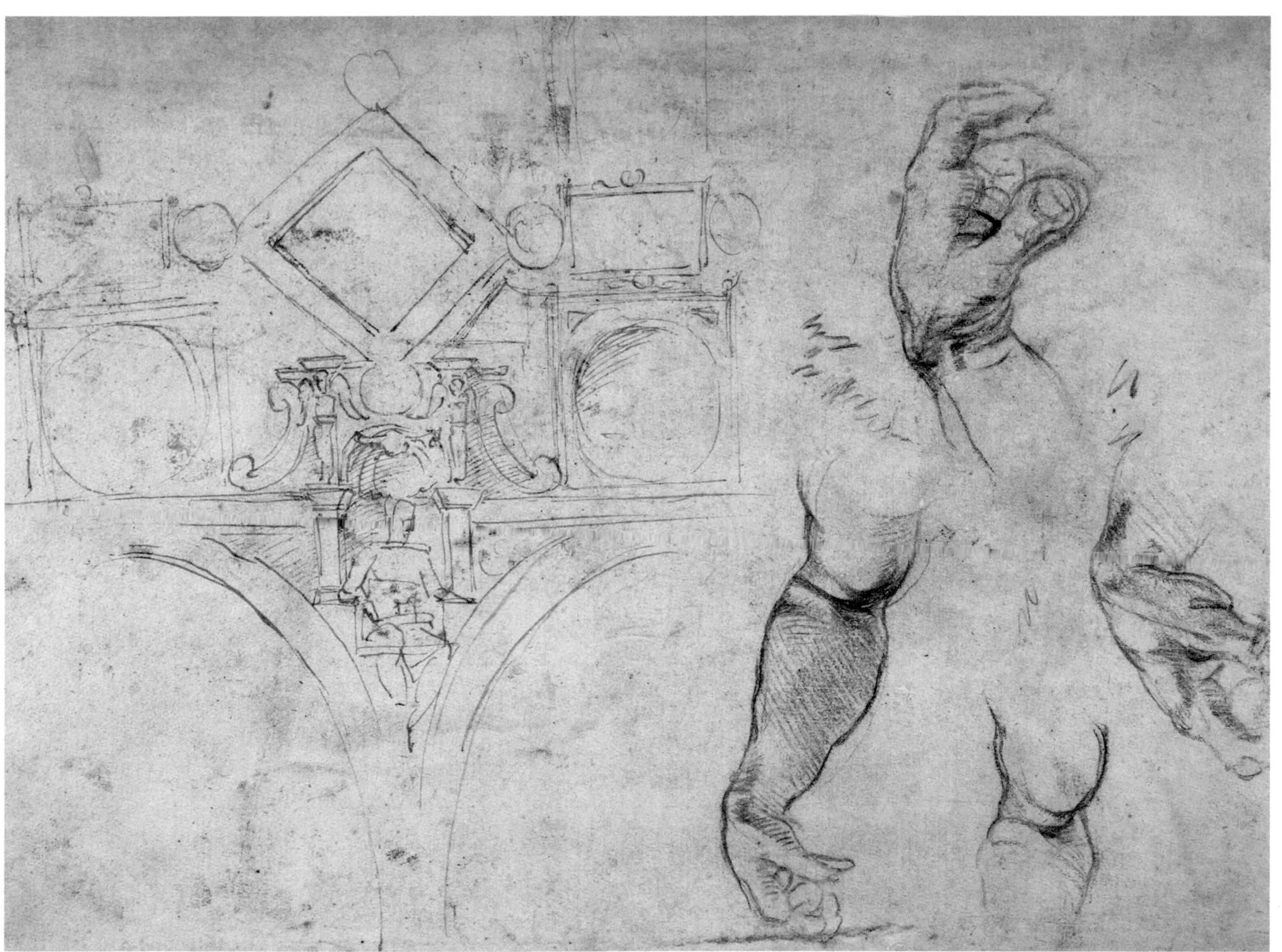

Study for The Annunciation
Red chalk on paper
British Museum, London

Study of head and shoulders
Pen and ink on paper
British Museum, London

Figure studies for a woman
Pen and ink on paper
British Museum, London

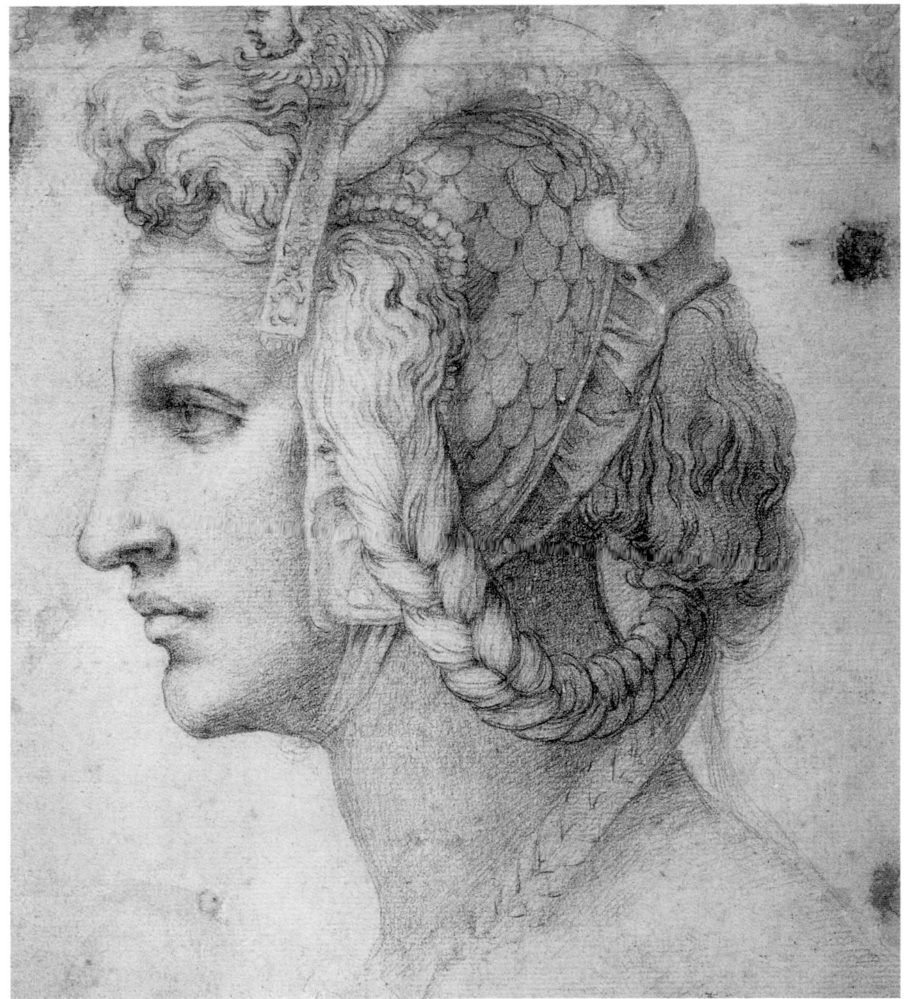

Study of a head
Pencil on paper
British Museum, London

OPPOSITE LEFT

The Alchemist

Pen and ink and pencil on paper

British Museum, London

The title of this sketch is suggested by Tolnay and is one of a number offered, based on whether he is carrying a sphere or a skull.

OPPOSITE RIGHT

Studies of male nudes

Pen and ink on paper

British Museum, London

LEFT

Male figure studies

Pen and ink on paper

British Museum, London

RIGHT

Study of a man shouting

Charcoal on paper

Gabinetto dei Disegni e Stampe, Uffizi, Florence

OPPOSITE LEFT

Virgin and Child

Pencil on paper

Louvre, Paris

OPPOSITE RIGHT

Sketch of a male head and two legs

Charcoal on paper

Gabinetto dei Disegni e Stampe, Uffizi, Florence

Page from a sketch book with figure studies and notes
Pen and ink on paper
British Museum, London

Zenobia, Queen of Palmyra, Syria (3rd century AD)
Charcoal on paper
Gabinetto dei Disegni e Stampe, Uffizi, Florence

OPPOSITE LEFT

Two Sketches of legs

Charcoal on paper

Gabinetto dei Disegni e Stampe, Uffizi, Florence

OPPOSITE RIGHT

Sketch of torso

Charcoal on paper

British Museum, London

LEFT

Head of a satyr

Pen and ink on paper

Louvre, Paris

RIGHT

Study of a head

Sanguine

Casa Buonarroti, Florence

OPPOSITE LEFT

Study for The Sacrifice of Isaac by Abraham *(1532–33)*

Black pencil, ink and sanguine

16 x 11 1/3in (41 x 29cm)

Casa Buonarroti, Florence

OPPOSITE RIGHT

Anatomical study: a man kneeling, back facing *(c. 1530)*

Black pencil, 10 1/8 x 7in (26 x 18cm)

Casa Buonarroti, Florence

Anatomical study

Black pencil

Casa Buonarroti, Florence

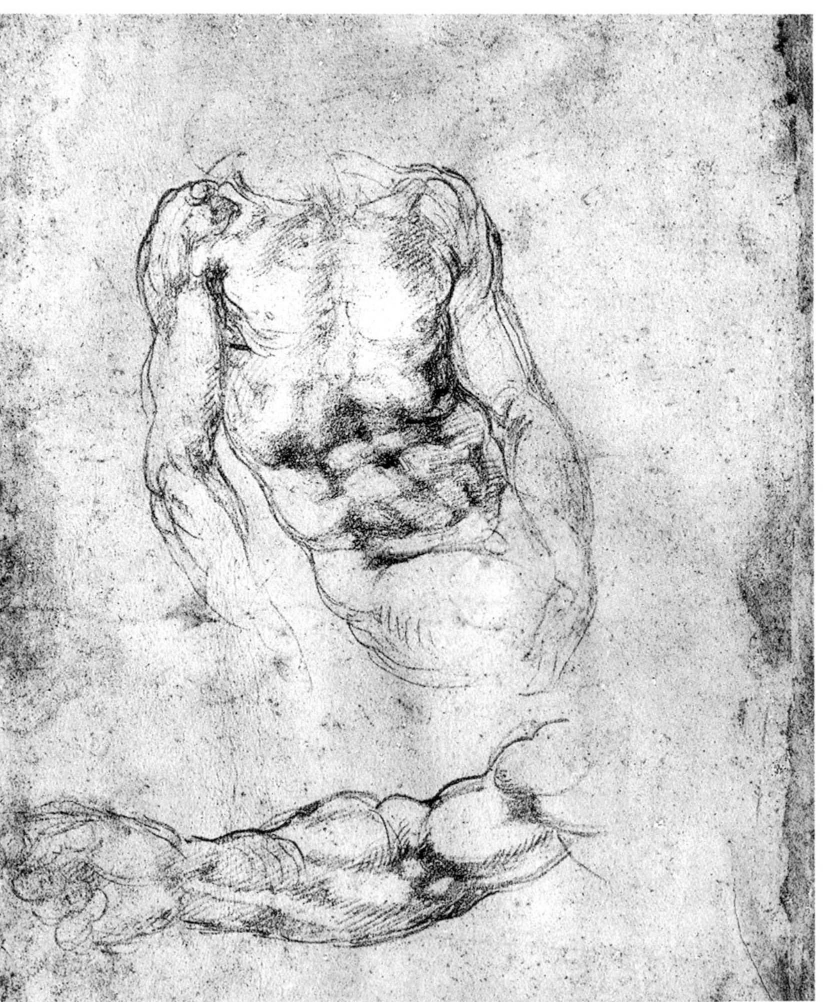

Study for The Last Judgement

Pencil on paper

British Museum, London

Study for an Ascension
Pencil on paper
British Museum, London

Figures for The Lamentation over the Body of Christ
Pencil on paper
British Museum, London

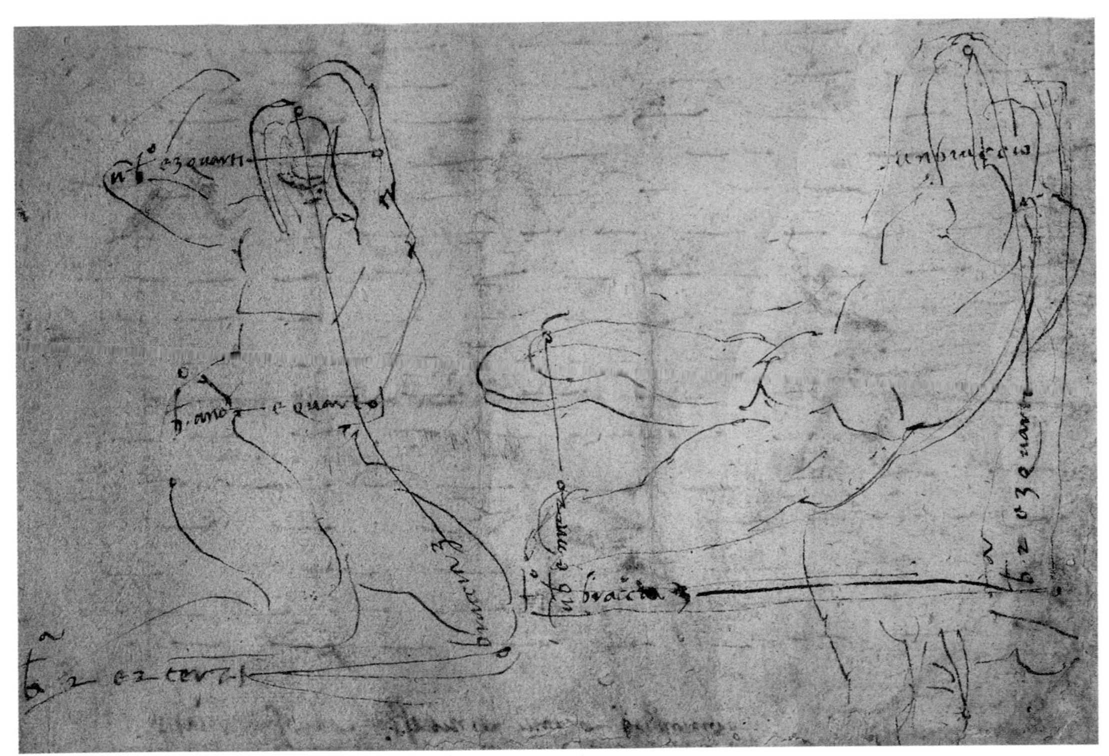

OPPOSITE LEFT
Study of three crucifixes
Red chalk on paper
British Museum, London

OPPOSITE RIGHT
Christ on the Cross
Red chalk on paper
British Museum, London

LEFT
Study for river god
Pen and ink on paper
British Museum, London

RIGHT

Study of a head

Red chalk on paper

British Museum, London

OPPOSITE LEFT

Study of Lazarus and two attendant figures

Red chalk on paper

British Museum, London

OPPOSITE RIGHT

Head of a bearded man shouting

Red chalk on paper

Ashmolean Museum, Oxford

Chapter Five

The Architecture of Michelangelo

OPPOSITE

The Cathedral Church of St. Peter, Rome *(mid-16th–17th centuries)*

The replacement of the old basilica of Constantine was the ambition of several popes and many designers of whom Michelangelo was just one. Bramante and Raphael had produced earlier designs and Antonio da San Gallo the Younger preceded Michelangelo as chief architect. Michelangelo did not approve of his design and made another when he reverted to Bramante's intention.

As a result, the origins of the present church are somewhat mixed. It is important to note this since it is usual to claim that only the dome is Michelangelo's. While this is not so it is undoubtedly his most individual single contribution, though it was finished after his death with slight modifications.

Considering the enormous painting and sculptural programmes outlined above it is astonishing to find that Michelangelo had either the time or the opportunity to acquire the qualifications to undertake any architectural work. That he was appointed chief architect for the new St. Peter's by Pope Paul III in 1546, after the death of Antonio da San Gallo the Younger, will make it clear that whether he was qualified or not was of no great significance: his reputation as the greatest artistic figure of his day was universally accepted and it was assumed that he could, if he wished, do anything. It is indeed true that his contribution to Renaissance architecture, while not as extensive as painting and sculpture is in many ways as important. After he had settled in Rome in 1534, he was soon acknowledged as the greatest artistic figure of the Renaissance. Readers may be suspicious or bored by these constant superlatives, but be assured that they are not casually or lightly bestowed.

Michelangelo's most famous architectural design was for the dome of St. Peter's and was intended to surmount the body of the basilica designed by Bramante, which had replaced an earlier planned design by Raphael. Michelangelo modified Bramante's design, intending to provide a centrally planned church and made designs for the interior which were partially carried out. The central plan was subsequently replaced by the extension of a nave, atrium and façade in the 17th century designed by Carlo Maderna. The disappointing effect of this was to diminish the intended dominance of the structure by the dome; the additions pull the front façade forward, partially obscuring the dome and diminishing its effect. Michelangelo worked on a partial redesign of the body of the basilica of St. Peter's for the next 17 years until he died in 1564, and the dome was completed after his death by Della Porta with some small modifications.

Some of Michelangelo's major sculptural commissions involved the use of architectural detail and he became familiar with the use of classical decorative elements and their possibilities. The great unfinished tomb of Julius II, for which the *Moses* was intended as a centrepiece, was planned as a large decorative architectural feature for St. Peter's but the plan was changed and the work, uncompleted at Michelangelo's death, was placed in the church of San Pietro in Vincoli.

Michelangelo was also commissioned to undertake another memorial tomb, this time in Florence for his

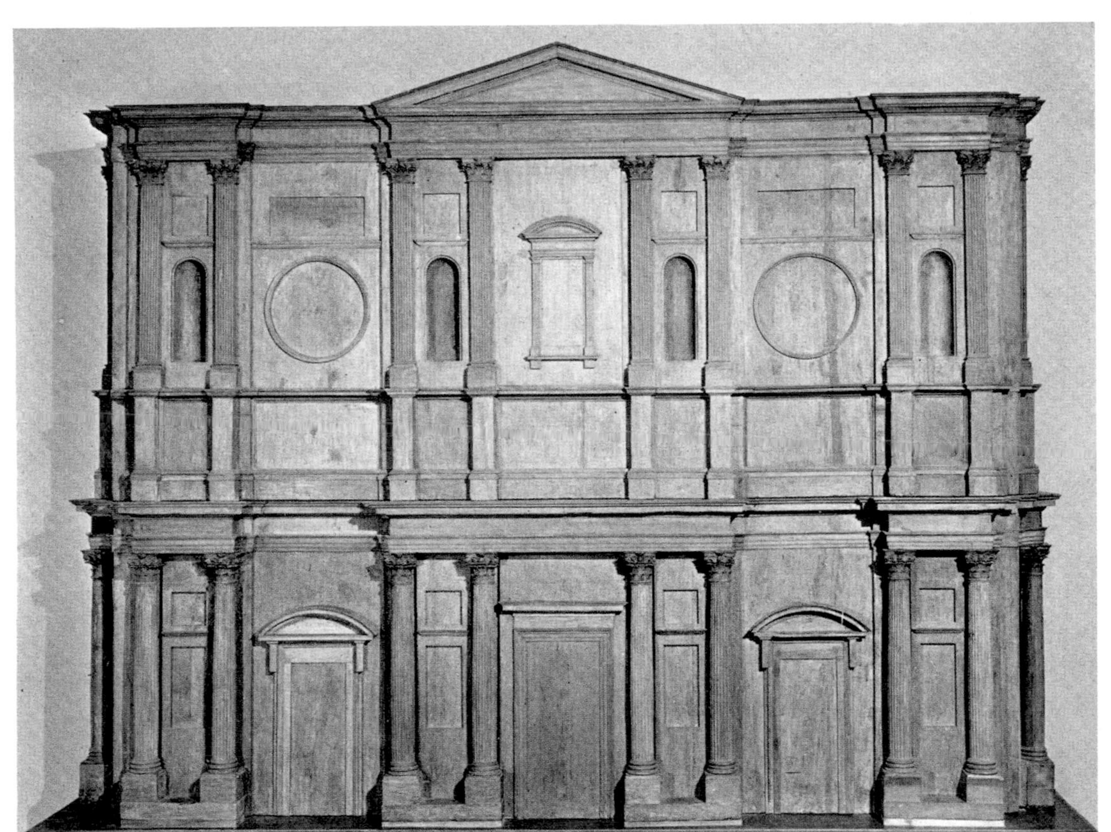

OPPOSITE

The Church of San Lorenzo, Florence (1441)

The design of the church by Filippo Brunelleschi was an enlargement of an earlier parish church in one of the richest districts of Florence. His first contribution was the design for the sacristy (now known as the Old Sacristy) and the building he envisaged was never realized, as is evidenced by the front view here. The dome seen rising above and the architecture surrounding it is Brunelleschi's contribution. What is important here is that Michelangelo was commissioned to design the front and produced a number of designs which included sculptures. A drawing of the architectural elements appears on page 385.

LEFT

Model of the façade of San Lorenzo

Casa Buonarroti, Florence

Church of San Lorenzo, Florence
Interior view of the Old Sacristy (1418–29)

The design by Filippo Brunelleschi of the sacristy in San Lorenzo was the basis for the architectural work that Michelangelo introduced in the New Sacristy in which the important tombs of Lorenzo de' Medici, duke of Urbino and Giuliano de' Medici, duke of Nemours were designed by Michelangelo.

Design for the façade of San Lorenzo by Michelangelo
Casa Buonarroti, Florence

Michelangelo made a number of drawings for the façade and a wooden model (page 383). He intended to fill the niches with sculptures, but like so many of his commissions it remained only a project.

important patrons the Medici. This, too, like the Julian tomb, was a combined architectural and sculptural structure and was to be placed in the New Sacristy in the church of San Lorenzo in Florence. The Old Sacristy had been designed by Brunelleschi and the New Sacristy was a near replica by Michelangelo to house four Medici tombs, only two of which were completed.

His most important fully architectural work in Florence was the Laurentian Library commissioned by the Medici Pope Clement VII and located within the cloisters of San Lorenzo to house the collection of books and documents collected by the Medici family. Work began in 1524 but was not completed when Michelangelo left for Rome in 1534, where he remained for the rest of his life. The library was finished to his design after his death. Michelangelo's influence in the development of the art of the High Renaissance into Mannerism is evident in the details of the library, as discussed elsewhere.

Michelangelo's appointment as chief architect of St. Peter's confirms his importance in the religious architectural scene, while another commission from Paul III gave him the central role in official secular Roman architecture. Pope Paul III was determined to redevelop the piazza space at the top of the Capitoline Hill with the only remaining bronze statue from the days of imperial Rome as a centrepiece. Michelangelo was appointed to redesign the Capitol, historically the most important civic centre of classical Rome. He realized the psychological importance of the location as well as its physical dominance looking across the city and visible from most parts of it.

The focus that the square needed was provided by the classical bronze equestrian figure of the Roman emperor, Marcus Aurelius, which had survived only because it had been thought to be an effigy of Constantine. Although Michelangelo was initially against the proposal, he agreed and designed an elliptical pedestal on which it was to be placed. It was located in the centre of the large piazza which contained only the ruins of its classical origins and the remains of the medieval Palazzo del Senatore. Michelangelo's task was to reinstate the Capitol as the centre of Roman civic pride.

He made designs for two identical facing palazzos and a modern redesign of the Palazzo del Senatore;

Church of San Lorenzo: the New Sacristy *(details of tombs)*

The sculptural work that Michelangelo produced for the tombs of Lorenzo and Giuliano de' Medici (pages 212–213 and 218–223) has been considered earlier, though the architectural context in which they were placed, although part of Michelangelo's design, is often overlooked. These two views may be considered in relation to the design by Brunelleschi for the Old Sacristy (page 384).

Church of San Lorenzo, Florence, Loggia delle Reliquie *(1533)*

The loggia is a lesser known work by Michelangelo. Situated above the main door of San Lorenzo, it is repository for holy relics.

A drawing for the Loggia

OPPOSITE and LEFT
The Laurentian Library *(1524–34).*

The Medici Pope Clement VII commissioned Michelangelo in 1524 to prepare plans for a new library within the cloisters of San Lorenzo to house the books and manuscripts belonging to the family. Although the work began that year it was suspended two years later, resumed in 1530 and again suspended in 1534. It was resumed in 1550 when the direction of the project was assumed by the architect Bartolommeo Ammanati. Michelangelo had no further part in the building but it was completed to his design after his death.

Michelangelo had conceived the vestibule (left) as rising eventually to three storeys, and as a preludium, designed to transport the scholars from the mundane outer world to the peaceful scholarly life within the library. The tall vestibule contains a triple staircase which rises to the reading room (opposite), giving a visual introduction as indicated in the illustration. The design has elements of Mannerism, soon to replace the classical restraint of the High Renaissance.

Staircase of the Laurentian Library

although nothing was finished in his lifetime, and proposals for changing his designs were made, his surviving friends ensured that they were completed almost as he had intended. The elliptical ends of the equestrian statue pedestal that he had made indicate his intention to emphasize the elliptical form in the piazza paving plan. The two new palazzi, facing each other, were placed at an angle which produced a trapezoid narrowing towards the steps up to them. The remaining side was closed with a balcony and steps and the whole space created, open to the sky, has something of the effect of a modern stadium in classical dress and is in Italy described as a *piazza salone*, an open-air room.

The finished piazza, bounded on three sides by great palaces, the Palazzo del Senatore, the Palazzo dei Conservatori and its twin Palazzo Nuovo, now the Palazzo del Museo Capitolino, and with the fourth narrower side facing towards Rome, the greatest city of ancient times and with nothing remotely religious within its boundaries, resonates with the sense of empire and civic pride. This piazza has become the basic model for many others but none has equalled its atmosphere of imperial power.

Other smaller commissions were undertaken at the request of Pope Paul III, a Farnese, including work on the Farnese Palace designed by Antonio da San Gallo the Younger.

THESE PAGES and OVERLEAF
Palazzo Farnese, Rome
Façade main portal 1546
Courtyard top storey 1548

The Palazzo Farnese was begun in 1517 to the design by Antonio da San Gallo the Younger, redesigned in 1534 and 1541, modified under Michelangelo from 1546 and completed in 1589. It is the most splendid of the Renaissance palaces in Rome.

Michelangelo was appointed in 1546 by Paul III to complete the unfinished building. This involved the window over the main portal, the great overhanging cornice, the upper storey in the courtyard and other internal details

The wide façade (185ft/56m) has three storeys with 14 windows on the

Continued overleaf

third storey and 12 on the second and offers a repetitive image held by a heavy cornice so that the bolder more ornate main entrance façade and decorative arch surmounted by the window by Michelangelo enlivens the whole effect.

The addition of rustication and elaborated first-storey windows is somewhat constrained by the close windows on the ground level.

The third storey of the courtyard was also the work of Michelangelo and although the basic pattern was set by the lower storeys, the sensitivity of Michelangelo's classicism is apparent.

THE CATHEDRAL CHURCH OF ST. PETER, ROME

When, in AD 313, the Roman Emperor Constantine formally recognized Christianity as a religion legally permitted within the Roman Empire, he initiated the process of transforming the whole of the Roman Empire into a Christian community. The persecution of Christians ceased and in 333 Constantine established Christianity as the official religion of the Roman Empire. In Rome he began the construction of the first church dedicated to St. Peter, near to the supposed site of his martyrdom and above the cemetery where he was believed to have been buried. Although there is no record of St. Peter's time in Italy, the site became the home of the Roman Church and St. Peter's church its greatest monument.

Part of the tradition also makes St. Peter the first bishop of Rome and the authority assumed by all subsequent popes, through what is known as the Apostolic Succession, descends from him, the ultimate interpretation of the Roman Catholic faith being invested in each pope when he is elected.

The elevation of Nicholas V in 1447 resulted in the start of the long process of replacing Constantine's old basilica, which had become dilapidated and dangerous

(more than one pope had had a narrow escape from falling stonework). Despite this, no pope had had the courage to even consider replacing such a revered building with so much history. Charlemagne had been crowned Holy Roman Emperor there on Christmas Day AD 800, a significant moment in the political structure of the modern church and state relationship which eventually spread throughout Christendom.

Pope Nicholas began a great programme of rebuilding and restoration, with St. Peter's at its centre. However, even Nicholas did not have the confidence to totally demolish the old basilica and ordered a new building to be constructed around it. In fact, the old basilica stood there crumbling away throughout all the subsequent building activity.

Bernardo Rossellino, sculptor and architect, was contracted and the building of the enormous sanctuary end of the new church began. Later popes interrupted this work but it remained standing and confirmed the scale to which the later church would be constructed. Consequently, St. Peter's not only became by far the largest of all Christian churches but also the greatest building enterprise in the whole of Europe during the period. Hundreds of workers were employed and the church became either the centre of intense activity or of temporary abandonment from the mid-15th century until it was finally completed in the 17th century.

OPPOSITE

The Cathedral Church of St. Peter, Rome *(mid-16th–17th centuries)*

Interior of the dome

LEFT

Drawing of the dome of St. Peter's by Michelangelo

The Cathedral Church of St. Peter, Rome

The colonnade to the left was designed by Gian Lorenzo Bernini and surmounted by figure sculptures; but the effect is to further diminish the impact of Michelangelo's dome.

Successive popes, although they made plans, did not continue work on St. Peter's and it was not until the early 1500s under Julius II that the building programme was purposefully carried forward. Julius II was a powerful, demanding patron of the arts and had commissioned Michelangelo to undertake the Sistine Chapel ceiling and his personal mausoleum to be placed in the new St. Peter's. He was also known as the Warrior Pope for his military campaigns, notably against Bologna, which he annexed to the Papal States. Under his papacy the Papal States became dominant in Italy and an important European power

Pope Julius put Donato Bramante in charge of the building of St. Peter's; Bramante took the bold decision, agreed by Julius, to have the old building demolished and produced a design incorporating Rossellino's earlier great structure. Work began in April 1506.

Julius died in 1513 and Bramante less than a year later. By that time the old church had been partly demolished and work begun on the new structure. But after Julius died work failed to progress for another 30 years until the pontificate of Paul III, a dedicated reformer, informed Humanist and devout Christian. He

PRINCIPIS APOST PAVLVS V BVRGHESIVS ROMANVS PONT MAX AN M XII PONT VII

The Cathedral Church of St. Peter, Rome

OPPOSITE LEFT
Plan drawing of a buttress with twin columns for the drum of the dome of St. Peter's

OPPOSITE RIGHT
A wooden model of the 16th-century dome designed by Michelangelo is housed in the Vatican Museum

greatly admired Michelangel and appointed him in 1546, when he was aged 72, architect-in-chief of St. Peter's. Michelangelo was reluctant to undertake this protracted and daunting programme on which very little had been done for 40 years and would have preferred to have returned to the sculptural contracts that remained unfinished. He accepted the commission, however, with the proviso that he would receive no payment for it.

First and foremost a sculptor, architecture was something of a sideline as far as Michelangelo was concerned; indeed, most of his architectural undertakings occurred later in his career. But in the end he was unable to refuse the challenge. Paul, aware of the many problems Michelangelo had had with Pope Julius over the Sistine ceiling, gave him full permission to 'change the model, form and structure at will'. With this authority, and the fact that he was under no finanancial obligations, Michelangelo now had remarkable freedom, which enabled him to make his own decisions and gave him the upper hand over envious colleagues.

Michelangelo worked on the church for the rest of his life, amending the design of his immediate predecessor, Antonio da San Gallo the Younger. However, he decided it was lacking in the grandeur the subject demanded and returned to Bramante's design which he believed to be superior, being 'clear, straightforward, luminous, and isolated from the Vatican Palace all around'. He succeeded in completing much of the central part of the church although the dome was not completed until 1590, finished by others but to Michelangelo's design.

The completed church is not as intended by Michelangelo. When Pope Paul V was elevated in 1605 he ordered the demolition of the still-remaining part of Constantine's basilica and a competition for the design of the new façade was won by Carlo Maderna, then architect of St. Peter's. Michelangelo's centrally-planned church was changed from a Greek to a Latin cross layout and the eastern arm was extended by an atrium, creating the long nave of the present church. In 1612 he added a long façade which extended much wider than the nave. The effect on Michelangelo's work was that the dome could not be seen from any distance less than a quarter of a mile away and the interior was altered from a basilical form to have a directional axis from entrance to altar. This was more suitable for long ceremonial processions than Michelangelo's design would have been.

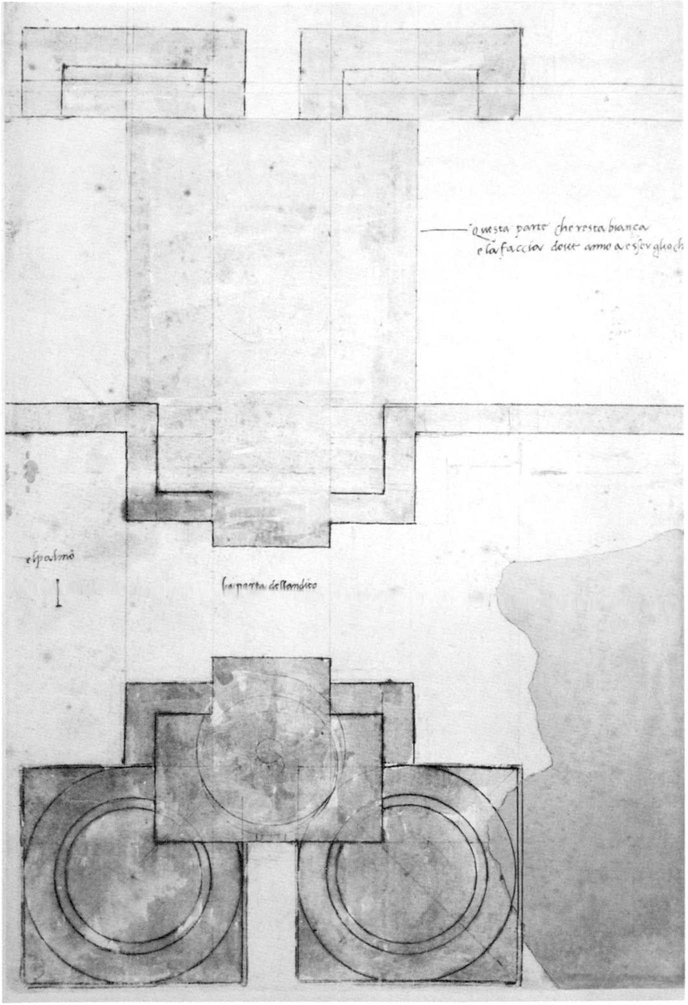
Questa parte che resta bianca
e la faccia dove anno a esser gli och

RIGHT

The dome of St. Peter's from the Vatican gardens

OPPOSITE

Swiss Guards of the Vatican City, Rome

Swiss Guards dressed in their traditional uniforms, the design of which has been attributed to Michelangelo.

The present character of the church was determined by further internal and external alterations by Gian Lorenzo Bernini (1598–1680), the greatest master of the Italian Baroque, who became architect of St. Peter's at the age of 31 in 1629. He had already achieved success as a sculptor by the age of 19 – an early achiever like Michelangelo but with a very different extravert temperament. Internally, Bernini added an elaborate Chair of St. Peter in the apse, a baldacchino, or ceremonial canopy, over the papal altar directly beneath Michelangelo's dome, the columns of which frame the best view of the apse. Externally he added the great elliptical piazza which fronts the church, at the centre of which was placed an ancient Egyptian obelisk. The piazza colonnades are surmounted by figure sculptures but the effect is to further diminish the impact of the dome (page 400). Nevertheless, in removing the indeterminate approach that had previously been there and replacing it with an expansive controlled public space, he added a sense of separateness and dignity that the church did not have before.

Although the majesty of St. Peter's owes most to Michelangelo, Bernini's contributions probably have more emotional impact on the visitor today.

Church of St. Peter's, Rome

This view offers an unusual opportunity to see the proportions of the elements of St. Peter's more distinctly than is possible from the ground, either from afar or close up. The large façade obscures the intended effect by the earlier designers, including Raphael, Bramante and Michelangelo, which was to have been a Greek Cross church with no long nave which was to have culminated in a drum and dome. From the ground the drum is not visible and the dominance of the dome, apparent here, is greatly diminished. However, it is possible in this view to see the relationship of the church with the Vatican City on the right.

RIGHT

Piazza del Campidoglio, Rome

OPPOSITE LEFT

Equestrian statue of Marcus Aurelius

OPPOSITE RIGHT

Plan of the piazza

The commission given to Michelangelo by Pope Paul III to design the Capitol, historically the civic centre of classical Rome, was of great significance and its importance was still alive in the minds and hearts of the Renaissance citizens despite its undistinguished architectural character. Michelangelo was influenced by this and understood the importance of the site. His first design element was to place the classical equestrian statue of Marcus

Continued on page 410

The Capitol, Rome

From his arrival there in 1534 Michelangelo spent the rest of his life working in Rome. After the rebuilding of St. Peter's the most important architectural programme was the refurbishment of the Capitol and that was also entrusted to him.

Although the Campidoglio on the Capitoline Hill has been considered, the individual buildings and much of

AREAE·CAPITOLINAE·ET·ADIACENTIVM·PORTICVVM·SCALARVM·TRIBVNALIVM·EX·
MICHAELIS·ANGELI·BONAROTI·ARCHITECTVRA·ICHNOGRAPHIA
ROMAE·ANNO·∞ D LXVII

Aurelius on an elliptical base. This determined the character of the whole design which took the form of a large oval piazza bounded by three great palaces, the Palazzo del Senatore, the Palazzo Nuovo (Palazzo del Museo Capitolino) and the Palazzo dei Conservatori, planned to form a narrowing boundary looking towards Rome. The patterned pavement was also to Michelangelo's design. The work was not completed in his lifetime but to his basic intention later on.

OPPOSITE
View across the piazza towards the steps with the statues in the foreground. In the background is the Palazzo dei Conservatori which is covered in scaffolding.

the design of the piazza, have not been examined.

The only palazzo on the Capitoline Hill dating from Michelangelo's lifetime is the Palazzo dei Conservatori, construction of which began in 1561. The Senatore dates from the medieval period and was modified by Michelangelo and others while the Palazzo Nuovo (as it was then called) had not been started when Michelangelo died, but was built later to his Conservatori design.

The most important single design and the basis for two buildings on the piazza is the Conservatori, which replaced a *quattrocento* palace. The new building was finished in 1584 and its partner, the Palazzo Nuovo, between 1603 and 1654. The new façade included massive pier pilasters rising to the full height and surmounted by an impressive cornice, balustrade and statuary. The façade was given a large central window which Michelangelo would probably not have liked. Michelangelo's colossal pilasters did not precisely correspond with the classical pattern but they set a fashion in Europe which lasted for over 200 years.

The Palazzo Nuovo followed the design of the Conservatori and was placed at a similar angle to the Senatore.

The scheme for the restoration of the Palazzo del Senatore was planned in the 1540s but it was not funded until the design for the whole of the area, including the piazza and an enlarged base for the statue of Marcus Aurelius, was agreed by Pope Pius IV. Michelangelo's design for a double stairway in front of the Senatore was begun in the 1540s and the restoration work around 1561–64, Tommaso Cavalieri having been placed in charge. The palazzo was given a facing of pilasters to link the *piano nobile* with a new portal at the top of the double staircase. The present bell tower is not part of Michelangelo's design, although he intended one, but was designed and completed in 1583 by Longhi. The whole façade was finished by about 1600.

The piazza itself became a model for future public squares and Michelangelo's design for the paving has been replicated using different patterns and to the extent of including a separate central sculpture. The essence of Michelangelo's designs is symmetry and he likened it to the human body – a similar hand on both sides. As mentioned earlier, the form is trapezoidal and the elliptical pattern of the paving, reminiscent of an egg, suggests the centre of the world which, of course, is Rome.

MUSEI CAPITOLINI
PALAZZO DEI CONSERVATORI

MUSEI CAPITOLINI
PALAZZO NUOVO

OPPOSITE
The Palazzo Nuovo (Musei Capitolini) *1603–54*

LEFT
The steps and ramp dating from 1536 which lead up to the Piazza del Campidoglio. The statue is of a Dioscuro, a son of Leda and Zeus.

The Palazzo del Senatore on the Piazza del Campidoglio, Rome
(completed 1600)

Florence Cathedral (Santa Maria del Fiore)

Due to Brunelleschi's great dome (1420–34), the duomo is regarded as one of the greatest of the incipient Renaissance. The Baptistery is noted for the workmanship of its bronze doors which were added in the 14th and 15th centuries by Andrea Pisano and Lorenzo Ghiberti. In 1514, due to its threatened collapse, Michelangelo introduced an iron chain around the base of the dome, together with ornamentation

Porta Pia, Rome *(1561–64)*

The Porta Pia was built between the above dates but modifications to it were made later and in the 19th century when an upper storey was added. According to Vasari, Michelangelo made a number of designs of gateways but only the Porta Pia was built. It was designed to be the culmination of the straight road that Pope Pius IV himself had built.

The Architecture of Michelangelo

Michelangelo's Architectural Drawings

Drawings made for artistic purposes in respect of painting or sculpture are different in purpose from architectural drawings and the observations made earlier concerning artistic drawings do not closely relate to the drawings reproduced on the following pages: some further comments are therefore necessary.

Architecture is regarded as an art form but it is different in nature from all others in that its essential existence is the result of a practical social need rather than inspired self-interest. Architecture only exists because it is useful. As has been noted earlier in an observation of John Ruskin's, this only means a structure that we call a building. The art element, the aesthetic content, turns it into architecture. It is the art element that these drawings reflect. However, this is constricted mainly, although not entirely, to visual surface treatment.

Over the centuries, architectural surface treatment has changed and one of the several dramatic changes took place between the Medieval and Renaissance periods when a style of visual treatment inspired by the Christian religion was replaced by a return to one developed in the pre-Christian classical societies. This resulted in a 'classical' style in the Renaissance and the architects spent much time learning the rules of proportion and standard forms of decoration that had been used in Greek and Roman societies. This resulted in careful copying of classical buildings and classical drawings of buildings based on the publication of instructional and informational volumes on style. These ranged from the earliest work of Vitruvius (c.90–20 BC), his *De Architectura*, to such works as the Ten Books of Architecture of Leon Battista Alberti (1404–72) and the later Sebastian Serlio, a contemporary of Michelangelo, who was the author of *L'Architettura* and one of the most important theoreticians of the Renaissance.

Michelangelo never regarded himself as a 'professional' architect but he had a deep interest in proportion and detail and the standards that following the classical style demanded. As a result, his architectural drawings are careful and measured, obeyed the rules and calculated for a specific use. They are, despite Michelangelo's assertion that he was not an architect, professional designs, and should be regarded as such. The selection that follows establishes this.

Architectural drawing
Pen and ink on paper
British Museum, London

Architectural study
Red chalk on paper
British Museum, London

Studies for a capital
Pen and brown ink on paper
British Museum, London

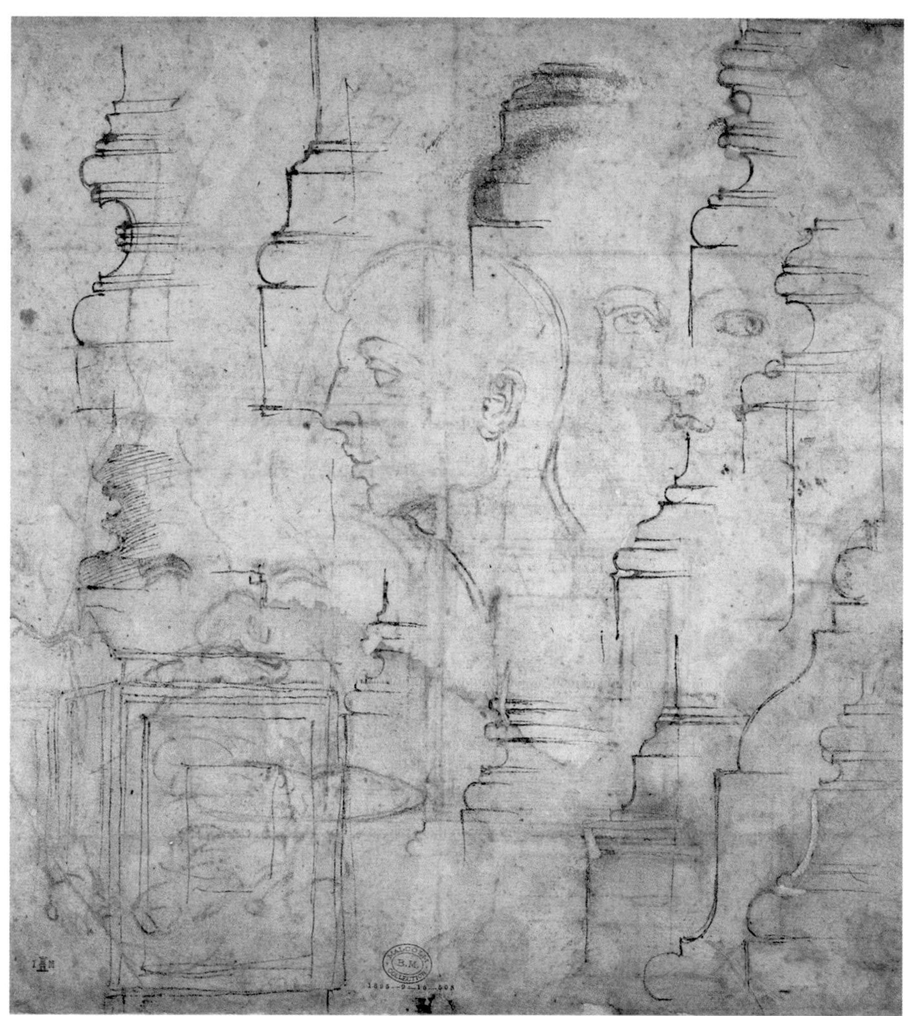

Sketches of a column with faces

Pen and pencil on paper

British Museum, London

Study for a window

Pen and ink on paper

British Museum, London

Study of column capitals
Coloured pencil
British Museum, London

Roughly-sketched designs for furniture and decorations
Pen and ink on paper
British Museum, London

Chapter Six

The Poems of Michelangelo

The letters and writings of Michelangelo add an interesting and significant contribution to his creative output, though they were only known to a small circle of friends during his lifetime; it could not be claimed that he was a professional writer. However, and among all his other talents, he was also known as a poet. Although there were plans to publish his poetry during his lifetime they were printed in a 'slightly revised' form by a grand-nephew in 1623. After a period of obscurity they were published again in *The Romantic Age of Poets*, appropriately at the time of Keats and Shelley. The first translations were in French and German and in 1833 an appreciation was published in French which presented them as intimate confessions.

Michelangelo wrote in the Tuscan dialect and the muscular intensity of his words are as powerful as his artistic statements, though may have lost something in translation. In his early poems he expresses the sensual responses of youth, while in his maturity the tragic aspects of love come to the surface in his poems addressed to Tommaso Cavalieri, the beautiful youth, the embodiment of his passion for physical beauty and perfection, in an example of what may be termed Platonic love. Later, his intense relationship with Vittoria Colonna is expressed in terms of almost spiritual adoration verging on a religious experience. In the last poems, the new insights into Christianity which she had given him, her death and his own self-doubt, prompted poetic invocations directed to God in His mercy.

Michelangelo's poems, directed towards his two most intimate friends, reveal the conflict between sacred and profane love which may not ever have been resolved.

Vittoria Colonna (c.1492–1547)

Michelangelo was one of a circle of Vittoria's friends who were concerned with the problem of salvation and the possibility of direct communication and contact between the individual and God. They were in favour of religious reform and their discussions appeared to favour a more severe Protestantism. Michelangelo was passionately involved with Vittoria and loved her deeply. Whether this love was physical or like that of a son for his mother is open to conjecture, but he was certainly desolated when she died.

Tommaso de' Cavalieri

It is said that Cavalieri was one of Michelangelo's reasons for going to Rome in 1534, Michelangelo having reputedly met him in Rome in 1532 when he was much attracted to him. Cavalieri came from an old Roman family, was unusually intelligent and had great physical beauty. He was also interested in the arts and the two formed a close friendship based on mutual esteem. Michelangelo taught Cavalieri to draw and wrote poems to him of Petrarchian love and passion and Cavalieri even assisted in the supervision of the Campidoglio. Cavalieri was with Michelangelo when he died and attended his funeral.

Again, it is not known if there was a physical element to their relationship. However, some of Michelangelo's sonnets, reproduced below, were once the subject of a deliberate attempt to present them as heterosexual. Since the 19th century, however, and J.A. Symonds' study of the subject, their homoerotic nature has come to the fore.

Michelangelo

To Tommaso de' Cavalieri

A Che Piu Debb'io

Why should I seek to ease intense desire
With still more tears and windy words of grief,
When heaven, or late or soon, sends no relief
To souls whom love hath robed around with fire.

Why need my aching heart to death aspire,
When all must die? Nay death beyond belief
Unto these eyes would be both sweet and brief,
Since in my sum of woes all joys expire.

Therefore because I cannot shun the blow
I rather seek, say who must rule my breast,
Gliding between her gladness and her woe?

If only chains and bands can make me blest,
No marvel if alone and bare I go
An armed Knight's cantive and slave confessed.

Veggio nel Tuo Bel Viso

From thy fair face I learn, O my loved lord,
That which no mortal tongue can rightly say;
The soul imprisoned in her house of clay,
Holpen by thee to God hath often soared:

And tho' the vulgar, vain, malignant horde
Attribute what their grosser wills obey,
Yet shall this fervent homage that I pay,
This love, this faith, pure joys for us afford.

Lo, all the lovely things we find on earth,
Resemble for the soul that rightly sees,
That source of bliss divine which gave us birth;

Nor have we first fruits or remembrances
Of heaven elsewhere. Thus, loving loyally,
I rise to God and make sweet death by thee.

Non Vider gli Occhi Miei

No mortal thing enthralled these longing eyes
When perfect peace in they fair face I found:
But far within, where all is holy gound,
My soul felt Love, her comrade of the skies:

For she was born with God in Paradise;
Nor all the shows of beauty shed around
This fair false world her wings to earth have bound;
Unto the Love of Loves aloft she flies.

Nay, things that suffer death quench not the fire
Of deathless spirits; nor eternity
Serves sordid Time, that withers all things rare

Not love but lawless impulse is desire:
That slays the soul; our love makes still more fair
Our friends on earth, fairer in death on high.

Sonnet in honour of Dante

From heaven he came, in mortal clothing, when
All that was worst and best has been observed
Living, he came to view the god he served
To give us the entire, true light again.

For that bright star which with its vivid rays
Picked out the humble place where I was born –
For this, the world would be a prize to scorn;
None but its maker can return its praise.

I speak of Dante, he whose work was spurned
By the ungrateful crowd, those who can give
Praise only to the worthless, I would live

Happy were I but he, by such men scorned,
If, with his torments, I could also share
His greatness, both its joy and exile bear.

An example of a comic (*buffo*) rhyme in the shape of a stanza parodying a declaration of love

When I behold your pointed dugs, I see
Two ripe cucumbers in a sack of gunny
And soon go up in flame, like a fusee.
The hoe has bent my back – 'tis scarcely funny
But were I still just as I used to be,
I chase you like a cur. You draw as honey
Draws the bee. How easy then it seemed –
What would today quite marvellous be esteemed.

A poem to a young woman

How much a garland pleases when it lies,
Woven with flowers, upon some golden hair;
It seems as if each blossom thrusts and tries
To be the first to kiss that forehead fair.

Content all day long that garment is
Which spreads itself but first clings to her breast.
The golden thread asks nothing but to rest,
Touching her cheeks and throat with tenderness.

More honoured still that ribbon which can lie
Gilded and shaped in the most cunning fashion
Touching the breast which it so carefully laces.

And that small belt that knots so easily
Seems to declare, 'Unceasing my caresses'.
Would that my arms might join in such a passion!

Renowned and beautiful sonnet to Cavalieri

If love is chaste, if pity comes from heaven,
If fortune, good or ill, is shared between
Two equal loves, and if one wish can govern
Two hearts, and nothing evil intervene:

If one joins to bodies fast for ever,
And if, on the same wings, these two can fly,
And if one dart of love can pierce and sever
The vital organs both equally;

If both love one another with the same
Passion, and if each other's good is sought
By both, if taste and pleasure and desire

Bind such a faithful love-knot, who can claim
Either with envy, scorn, contempt or ire,
The power to untie so fast a knot?

Chronology

Michelangelo

1475 Born on 6 March in Caprese.

1481 Francesca Neri di Miniato del Sera Michelangelo's mother, dies.

c.1485–c.88 Attends the school of the humanist Francesco da Urbino. Michelangelo's father remarries.

1488 Michelangelo becomes an apprentice in the workshop of painter Domenico Ghirlandaio.

c. 1490–92 Worked for the Medici household It is likely that he produced the *Madonna della Scala* and the *Battle of the Centaurs*.

1492 Lorenzo de' Medici dies.

1494 The Medici are expelled from Florence.

1494–95 Michelangelo works in Bologna where he carves figures for the tomb of St. Dominic.

1495 Returns to Florence, which is heavily under the influence of the Dominican preacher Girolamo Savonarola. Works include *St. John the Baptist* and the *Sleeping Cupid*.

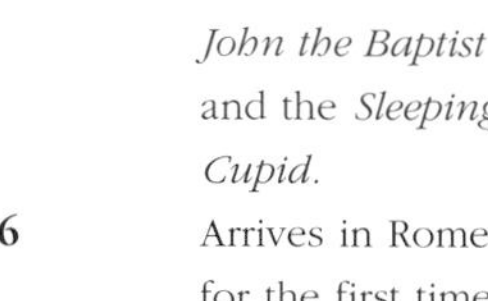

1496 Arrives in Rome for the first time on 25 June.

1496–1501 Still in Rome, his works include *Bacchus*, the *Pietà and the Bruges Madonna*.

1501 Returns to Florence where he is contracted to carve figures for the Piccolomini altar and is also commissoned to carve the statue of *David*.

1503 Is given a large commission for the twelve apostles, including *St. Matthew*, for Florence cathedral.

c. 1503–05 Works include the *Doni Tondo*, *Taddei Tondo*, and *Pitti Tondo*.

1504 *David* is completed. He is commissioned to paint the *Battle of Cascina.*

1505 Michelangelo is summoned to Rome where he is commissioned to create the tomb for the Pope Julius II. He travels to Carrara's quarries where he spends many months selecting marble for the tomb.

1505–45 Michelangelo works sporadically on Julius II's tomb, working in both Rome and Florence. He carves *Moses*, the *Dying* and *rebellious Slaves*, other Slave figures and *Rachel* and *Leah*.

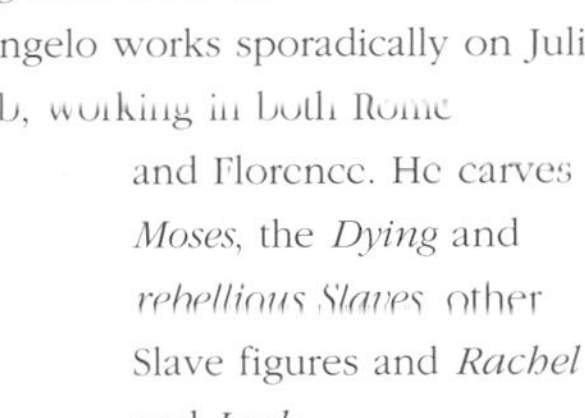

1506 In April he is in Florence. In November he meets Pope Julius II in Bologna. Julius commissions him to design a bronze statue of himself which is subsequently destroyed.

1508 Returns to Florence in February. Once again Pope Julius II summons him to Rome where he is commissioned to paint the greatest work of his life the ceiling of the Sistine Chapel which he starts in May.

1508–12 Michelangelo is tied to Rome for the next four years working on the Sistine Chapel painting which he completes in October 1512.

1513 Pope Julius II dies. Giovanni de' Medici is elected as Pope Leo X. Michelangelo signs a further contract for the tomb of Pope Julius II.

1514 Commissioned for *Christ with the Cross (Risen Christ)* and the chapel of Pope

Chronology

Leo X in Castel Sant' Angelo, Rome.

1516 In July he returns to Florence where he is commissioned to erect the façade of the Medici church of San Lorenzo in Florence. He signs a third contract for the tomb of Pope Julius II.

1516–19 Michelangelo makes many visits to the quarries at Carrara and Serravezza to select marble for the San Lorenzo façade.

c. 1517 Commissioned to design the *Kneeling Windows* for the Medici Palace.

1519 Commissioned to design the New Sacristy, or Medici Chapel, for San Lorenzo.

1520 The contract for the San Lorenzo façade is cancelled. Michelangelo starts work on the Medici Chapel tombs.

1521 Pope Leo X dies.

1523 Giulio de' Medici is elected pope as Clement VII.

1524 Commissioned to design the *Laurentian Library* at San Lorenzo.

1527 Sack of Rome on 6 May. Medici are exiled from Florence on 17 May.

c.1525–30 Michelangelo works on *Apollo/David*.

1527–30 Florence becomes the last republic. He is commissioned to carve Hercules but is is never fulfilled. Michelangelo designs and builds fortifications.

1529–30 Florence is under siege by the combined forces of Pope Clement VII and the Holy Roman Emperor Charles V.

1532 He visits Rome where he meets Tommaso de' Cavalieri. He gives Cavalieri gifts of drawings and poems. Signs new contract for the tomb of Pope Julius.

1533 Reliquary loggia in San Lorenzo completed.

1534 Pope Clement VII dies. Alessandro Farnese is elected as Pope Paul III. Michelangelo leaves Florence, never to return. The *Medici*

Michelangelo

Madonna and *Victory* are left incomplete in his Florentine workshop. For the next 30 years until his death he remains in Rome.

1535 Starts painting the *Last Judgment* in the Sistine Chapel. Meets Vittoria Colonna.

1538 Begins work on the Campidoglio on the Capitoline Hill.

c. 1540 Works on the bust of *Brutus.*

1541 Completes the *Last Judgment.*

1542 In August he signs a contract for the final version Pope Julius' tomb as agreed by his heirs. Begins work on the Pauline Chapel.

1545 The tomb of Julius II is completed and installed in San Pietro in Vincoli, Rome. Still working on the Pauline Chapel frescoes until 1550.

1546 Michelangelo's chief architect Antonio da San Gallo dies. San Gallo worked on St. Peter's and the Farnese Palace.

1547 Vittoria Colonna dies. Michelangelo starts work on a Pietà for his own tomb which he abandons c.1555.

1553 Ascanio Condivi's *Life of Michelangelo* is published. Starts work on the Rondanini *Pietà*

1559–60 Designs for San Giovanni dei Fiorentini, Rome.

c. 1560 Commission for the Sforza Chapel in Santa Maria Maggiore, Rome.

1561 Commissions for the Porta Pia and Santa Maria degli Angeli in Rome.

1564 February 18. Dies at home in Rome.

Bibliography

A number of books that will provide interesting further information on the subjects considered in this book are listed below. The bibliography of the Renaissance and the life of Michelangelo is so extensive that to attempt cover them completely would cause more problems than it would solve, since choices by the interested but new reader would inevitably be random. Bear in mind that the few titles listed will themselves contain reading lists of further books ad infinitum. Consequently the titles listed are a suggested starting point.

The books are selected under three headings: The Renaissance; Art and Architecture in the Renaissance; and Michelangelo.

The Renaissance

Jacob Burckhardt: *The Civilization of the Period of the Renaissance in Italy*, Phaidon.
E.H. Gombrich: *Gombrich on the Renaissance* (3 volumes), Phaidon.
Edgar Wind: *Pagan Mysteries of the Renaissance*, Faber.
Christopher Hibbert: *The Rise and Fall of the House of Medici*, Allen Lane/Penguin.
Hutchinson Encyclopedia of the Renaissance, Helicon.
John Hale: *The Civilization of Europe in the Renaissance*, Harper Collins.
Baldassare Castiglione: *The Book of the Courtier.*
Niccolò Machiavelli: *The Prince*; *The History of Florence.*
Villari: *Life and Times of Niccolò Machiavelli.*
J.C.L. Sismondi: *A History of the Italian Republics.*
Michael de la Bedoyère: *The Meddlesome Friar* (Savonarola and Alexander VI)
C.S. Gutkind: *Cosmo de' Medici (Pater Patriae).*
Y. Maguire: *The Women of the Medici.*
J.A. Symonds: *The Renaissance in Italy.*
Benvenuto Cellini: Autobiography.
H.M. Vaughan: *The Medici Popes.*
Bertrand Russell: *History of Western Philosophy* (Sections on the Classical and Italian Renaissance).
Pope-Hennessy: *The Portrait in the Renaissance.*

Michelangelo

Art and Architecture in the Renaissance

Leon Battista Alberti: Ten Books of Architecture; and other books on painting.

John White: *The Birth and Rebirth of Pictorial Space.*

Nicholas Pevsner (editor): *The Pelican History of Art* (the volumes concerned with the period).

Anthony Blunt: *Artistic Theory in Italy, 1450–1600.*

Walter Pater: *The Renaissance: Studies in Art and Poetry.*

Bernhard Berenson: *The Italian Painters of the Renaissance*; *The Florentine Painters of the Renaissance.*

Heinrich Wolfflin: *The Art of the Italian Renaissance.*

John Ruskin: *Modern Painters.*

S. Freedberg: *Painting of the High Renaissance in Rome and Florence.*

Michelangelo

There are many books on Michelangelo's life and the assessment of his artistic achievement takes various forms. Some are concerned with a particular aspect of his oeuvre, such as the ceiling of the Sistine Chapel, or his poetry. Most of them are adequate and accurate and some are imaginative and inspiring, making it less than easy to select essential further reading. The early biographers, like Vasari and Condivi, offer extremely interesting interpretations even though they are not always factually accurate.

Later writers, with more tested information available to them, are likely to be accurate and, with the range of Michelangelo's achievement becoming more widely understood, have often emphasized some aspect of his career rather than attempt an overall picture.

Some suggested authors are listed below without titles, since most will be identified by the name Michelangelo. Where they have a particular emphasis on one aspect of his work this is identified in brackets.

John Addington Symonds (life and sonnets)

C. Heath Wilson (19th-century study)

Romain Rolland

Georg Brandes (poems and letters)

F. Harrt

C. Tolnay (major authority); Life in 5 volumes

J. Wild

Index

Page numbers in italics refer to illustrations

Index

Acknowledgements

The Publishers wish to thank the following for providing photographs, and for permission to reproduce copyright material. While every effort has been made to trace and acknowledge copyright-holders, we wish to apologise whould any omissions have been made.

AA Photo Library: Pages 28, 79, 127, 128, 148, 172
©Adam Woolfitt/CORBIS: Page 236 left
©Araldo de Luca/CORBIS: Page 191, 208 both, 209, 414-415,
©Archivo Icongrafico, S.A./CORBIS: Page 194 right, 195 left
©Arte & Immagini Srl/CORBIS: Pages 24, 75, 199 right, 200 right, 201, 239 both, 240, 241 both, 242 both, 244, 245 both, 246 both, 247
Ashmolean Museum, Oxford/The Bridgeman Art Library, London: Pages 353, 379 right
Bargello, Florence, Italy/The Bridgeman Art Library, London: Pages 166, 198, 248, 249
©Bettmann/CORBIS: Pages 25, 205
Brancacci Chapel, Santa Maria del Carmine, Florence, Italy/The Bridgeman Art Library, London: Page 60
The Bridgeman Art Library, London: Pages 6, 27, 55, 99, 153, 202, 203, 206 left, 207 both, 210, 218, 220, 222, 257, 381, 384, 386 left, 390, 391, 396, 397, 408
British Museum, London: Page 129
British Museum, London/The Bridgeman Art Library, London: Pages 32, 33, 35, 40, 42, 43, 56, 58, 69, 83, 121, 122, 132, 158, 159, 224 right, 283, 311, 329, 346, 349, 350 both, 351, 353, 354, 355, 357, 358, 359, 360, 361, 362 both, 363, 366, 368 both, 373, 374, 375, 376 both, 377, 378m 379 left, 419, 420, 421, 422, 423, 425, 426
Capella Paolina, Vatican, Italy/The Bridgeman Art Library, London: Pages 106, 107, 342 both, 343, 344 both, 345
Casa Buonarotti, Florence, Italy: Pages 96, 162, 173, 370, 371 both, 372, 383, 385
Casa Buonarotti, Florence, Italy/The Bridgeman Art Library, London: Pages 164, 165, 170, 194 left
Castello Sforzesco, Milan, Italy/The Bridgeman Art Library, London: Pages 226 both, 227 right
Central Saint Martin's College of Art and Design/The Bridgeman Art Library, London: Page 66
Church of San Domenico, Bologna, Italy/The Bridgeman Art Library, London: Page 73, 74
Copplestone, Trewin: Pages 44, 47, 65, 80, 85, 144 left, 176 both, 177 right, 181, 182 both, 392, 398, 409 left
Cortauld Gallery, London/The Bridgeman Art Library, London: Pages 41
©David Lees/CORBIS: Pages 195 right, 197, 214, 215, 216, 217
Duomo, Sienna, Italy/The Bridgeman Art Library, London: Pages 188, 189 both
Edifice © Darley: Page 20
Edifice © Kim Sayer: Page 416
Edifice © Lewis: Page 94
Edifice © Lewis/Darley: Page 401
Edifice © Philippa Lewis: Pages 139, 411, 412, 413
©Francis G. Mayer/CORBIS: Pages 234 left, 235
Fratelli Fabbri, Milan, Italy/The Bridgeman Art Library, London: Page 145
Gabinetto dei Disegni e stampe Uffizi, Florence, Italy: Page 369
Gabinetto dei Disegni e stampe Uffizi, Florence, Italy/The Bridgeman Art Library, London: Pages 61, 273, 319, 319 both, 364, 365 right, 367
Galleria degli Uffizi, Florence, Italy/The Bridgeman Art Library, London: Pages 86, 169,

Acknowledgements

356 left 403 left

Galleria dell'Accademia, Florence, Italy/The Bridgeman Art Library, London: Pages 3, 171, 177 left, 179, 180, 183, 185, 186-7 all, 200 left, 238

Galleria dell'Accademia, Venice, Italy/The Bridgeman Art Library, London: Page 76

K & B News Foto, Florence/The Bridgeman Art Library, London: Page 382

Kunsthistorisches Museum, Vienna, Austria/The Bridgeman Art Library, London: Page 114

The Louvre, Paris, France: Pages 113, 225

The Louvre, Paris, France/The Bridgeman Art Library, London: Pages 237 both, 250 both, 251, 365 left

Kersting, A.F.: Pages 22-23, 84, 108, 133, 134, 136, 144 right, 146, 147, 149, 150 both, 151, 152, 155, 404

©Massimo Listri/CORBIS: Page 403 right

©Michael Lewis/CORBIS: Page 174

©Michael Maslan Historic Photographic/CORBIS: Page 417

©MIT Collection/CORBIS: Pages 406-407

Musée Conde, Chantilly, France/The Bridgeman Art Library, London: Pages 5, 31

Musée des Beaux-Arts, Lille, France: Page 399

Museo dell'Opera del Duomo, Florence, Italy/The Bridgeman Art Library, London: Pages 230, 231, 232 both, 233 both

Museo di Firenze, Comera, Florence, Italy/The Bridgeman Art Library, London: Page 71

Musio Nazionale del Bargello, Florence, Italy: Page 72

National Gallery, London/The Bridgeman Art Library, London: Pages 262, 263, 264, 265

New Sacrisity, San Lorenzo, Florence, Italy/The Bridgeman Art Library, London: Page 213

Palazzo Medici-Ricardi, Florence, Italy/The Bridgeman Art Library, London: Page 4

Palazzo Vecchio, Florence, Italy/The Bridgeman Art Library, London: Pages 12, 116, 243 right

©Philadelphia Museum of Art/CORBIS: Page 236 right

Pitti Palace: Page 81

Private Collection/The Bridgeman Art Library, London: Page 348

©Richard T. Nowitz/CORBIS: Page 104

Royal Academy of Arts, London/The Bridgeman Art Library, London: Pages 167, 168

San Pietro in Vincoli, Rome, Italy/The Bridgeman Art Library, London: Pages 163, 204

Santa Maria delle Grazie: Page 111

Santa Maria Novella, Florence, Italy: Pages 50, 51

Santa Maria Novella, Florence, Italy/The Bridgeman Art Library, London: Page 45

© Ted Spiegel/CORBIS: Pages 10, 227 left, 394, 395

© TRIP/Michael Taylor: Page 38

© TRIP/P. Petterson: Pages 92-93

Uffizi Gallery, Florence, Italy: Page 252, 254, 255, 256

©Underwood & Underwood/CORBIS: Page 405

Vatican Museums and Galleries, Vatican City, Italy: Pages 266, 267, 268 both, 269, 270 274-5, 276, 277 both, 284, 285, 286 both, 287 both, 294 both, 295 both, 296-297 298, 299, 301, 302, 306, 307, 308, 309, 310, 312, 313, 314, 315, 316, 317, 318 both

Vatican Museums and Galleries, Vatican City, Italy/The Bridgeman Art Library, London: Pages 17, 89, 103, 106, 107 131, 156-157, 272, 274, 278-279, 280, 281, 282, 289, 290, 291, 293, 294, 304-305, 310, 316, 317, 318 right 321, 322, 323, 324, 325, 326, 327, 328,330, 331, 332, 333, 334, 336, 337, 338, 339, 340, 341